W9-ANI-944

Social Reconstruction Learning

This volume argues that educational problems have their basis in an ideology of binary opposites often referred to as dualism, which is deeply embedded in all aspects of Western society and philosophy, and that it is partly because mainstream schooling incorporates dualism that it is unable to facilitate the thinking skills, dispositions and understandings necessary for autonomy, democratic citizenship and leading a meaningful life. Drawing on the philosophy of John Dewey, feminist philosophy, Matthew Lipman's Philosophy for Children program, and the service learning movement, Bleazby proposes a social reconstruction learning approach to schooling, in which students engage in philosophical inquiries with members of their community in order to reconstruct real social problems. *Social Reconstruction Learning* argues that this pedagogy can better facilitate independent thinking, imaginativeness, emotional intelligence, autonomy, and active citizenship.

Dr. Jennifer Bleazby is a lecturer in the Faculty of Education at Monash University. Her recent publications include "Dewey's Notion of Imagination in Philosophy for Children", *Education and Culture* 28(2), and "Overcoming Relativism and Absolutism: Dewey's Ideals of Truth and Meaning in Philosophy for Children", *Educational Philosophy and Theory* 43(5).

Routledge International Studies in the Philosophy of Education

Social Reconstruction Learning

Dualism, Dewey and Philosophy in Schools

Jennifer Bleazby

 Routledge
Taylor & Francis Group

NEW YORK   LONDON

First published 2013
by Routledge
711 Third Avenue, New York, NY 10017

Simultaneously published in the UK
by Routledge
2 Park Square, Milton Park, Abingdon, Oxon OX14 4RN

*Routledge is an imprint of the Taylor & Francis Group,
an informa business*

© 2013 Taylor & Francis

Library of Congress Cataloging-in-Publication Data
Bleazby, Jennifer.
    Social reconstruction learning : dualism, Dewey and philosophy in
schools / by Jennifer Bleazby.
        p. cm. — (Routledge international studies in the philosophy of
education ; 29)
    Includes bibliographical references and index.
    1. Education—Philosophy. 2. Dualism. 3. Dewey, John, 1859–
1952. 4. Philosophy—Study and teaching—United States. 5. Thought
and thinking—Study and teaching. I. Title.
    LB14.7.B58 2013
    370.1—dc23
    2012031138

ISBN: 978-0-415-63624-7 (hbk)
ISBN: 978-0-203-06911-0 (ebk)

Typeset in Sabon
by IBT Global.

Printed and bound in the United States of America on sustainably sourced
paper by IBT Global.

For my Dad

Contents

Acknowledgments

I wish to thank my friends and family for their support, love and encouragement, especially Peter Bleazby, Belinda Bleazby, Shane Bleazby and Jesse Toby. I am also grateful to my students, especially my year 11 and 12 philosophy students, who influenced some of the ideas in this book and provided me with many good examples of the benefits of classroom philosophical inquiries.

The ideas and arguments in this book began as an Honours thesis and were later developed as a PhD thesis. I am indebted to my honours supervisor, the late Ross Philips, who introduced me to Philosophy for Children and provided invaluable feedback on very early versions of ideas contained within this book. I am also grateful to my PhD supervisor, Philip Cam, who introduced me to the philosopher John Dewey and read and provided feedback on drafts of most of the chapters in this book. Advice and feedback from the following people has also enabled me to develop and improve the ideas and arguments presented in this book: Gilbert Burgh, Rosalyn Diprose, Megan Laverty, Ann M. Sharp, Tim Sprod, Maurizio Toscana and many anonymous reviewers. The School of Philosophy and the Faculty of Arts and Social Sciences at the University of New South Wales and the Faculty of Education at Monash University have provided resources and support which enabled the writing of this book.

Parts of this book have previously been published in abridged and modified forms. An abridged version of Chapter 3 was published as "Overcoming Relativism and Absolutism: Dewey's Ideals of Truth and Meaning in Philosophy for Children", *Educational Philosophy and Theory*, 2011, 43(5). Parts of Chapter 4 will be published as "Dewey's Notion of Imagination in Philosophy for Children" in a forthcoming edition of *Education and Culture*, 2012, 28(2). An abridged version of Chapter 6 was published as "Autonomy, Democratic Community, and Citizenship in Philosophy for Children: Dewey and Philosophy for Children's Rejection of the Community/Individual dualism", in *Analytic Teaching*, 2006, 26(1). Parts of Chapter 7 appeared as "Reconstructing Gender in the Philosophy for Children Program" in *Thinking: The Journal of Philosophy for Children*, 2008, 19(2–3). I am grateful to the editors who have granted permission for parts of these publications to be reused here.

Introduction

Many of the criticisms made of modern schooling appear to be incompatible with each other or even contradictory. For example, it is often argued that schools promote individualism and competitiveness and, as a consequence, students lack altruism and social skills, having no sense of themselves as connected to other people. This is said to be reflected in problems such as the prevalence of bullying and juvenile crime, young people's lack of a sense of civic duty and the increasingly self-absorbed and narcissistic attitude exhibited by many young people today (e.g., see Twenge and Campbell 2009). If it is true that schools fail to promote a sense of community, one would expect that their focus on the individual would at least mean that they foster independent thinking and autonomy. Yet another common criticism of schools is that they fail to promote the thinking skills needed for autonomy, self-motivation and purposeful, self-directed action because their primary goal is to transmit established bodies of knowledge into the heads of passive students. This is in spite of the fact that it is now common for official curriculum documents to prescribe the teaching of thinking skills, and many teachers claim to deliberately foster independent thinking. In fact, some people even claim that schools focus so much on teaching thinking skills that they no longer teach enough disciplinary knowledge and, as such, young people lack fundamental knowledge about the world they live in. For example, E. D Hirsch (1988, 1996) argues that progressive educational ideas, which he largely attributes to Dewey and Rousseau, now dominate schooling in the United States. Progressive educational ideas include student-centred learning, differentiated curricula, problem- and inquiry-based learning, constructivist notions of knowledge, project-based learning and experiential or 'hands on' learning, and a focus on the development of general capabilities, like thinking skills. According to Hirsch (1988, 1996), the predominance of such educational methods, which he believes focus on teaching skills rather than content, is the reason young Americans are "culturally illiterate". However, other educationalists maintain that while progressive ideas are common in official curriculum documents and educational policies, they have had little to no impact on actual classroom practice (e.g., Yates 2011, 34; Lagemann 2000; Buras 1999; Tanner 1997, 11). How is it that some educational experts can believe that modern schools focus so much on teaching thinking skills that they fail to teach content, while others maintain that schools focus so much on transmitting facts that they fail to teach students how to think for themselves? How can schools be seen to focus on the individual to such an extent that they fail to foster community, while also being seen as failing to teach the very thinking skills needed for independence and autonomy?

Another common criticism of modern schools is that they focus on both the acquisition of knowledge and the development of rationality to such an extent that they devalue or exclude other valuable capabilities, such as emotional intelligence, imaginativeness and practical skills. The apparent devaluation of these other attributes in favour of rationality is sometimes considered to be particularly problematic for the education of girls and women. It is thought that schools discriminate against females because they privilege an abstract, rationalistic, theoretical and individualistic notion of thinking that is inherently 'masculine'. Furthermore, the attributes that schools supposedly exclude and devalue are traditionally considered feminine (e.g., the emotions and imagination). However, such arguments are in direct conflict with research claiming that schools discriminate against males because curricula and pedagogies are becoming increasingly 'feminised'. In particular, it is claimed that English curricula and pedagogy emphasise the imagination, emotionality, personal relationships, group work and discussion, which favours girls, excludes boys and is part of the reason boys are reluctant readers and don't perform as well on standardised literacy tests. How can schools be seen to simultaneously discriminate against both females and males for opposing reasons? Furthermore, how can schools be accused of failing to teach thinking skills and disciplinary knowledge by some scholars, while being seen by others to focus so much on knowledge and reasoning that they marginalise other valuable attributes like emotion and imagination?

It may seem that schools cannot possibly be responsible for such an abundance of seemingly incompatible problems. The obvious response is that not all these criticisms are equally warranted. However, I believe that they are all warranted to some extent and that they all reflect serious educational problems. I will argue that such problems have their basis in a philosophical tradition often referred to as dualism. Dualism refers to a system of interlocking oppositional pairs, including Reason/emotion, Reason/imagination, Reason/experience, public/private, mind/body, theory/practice, subject/object, individual/community, universal/particular, abstract/concrete, absolute/relative and male/female. These dualisms are deeply embedded in all aspects of Western society and philosophy, influencing many of our dominant beliefs, values and practices. For example, those attributes on the left are traditionally associated with masculinity, truth, knowledge, personhood, citizenship and education. They are traditionally opposed to, and considered superior to, the 'feminine' attributes on the right. Thus, many feminists have argued that these dualistic pairs legitimise patriarchy and other hierarchical social structures.

Many philosophers, notably feminists, continental philosophers and pragmatists, have argued that these dualisms are problematic because they claim to separate and oppose that which is actually interdependent and interconnected. John Dewey argues that the attributes that make up these dualistic pairs are operationally co-dependent. Knowledge, truth, meaning, autonomy, personhood and citizenship involve these various attributes functioning simultaneously and interacting with each other. For example, according to Dewey, we can't exclude the emotions from reasoning because reason and the emotions provide each other with their cognitive force and practical value. In trying to suppress the emotions in the process of reasoning, we effectively render reasoning defective. Thus, dominant dualistic ideals of knowing, learning, autonomy and citizenship are problematic because they attempt to suppress or exclude valuable and essential attributes and processes. Consequently, the attributes that are included in the epistemological and educational terrain, such as reason and individuality, are rendered incomplete and problematic because they are operationally co-dependent on other excluded attributes, such as the emotions and imagination.

I will argue that the incorporation of these dualisms into dominant educational theories and practices is, at least, partially responsible for the types of educational problems described above. Dualism explains how dominant educational practices can give rise to seemingly incompatible problems. For example, while many teachers do focus on the teaching of thinking skills, they often assume a dualistic notion of reason that is opposed to emotion and imagination. If reason is operationally co-dependent on the emotions and imagination, not only will these teachers fail to facilitate emotional intelligence and imagination, they will actually fail to teach reasoning skills too. For the same reason, schools that aim to facilitate individuality and autonomy, at the expense of community and connectedness, ultimately fail to facilitate both because individuality and autonomy can only be developed within community.

Thus, the aim of this book is to outline the problematic nature of various dualisms and explain how they have influenced dominant educational ideals and practices, while also outlining and developing an alternative, non-dualistic pedagogy and philosophy. This alternative will integrate the philosophy of John Dewey; Philosophy for Children (P4C), which is actually based on Deweyian ideals; and a particular type of service learning that has a critical and social justice orientation. This alternative educational ideal will be referred to as social reconstruction learning.

The term 'Philosophy for Children' is interpreted and used in a variety of ways. Philosophy for Children has evolved from a curriculum and pedagogy originally developed by Matthew Lipman in the 1970s. Lipman's curriculum and pedagogy introduces the pragmatist idea of the Community of Inquiry and the methods and subject matter of philosophy into the classroom, with the primary aims of fostering reflective thinking, the construction of meaning and the skills and dispositions associated with a Deweyian notion of democracy. While pragmatists like Dewey and Peirce emphasised scientific inquiry as the model of reflective thinking, Lipman integrates the Community of Inquiry with the subject matter of philosophy. Lipman (2003) argues that the discipline of philosophy is best equipped to foster the development and improvement of thinking, as well as the attitudes and skills associated with democracy. Two of the key educational advantages of philosophy as a subject matter include its very contentious nature, which provokes inquiry as a means to working through problems, and its focus on metacognition, especially in its sub-discipline of logic, which provides students with the tools and language needed to undertake procedural inquiries—inquiries into the nature of thinking itself.

Lipman's original curriculum consists of a series of specially written narratives for elementary and secondary school students, with accompanying teacher's guides that are intended to provoke philosophical inquiry. A typical P4C class involves students and the teacher sitting in a circle and jointly reading aloud a narrative, containing philosophical themes. Students then take turns formulating questions provoked by the stimulus material. The questions are often written on butcher's paper (so they can be kept) with each student's name recorded next to their question. The community then takes a vote on which question they will inquire into first. Thus, in this sense, P4C is student-centred because the students' interests, concerns and questions help set the agenda for inquiry. However, it is not entirely student-centred in that the teacher is responsible for selecting the stimulus material and facilitating the inquiry, including guiding the formulation of suitable student questions. Once the agenda has been set, the students take turns contributing possible solutions, further problems or questions, examples, arguments, opinions, criticisms, reasons, analogies, criteria for making judgments and so on. The aim is to develop a better understanding of the issue and some form of a solution or settlement to the problems raised. Broadly, the aim is to construct meaning that will lead to more reflective and intelligent action (Lipman 2003; Splitter and Sharp 1995; Sharp 1987). One of the intended outcomes of P4C is that the community members will come to realise that they are dependent on the procedures of inquiry and on each other's contributions in order to construct meaning and develop thinking skills. As a result of this realisation, which is also facilitated by teacher prompting, students come to understand that they must be reasonable, trusting, caring, empathetic and supportive even when being critical of each other because they need to create an environment in which each and every participant feels safe to contribute ideas and perspectives so as they can construct more objective meanings, solve the problems explored and learn. Often, the first classroom Community of Inquiry involves a collaborative investigation and construction of some general procedures or rules to guide the communal inquiry (e.g., taking turns to speak, listening attentively to each other, providing reasons for opinions, not ridiculing contributions, etc). However, these procedures always remain open to inquiry and reconstruction. Such procedural inquiry is a highly valued and defining feature of the Community of Inquiry. Not all P4C teachers necessarily follow these exact procedures, and this is not all that P4C consists of. P4C often involves the use of a host of other activities and resources, including many conceptual analysis and logic-based activities and exercises (e.g., Cam 1995, 2006; Golding, 2002, 2005b, 2006). The fact that members of the classroom Community of Inquiry have a shared interest and goal, common procedures and a recognition of their interdependence is thought to foster the kind of democratic community that Dewey promoted—a community that values inquiry, diversity, inclusivity and the collaborative reconstruction of experience as a means to fostering human flourishing.

While I will draw heavily upon Lipman's own writings, when I use the term 'Philosophy for Children' I will not strictly be referring to Lipman's program with its associated books and teacher's manuals. While many of these books and teacher's guides are valuable, they are not essential for promoting philosophical, communal inquiry in schools. All school subjects contain philosophical elements, and philosophical inquiry can be stimulated by a variety of sources and experiences, including contemporary social issues, personal experiences, the media, artworks, experiments, practical activities, excursions and so on. Furthermore, the term 'Philosophy for Children' is now commonly used to refer to a whole approach to learning and doing philosophy, which more broadly focuses on communal inquiry and philosophical thinking. It will be argued that the type of philosophical community of inquiry promoted by P4C is an educational, philosophical and political ideal that overcomes many of the problems with existing educational, philosophical and political ideals and practices. In order to distinguish between the broader sense in which I will be using the term 'Philosophy for Children' and the original P4C curriculum, the latter will be referred to as Lipman's P4C curriculum.

The following chapters provide a detailed analysis of the ideals of thinking, truth, knowledge, meaning, the self, autonomy, the emotions, the imagination, experience, community and citizenship that P4C assumes. It will be shown that these ideals effectively deconstruct many of the problematic dualisms embedded in other philosophical and educational ideas and practices. P4C's anti-dualism stems from its Deweyian roots. As Lipman himself acknowledges, P4C "is built unapologetically on Deweyian foundations" (2008, 150).[1] However, Lipman never provided an in-depth explanation of Dewey's influence on P4C. Thus, a detailed account of how P4C assumes many aspects of Dewey's epistemology, metaphysics, political philosophy, theory of logic, ethical ideals, psychology and educational ideas will be given here. Dewey describes inquiry as the means by which individuals construct meaning through reconstructing problematic experiences. He argues that meaning can only be acquired in inquiries that involve a constant interaction and continuity between mind/world, mind/body, self/other, Reason/experience, abstract/concrete, theory/practice, Reason/ emotion, Reason/imagination, subject/object and individual/community. Consequently, inquiry and knowledge is not purely objective, abstract and absolute, but subjective-objective, concrete-abstract, theoretical-practical, rational-emotional and so on. Dewey's philosophy has much in common with the many contemporary feminists who also reject dualism and emphasise the concrete, embodied, contextual and social nature of inquiry and meaning. Unlike Dewey, these feminist philosophers also emphasise the gendered nature of dualism, which enables a consideration of how such dualisms underpin gender problems in education and philosophy. Throughout the book, Dewey's philosophy will be integrated with the ideas of many feminist theorists, notably Val Plumwood, Lorraine Code, Sandra Harding, Carol Gilligan, Belenky et al., Evelyn Fox Keller and Alison Jaggar. It will be shown that it is because P4C assumes this non-dualistic philosophy that it is able to overcome many of the problems that characterise mainstream education.

In order to understand how Dewey and P4C overcome these problematic dualisms, it is first necessary to understand the nature of dualism. In Chapter 1, feminist and Deweyian critiques of traditional Western epistemology and philosophy will be used in order to explicate the problematic nature of the dualistic relationship.

A general overview of Dewey's philosophy will be given in Chapter 2, with a focus on his rejection of key dualisms. In the remaining chapters, a more detailed analysis of Dewey's rejection of particular dualisms will be given, namely, absolute/relative, Reason/imagination, Reason/emotion, individual/community and theory/practice dualisms. However, because Dewey's vast philosophical ideas are interdependent and mutually reinforcing, it is also necessary to first give a general overview of his philosophy. Dewey is frequently misunderstood, and one of the reasons for this is that the many integrated aspects of his philosophy, psychology and educational ideas are often studied and discussed in isolation.

Chapters 3–7 focus on different dualisms that are particularly problematic from an educational perspective. In Chapter 3, the focus is on absolute/ relative dualism, which incorporates various other dualisms, such as object/ subject, Reason/experience, mind/body and abstract/concrete. Such dualisms have given rise to two competing theories of truth and knowledge: relativism (including subjectivism) and absolutism. Both these theories are deeply problematic, and schooling that assumes either absolutism or relativism is unable to promote reflective thinking, autonomy, community, open-mindedness, objectivity, fallibilism, care, empathy or meaningfulness. Since the facilitation of such ideals and attributes is the goal of P4C, both relativism and absolutism are incompatible with P4C. An analysis of P4C will show that it incorporates a Deweyian pragmatist ideal of truth, which occupies a kind of 'middle ground' position between relativism and absolutism. It incorporates the best aspects of both theories: relativism's recognition of the concrete, constructed, subjective and fallible nature of truth claims, and absolutism's valuing of objectivity, general principles and methods of inquiry and communication that cross cultures, times and spaces. It will be argued that because P4C incorporates this Deweyian notion of truth it is able to facilitate a multitude of ideal, although seemingly incompatible, types of thinking, dispositions and social and philosophical ideals, whereas other dominant pedagogies have failed to do so.

Chapter 4 and 5 focus on the Reason/emotion and Reason/imagination dualisms. It will be argued that mainstream schooling incorporates these problematic dualisms and, as a consequence, is unable to facilitate inquiry, autonomy, community, caring thinking, empathy and democracy. This is because all reflective thinking and action is simultaneously imaginative, emotive, experiential and rational. Dewey's theories of emotion and imagination will be analysed at length in order to explicate the role of emotion and imagination in all inquiry and learning. As P4C promotes this Deweyian notion of inquiry, it is better able to facilitate the imagination and the emotions as essential aspects of all thinking and social life.

In Chapter 6, P4C's non-dualistic ideals of the self, autonomy, community, democracy and citizenship will be explored. Traditional notions of autonomy and citizenship are based on individual/community dualism. For example, the dominant notion of autonomy emphasises rugged individualism and self-sufficiency and is opposed to community and dependency. Communities are often thought to involve homogenisation and the loss of a separate self. It will be shown that such dualistic notions of autonomy and community are educationally and politically problematic. In contrast, P4C incorporates a Deweyian notion of the self as mutually dependent on others for growth and autonomy. Dewey argues that in order to think for oneself, one must be a member of a community and not just any community but a democratic community of inquiry, which is inclusive of differences and engages in inquiry with other communities. It will be shown that P4C's classroom Community of Inquiry is modelled on Dewey's notion of democracy and, as such, is well positioned to facilitate the development of autonomous individuals who recognise their interconnectedness with others.

In Chapter 7, I will examine how P4C's anti-dualism enables it to overcome some gender equity issues embedded in mainstream schooling. Given that mainstream philosophy has been accused of perpetuating patriarchal notions of knowing, the self, autonomy and citizenship, there are understandable concerns about the appropriateness of teaching philosophy to children. However, it will be shown that P4C doesn't promote 'masculine' notions of rationality or autonomy. Nor does P4C exclude the 'feminine' emotions, subjectivity, imagination and community from the epistemological and political terrain. These patriarchal ideas are reflected in many dominant educational ideas and practices. It will be shown that P4C overcomes dominant gendered epistemological and political ideas by assuming a Deweyian notion of thinking that is simultaneously reasonable, emotional, imaginative and experiential, as well as a social notion of the self and autonomy. This notion of thinking doesn't just apply to philosophy but epitomises good thinking in all disciplines. As a consequence, P4C possesses the potential to help improve the participation of females in math and science, as well as the participation of boys in the arts and humanities, especially in regards to the English curriculum and reading in general.

The final chapter will examine the problematic consequences of P4C's failure to fully overcome theory/practice dualism. As with traditional schooling, P4C privileges the theoretical over the practical. Theory/practice dualism is reflected in the traditional curriculum hierarchy where subjects most associated with the body, concrete experience and applied knowledge traditionally have the lowest status (e.g., vocational education, physical education, health, outdoor education, etc). P4C's focus on classroom dialogue and written texts rather than on applied knowledge and action means that it helps perpetuate the privileging of the theoretical, cognitive and the abstract. This is in spite of Lipman's awareness of Dewey's well-known commitment to overcoming theory/practice dualism in philosophy and education. The best known feature of Dewey's Laboratory School at the University of Chicago was the use of practical, 'hands-on' activities like sewing, building and gardening as a means to teach students traditional disciplinary content and skills in a contextualised and more meaningful manner. In theory, Lipman also rejects theory/practice dualism. However, P4C does not involve students participating in the type of active transformation of their environment that characterised learning at the Laboratory School. It will be shown that P4C's failure to overcome theory/practice dualism undermines its ability to foster reflective thinking, active citizenship, democracy and a pragmatic attitude that is essential for living a meaningful life. Drawing on the popular pedagogy known as service learning, a solution to P4C's problematic lack of practicality will be developed. Service learning involves students performing community service activities as a part of the learning process. The activities performed are embedded within the curriculum. However, there are two broad approaches to service learning identified in the literature: a traditional approach that focuses on civic duty and charity work and a critical approach focused on reconstructing real social problems. Only the critical approach, which has its roots in Dewey's educational ideas, critical pedagogy and the curriculum ideology known as social reconstructionism, is consistent with P4C's desirable educational goals. It will be argued that P4C can be improved by integrating it with this critical approach to service learning. P4C can also help overcome many of the problems that commonly plague critical service learning. This integrated pedagogy, which is referred to as social reconstruction learning, would involve students participating in philosophical communities of inquiry that extend beyond the classroom as a means to undertaking transformative action so as to reconstruct real social problems. Thus, it is argued that integrating P4C and critical service learning will better enable these two pedagogies to realise the Deweyian educational and political goals to which they both aspire.

1 The Problem of Dualisms

THE QUEST FOR CERTAINTY

Western philosophy and culture have been fundamentally shaped by a desire for certainty. As Dewey explains, "Man who lives in a world of hazards is compelled to seek for security", and the perennial assumption has been that only certainty, in the form of fixed and eternal truths, can provide such security (1930b, 7). A world that is constantly changing is unpredictable, can never be known in its entirety and, consequently, is difficult to manage and control. It is assumed that having certain knowledge of ourselves and the world would enable us to make reliable predictions and live in harmony with our environment rather than fear it. However, experience is corporeal and subjective, and it is experience of a world that is constantly changing, decaying and regenerating.

As such, the desire for certainty has given rise to the notion of an ultimate, eternal, fixed reality (Dewey 1930b, 23). Knowledge of such a reality could be absolute, universal and certain. However, we could not attain such knowledge through embodied experience. Thus, a notion of knowing has been devised that supposedly transcends the particularities and indeterminacies of concrete experience. This is the method of transcendental Reason, sometimes thought to be the only legitimate method of acquiring knowledge.[1] Reason is conceived of as a universal human faculty, located in a disembodied mind. Through Reason, the individual is meant to be able to transcend their embodied situatedness and objectively observe a fixed, eternal reality (Dewey 2004a, 252–255). While other attributes, such as the emotions, imagination and the senses, are also recognised as methods of acquiring information and organising thought, Reason has been conceived of as the only method *objective*, *abstract* and *universal* enough to endow us with untainted, "ultimately true representations of the one real world" (Lloyd 1984, viii). Many philosophers have been preoccupied with trying to understand this ultimate reality and, as such, preoccupied with perfecting the method of Reason, such as through identifying universal logical principles that thinking must adhere to in order to attain and preserve truth (Dewey 1930b, 19). As Dewey explains, it is in philosophy, more so than any other discipline, that the quest for certainty is apparent:

I do not doubt that there was a feeling before the rise of philosophy that the unalterably fixed and the absolutely certain are one, or that change is the source from which comes all our uncertainties and woes. But in philosophy this inchoate feeling was definitely formulated. It was asserted on grounds held to be as demonstrably necessary as are the conclusions of geometry and logic. Thus the predisposition of philosophy toward the universal, invariant and eternal was fixed. It remains the common possession of the entire classic philosophic tradition. (1930b, 23)

THE DUALISTIC NOTION OF REASON

This transcendental ideal of Reason is dualistic in that it is partially defined by its opposition to the emotions, imagination and experience—attributes considered too unreliable to be methods of knowledge acquisition (Dewey 2004a, 252–255). The senses are considered subjective and prone to illusion, while the emotions are thought to be idiosyncratic and are associated with the material body, which is concrete, situated and constantly changing. The imagination is deemed problematic because it is not constrained by reality and is associated with the emotions. Reason's supposed superiority over these other attributes is reflected in the work of many of the great philosophers, such as Descartes' well-known concerns about the reliability of sense experience and imagination:

> Our senses could quite often also mislead us . . . as when those with jaundice see everything as yellow, or when stars or other very distant bodies appear to us much smaller than they are. For after all . . . we ought never to let ourselves be convinced except on the evidence of our reason. And it is to be noted that I say 'our reason,' and not 'our imagination' or 'our senses'. (2006, 34)

Not only are the imagination, emotions and experience seen as inadequate methods of attaining knowledge, they are also considered to be distractions to Reason. This is reflected in Kant's discussion of the emotions:

> The impulses of nature [the passions, emotions], accordingly, are *obstacles* within man's mind to his observance of duty and forces (sometimes powerful ones) struggling against it. Man must, therefore, judge that he is able to stand up to them and subdue them by reason. (1964, 37)

In the dominant epistemological construct, which is highly influenced by Cartesian epistemology, these other methods of forming beliefs and organising information are seen as unreliable distractions that must be suppressed so that Reason alone can deliver us absolute knowledge. Consequently, the emotions, imagination, intuition and experience are conceived of as dualistically opposed to Reason. Since Reason is thought to provide certainty, while these other methods do not, Reason is considered superior to its oppositional partners and has a privileged role in defining them. Emotion, imagination and the senses are largely defined negatively, as 'not reason'—capacities incapable of providing us with knowledge and certainty (Gatens 1991, 92).

The Reason/emotion, Reason/experience and Reason/imagination dualisms interlock with other dualistic pairs central to this epistemological ideal, such as mind/body dualism. Since the body belongs to the material world, which is indeterminate and changing, it too is opposed to Reason. The body is also situated in that it must occupy a particular time and space. However, Reason is supposed to provide a transcendental 'god's eye view' of reality. Furthermore, because they involve feeling, the emotions are considered physiological and, consequently, the body is also associated with the emotions. Thus, Reason is thought to be situated in a 'disembodied mind'. As Dewey explains, the body is treated as merely a receptacle for the self-sufficient mind:

> Thought has been alleged to be a purely inner activity, intrinsic to mind alone; and according to traditional classic doctrine, "mind" is complete and self-sufficient in itself. Overt action may follow upon its operations but in an external way, a way not intrinsic to its completion. (1930b, 11)

It is not only those philosophers who adhere to a type of Cartesian dualism that accept this disembodied notion of mind. Even though most contemporary philosophers believe that the mind is physical (e.g., that is identical to the brain), much of their writing still implies a type of mind/body dualism. This is because, as Tanesini explains, even materialist accounts of the mind "do not consider properly the implications of the fact that we—our minds, our reason—are embodied" (1999, 216). These implications include the fact that an embodied mind is incompatible with the notion of universal, absolute, ahistorical and certain knowledge. The implication of an embodied mind is a more situated, concrete, emotional and subjective account of knowledge. As far as many materialist philosophers continue to reject such an account of knowledge or, at least, fail to fully comprehend its implications, they still embrace a form of mind/body dualism. Thus, the notion of universal and absolute knowledge still implies a disembodied mind, even when such a concept of mind is explicitly rejected.

Mind/body dualism is also closely connected to theory/practice dualism. Practical activity is dependent on the body and is directly concerned with concrete particularities and the material world. As such, practice is opposed to abstract theory, which is thought to be the product of pure cognition. Dewey describes the inferior status that practical activities have traditionally had:

Practical activity deals with individualized and unique situations which are never exactly duplicable and about which, accordingly, no complete assurance is possible. All activity, moreover, involves change. The intellect, however, according to the traditional doctrine, may grasp universal Being, and Being which is universal is fixed and immutable. Wherever there is practical activity we human beings are involved as partakers in the issue. All the fear, disesteem and lack of confidence which gather about the thought of ourselves, cluster also about the thought of the action in which we are partners. Man's distrust of himself has caused him to desire to get beyond and above himself; in pure knowledge he has thought he could attain this self-transcendence. (1930b, 10)

The mind/body, theory/practice, Reason/emotion, Reason/imagination and Reason/experience dualisms are at the centre of an extensive system of interlocking and mutually reinforcing dualistic pairs. This system underpins dominant ideas in Western epistemology and culture (Plumwood 2002, 20; F. Mathews 1998, 519). The following are other dualistic pairs in this system, some of which will be examined in detail throughout the book:

Male	Female
Reason	Intuition
Reason	Emotion
Reason	Sense Experience
Reason	Imagination
Master	Slave
Mind	Body
Individual	Community
Culture	Nature
Civilised	Primitive
Independence	Dependency
Adult	Child
Rationality	Animality
Form	Matter
Human	Animal
Spirit	Matter
General	Specific
Universal	Particular
Abstract	Concrete
Absolute	Relative
Theoretical	Practical
Self	Other
White	Black
Subject	Object
Public	Private
Production	Reproduction[2]

Those attributes on the left are associated with knowledge and all the things knowledge entails, such as personhood, autonomy, public life, education and citizenship. Those attributes on the right are thought to be opposed to knowledge, education, autonomy and so on.

Thus, the attributes associated with knowledge, autonomy, education and citizenship are also associated with masculinity, while the attributes opposed to knowledge are traditionally associated with women, non-whites, children and other marginalised groups. Many of the attributes opposed to knowledge and autonomy are also associated with the working class, including practicality, concreteness, dependency and the body (e.g., manual labour). This system appears to legitimise denying members of these groups full access to education, citizenship and public life. That is, dualism helps legitimise and naturalise the marginalisation and oppression of these groups and the superiority of white, Western, middle-class males (Plumwood 2002; Oliver 2002). If those who possess the capacity for Reason have access to knowledge, it follows that those same individuals should control and manage society. Those who don't have direct access to knowledge should presumably submit to those who do (Oliver 2002, 219; Plumwood 2002, 11). This idea is explicit in Plato's *Republic* (1998), where it is argued that the most capable Reasoners (the Guardians or Philosopher Kings) should rule over other groups in the state, who are more suited to bodily, practical activities (e.g., craftspeople, artisans, soldiers, merchants). Plato's just state mirrors his notion of the just person, whose capacity for reason should rule over other parts of the self, namely, the body and the passions.

While Dewey was aware of the way these dualisms were related to various types of social and political inequalities, this aspect of dualism has been more comprehensively explained by contemporary feminists. Dewey identified how this dualistic system, especially the theory/practice dualism, was related to class inequalities. However, he did not explicitly connect dualism to gender and racial inequalities, even though he was involved in these civil rights movements during his lifetime. He has been criticised for this oversight (see Laird 1988, 112). Nonetheless, Dewey's philosophy is highly compatible with many contemporary feminist philosophies. By integrating various feminist theories and Dewey's philosophy, we can more fully explain the epistemological, educational, political and social consequences of these dualisms and develop a method for reconstructing them.

THE NATURE OF THE DUALISTIC RELATIONSHIP

Feminist philosophers have also provided a more comprehensive and detailed analysis of the nature of the dualistic relationship than Dewey did. Understanding the nature of the dualistic relationship is important because characteristics of the relationship are also incorporated into dominant Western epistemology and culture, along with the dualisms themselves.

Articulating the nature of this dualistic relationship will also indicate a means for reconstructing dualism.

Dualism is not synonymous with merely dichotomous or oppositional thinking, which is actually a valuable analytic tool. As Plumwood explains,

> The term 'dualism' is often used in ways which do not distinguish it from dichotomy. But if we mean by "dichotomy" what is commonly meant, simply making a division or drawing a distinction, it is essential to distinguish between dualism and dichotomy. Equating them would either cripple all thought (if we were forced to abandon dichotomy along with dualism) or collapse the concept of dualism (if we were forced to retain dualism along with dichotomy). In either case escape form dualism becomes impossible. (2002, 22)

It is not the making of distinctions that is problematic but the nature of the distinction made and the way that distinction is treated which results in a relationship of domination.

First, the dualistic relationship is a *hierarchical* one. A dichotomy may oppose two categories that are considered to be equally valuable. However, in a dualistic relationship, one category is assumed to be superior to, and dominates, the other. In general, the superior nature of the attributes on the left side of the table of dualisms is justified on the grounds that those attributes are associated with knowledge, certainty and personhood. As we have seen, those attributes on the right side of the table are considered inferior, not only because they aren't associated with knowledge but also because they are seen as obstacles to attaining knowledge. Just as certainty is intended to provide control and domination over everything else, those attributes that enable certainty dominate those that are opposed to it.

The differentiation between the two categories in a dualistic pair also requires, not just a mere distinction, but complete separation, what Plumwood describes as '*hyperseparation*' or '*radical exclusion*' (2002, 24–26). Whereas any two opposites may be differentiated by the identification of one differentiating characteristic, in a dualistic relationship, the differences are magnified, maximised and emphasised. Any commonalities, continuity and similarities between dualistic opposites are denied or trivialised (Plumwood 2002, 24–25; F. Mathews 1998, 520). The purpose of this polarisation is to enforce the supremacy and domination of one faculty over the other. If one category in the dualism is to be superior and dominate the other it must appear to hold nothing in common with its inferior partner (Plumwood 2002, 25). Descartes' distinction between the soul and the body typifies hyperseparation: "the soul by which I am what I am, is entirely distinct from the body and is even easier to know than the body; and would not stop being everything it is, even if the body were not to exist" (2006, 24). Anything or anyone who seems to transgress the rigid boundaries of dualistic categories is either denied or labelled subversive, abnormal and problematic, such as individuals who don't adhere to dualistic gender categories.

In actuality, the attributes that make up these dualistic pairs are *interdependent*. First, because they are defined in opposition to each other, they are dependent on each other for their identity and definitional boundaries. The inferior attribute in the dualistic partnership is defined negatively as lacking the essential attributes of its dominant partner (Plumwood 2002, 26–27). The superior attribute is also partially defined via its exclusion of its inferior partner. Second, the two categories in a dualism are materially and/or operationally dependent on each other in that they cannot function properly or exist without each other. For example, the mind is materially dependent on the body for survival. Masters are dependent on their slaves in order to have their desires met and, as shall be argued throughout the following chapters, the experience, imagination, emotions and reason are operationally co-dependent in that neither one can produce meaning and knowledge without the others.

However, in order to remain dominant, the superior categories in a dualistic relationship must deny any definitional, material and functional dependency on their subordinate partner. Thus, another feature of the dualistic relationship is the *denial of interdependency*, which Plumwood calls 'backgrounding' (2002, 23–24). The dominate category makes its partner seem inessential or unimportant, or even denies its existence. It does this through "mechanisms of focus and attention" (2002, 23). The activities, services and attributes of the subordinate category are treated as the background of the dominate partner's foreground. This is exemplified by women's domestic and childrearing work, which is devalued and ignored even though the 'masculine' work of the paid labour force is dependent on it because 'women's work' provides healthy, effective workers. The definitional dependency of the superior attribute on its inferior partner is also denied. The dominant category is defined positively by distinct properties it possesses, while its inferior partner is negatively defined by the fact that it lacks such properties. For example, emotions are defined as not Reason, obstacles to Reason, while Reason is defined by the fact that it can deliver knowledge. Since the inferior category is denied positive traits, it lacks "internal boundaries" to define it. Rather it appears to be completely dependent on its dominant partner for meaning (Gatens 1991, 92–95). In contrast, dominant categories in the dualisms appear to have clear and definitive boundaries that distinguish them from other faculties or attributes.

Since the inferior category in dualistic relationships is constructed as devoid of positive properties, it is also thought to lack autonomy and intrinsic value. That is, any value it does have is *instrumental*, usually the services it provides its superior partner (Plumwood 2002, 27–28). For example, the body exists as an instrument which houses and protects the superior mind. Women exist as instruments for masculine desires and goals (i.e., reproduction, sexual gratification, domestic labour). Instrumentality legitimises the dualistic attributes of *mastery* and *domination*. The superior partner masters the use of its inferior instrument, shaping it to meet its own needs, such as culture's mastery of nature in order to utilise it for human consumption. However, since the superior partner denies its dependency on its inferior partner, its use of it must be made to seem inessential.

Finally, Plumwood argues that the dualistic relationship is characterised by the *homogenisation* or *stereotyping* of the inferior category, which is supported by the assumption that the inferior category lacks internal boundaries that define it (2002, 28–30). Hence, differences amongst instances contained within the inferior category are denied or ignored. This is most obvious with the members of marginalised social groups. As Plumwood points out, dominant cultures tend to perceive the diverse members of marginalised groups as fundamentally the same. For example, in Australia, all Aboriginal people are considered the same from the perspective of the dominant white culture, even though there are many different Aboriginal communities, languages and traditions, not to mention the differences between individuals themselves (Plumwood 2002, 28). Homogenisation, further supports the apparent inferiority, insignificance and instrumental value of the subordinate category in a dualism. The members of an inferior category are seen as interchangeable and replaceable commodities.

DUALISM IN EMPIRICISM AND SCIENCE

The focus on Reason may be taken to imply that dualism is only apparent in idealist or rationalism theories, which would mean that many contemporary philosophers are exempt from this critique. However, dualism is also apparent in empiricism and scientific methods of knowing, even though, on the surface, such epistemologies appear to reject Reason/experience, mind/body and culture/nature dualisms.

Keller explains how dominant scientific methods reflect dualistic ways of thinking. Drawing on the influential object relations psychoanalytic theory of Nancy Chodorow (1978), Keller argues that male psychological development gives rise to static notions of autonomy and objectivity (1985).[3] Static objectivity and autonomy involve the subject radically separating themselves from the objects of knowledge, including other people, so as to avoid affecting them or being affected by them. The aim is to know these objects as they are without contaminating them with one's own subjectiveness and situatedness. Thus, we must not only distance and separate ourselves from the objects of knowledge but also from our own feelings, concrete situatedness and interests (Keller 1985, 79). It is this ideal of disinterested, dispassionate, objectivity that legitimises claims of universal and absolute knowledge. Static autonomy is characterised by self-control, self-sufficiency, independence and rugged individualism. Static autonomy involves a subject that interacts with other people and objects in a defensive, controlling and dominating manner so as to protect its own autonomy and identity. Keller argues that this is reflected in the dominant ideal of scientific method. The object of scientific investigation is 'feminine' nature and science is conceived of as a means of dominating and mastering nature so that it can be used to fulfil human needs and desires (Keller 1985, 97–102; 123–124). Thus, even this empiricist epistemological ideal incorporate subject/object, self/ other and culture/nature dualisms, as well as the attributes of separation, mastery and domination, which characterise the dualistic relationship.

Furthermore, while empiricist ideals of knowing accept sense experience as a method of knowing, the ideal of experience they assume can be disembodied, transcendental and associated with the mind rather than the body (Dewey 2004a, 136–137). As such, even empiricism can perpetuate Reason/experience, Reason/emotion and mind/body dualisms. This is demonstrated by the traditional hierarchy of the senses. A disembodied notion of seeing traditionally trumps the other senses in terms of their epistemological value. Sight is considered the sense best able to provide the knower with objective, accurate and detailed representations of the external world. There are several reasons for this perennial belief.

First, seeing is thought to have an essentially spatial nature, in that it enables us to simultaneously perceive a "co-ordinated manifold of objects" located in different spaces (Jonas 1954, 509). In contrast, the other senses are essentially temporal in that they involve a perception of different, successive sensations. As Vesey explains, "It takes time to hear a tune or feel the shape of a statue, but one seems to be able to see a landscape instantaneously" (1967, 252). Thus, in temporal sense experiences, "the whole content is never simultaneously present, but always partial and incomplete" (1954, 508). In contrast, sight comes closer to enabling us to perceive things as complete, eternal, unchanging and co-existing (1954, 508, 513). Hence, sight provides the sensual basis for the notion of eternal and absolute truth.

Second, sight is seemingly more objective than the other senses. This is because "sight is the ideal distance sense", allowing for greater separation between the knower and the known than the other, more proximal senses (Jonas 1954, 517). Taste and touch are particularly problematic because they require physical contact between subject and object and are, therefore, presumed to be the most subjective and unreliable senses as there is no way for the knower not to affect what is known. In contrast, vision is thought to allow a subject to passively observe an antecedent reality without contaminating it:

> [I]n seeing I am not yet engaged by the seen object. I may choose to enter into intercourse with it, but it can appear without the fact of its appearance already involving intercourse. By my seeing it, no issue of my possible relations with it is prejudiced. Neither I nor the object has so far done anything to determine the mutual situation. It lets me be, as I let it be . . . While in touch subject and object are already doing something to each other in the very act in which the object becomes a phenomenal presence. (1954, 514)

Thus, seeing is thought to allow for the separation and control that characterises dualism. As Jonas states, seeing is a relation between a "self-contained object" and a "self-contained subject" (1954, 516).

The apparent lack of intercourse between subject and object also means that seeing can appear to be less corporeal, concrete and connected to the material world than the other senses, particularly those that require physical contact. As Vesey explains,

> One way in which seeing differs from feeling by touching is that if we feel something by touching it, our experience is of feeling it with a particular part of the body. Our visual experience, however, is not of seeing with our eyes. *We can imagine a disembodied mind having visual experiences but not having tactile ones*. Sight does not require our being part of the material world in the way in which feeling by touching does . . . Thus, the directness of seeing when contrasted with hearing, its non-involvement with its object when contrasted with feeling by touching, and its apparent temporal immediacy when contrasted with both hearing and feeling by touching are features that may partly explain the belief that sight is the most excellent of the senses. (1967, 252, italics added)

This is why seeing is commonly conceptualised as a mental, disembodied process that, of all the senses, comes closest to enabling us to transcend the particularities of the material world and acquire knowledge of abstract, atemporal and universal forms. As Keller and Grontowski note, this disembodied notion of seeing is captured in Descartes' claim that "[i]t is the soul that sees, not the eye" (1983, 215).

The epistemic privilege that sight has is reflected in the common use of visual metaphors to describe knowledge, truth and Reason. Knowledge is described as illuminating and enlightening. The most famous examples come from Plato's *Republic*, where the sun is given as a metaphor for the Good, with the Good being the most important of all Plato's forms. The Good is the form that gives all the other forms their value and makes knowledge of all the other forms possible. Just as the sun lights up the physical world, enabling us to see material objects, the form of the Good enables us to grasp all the other forms. In Plato's allegory of the cave, the prisoner escapes ignorance through escaping the darkness of the cave, going out into the light and looking up to the sun, consequently, gaining knowledge of reality. This disembodied notion of seeing is also reflected in sayings such as 'the mind's eye' and the 'eyes are the windows to the soul' (Keller and Grontowski 1983). Traditional empiricist theories of knowing are modelled on this ideal of seeing not embodied experience (Dewey 1930b, 26).

Not only is the notion of experience assumed by traditional empiricism typically disembodied, abstract and separational, but many empiricist epistemologies still privilege Reason. Dewey points out that according to traditional empiricism, which he refers to as 'sensationalism', our senses are unwittingly subject to stimuli caused by our external environment. The data received through the senses is considered to be raw, fragmented, particular and meaningless. It is commonly thought that in order to make sense of this raw data and intelligently respond to it, we must subject it to Reasoned analysis. Through abstracting from, conceptualising, integrating, organising and theorising the raw data of sense experience, Reason renders experience meaningful and useful. Hence, while experience is considered a passive activity of receiving information, Reason is considered an active, intellectual activity of making connections that give rise to meaning and knowledge (Dewey 2004a, 255–260). Experience and Reason are not thought to operate simultaneously as interconnected processes. The two processes are considered distinct with Reason occurring after and in response to sense stimuli, not as an aspect of experience. As Dewey states,

> [T]here was no need of thinking in connection with sense-observation; in fact, in strict theory such would be impossible till afterwards, for thinking consisted simply in combining and separating sensory units which had been received without any participation of judgment. (2004a, 258)

Thus, while experience is considered necessary for knowing, it is still the mind and Reasoning that turns concrete and particular sense experience into abstract, universal knowledge. Hence, even in many empiricist theories, mind/body and Reason/experience dualisms are maintained.

DUALISM IN EDUCATION

Problematically, dualism has also influenced dominant Western educational ideas and practices. One of the more conspicuous ways in which dualism has influenced schooling is in the traditional curriculum hierarchy. Some school subjects have maintained considerably higher status than others in Western society. At its very core, this traditional curriculum hierarchy reflects dualistic notions of knowledge because the top of the hierarchy is occupied by academic disciplines associated with abstractness, universal and absolute facts, rationality, theory and cognition, while those disciplines associated with concreteness, imagination, emotionality, practice, application and the body are located on the lower rungs of the hierarchy. Teese and Polesel (2003) describe how this curriculum hierarchy operates in senior secondary school curricula in Australia. At the top of the hierarchy are mathematics and the physical sciences (physics and chemistry). These subjects emphasise "abstraction from everyday life", consist of a supposedly universal "language of ideas (numbers, symbols, physical concepts)", and are seen as "comparatively stable and predictable" and as providing "a sense of certainty" (2003,

20–21). Their sense of certainty stems from their association with Reason and their apparent remoteness from concrete experience. As shall be argued in preceding chapters, all disciplines actually contain concrete, practical, imaginative and emotive dimensions. However, in subjects like mathematics and the physical sciences such 'inferior' attributes tend to be hidden, suppressed or denied. As Teese and Polesel explain, the theoretical content, formal operations and abstract concepts of these disciplines is deliberately stressed at the "price of ever greater remoteness from the external world" (2003, 21). Biology is the one science excluded from this top tier because it is undeniably associated with the body, the material world, reproduction and 'femininity'. This is suggested by an account of biology given in a 1959 report: "The passionate interest that many girls feel in living things can be as strong an educational incentive as the love of machines. It is not for nothing that biology is the main science taught to girls, as physics and chemistry are to boys" (Crowther Report, quoted in Scott 1980, 101). Biology has long been considered less academically demanding than the other sciences. In fact, when it was first introduced into the Australian school curriculum there was debate as to whether it was a science at all (Teese et al. 1995, 62). The traditional humanities also occupy a privileged place at the top of the curriculum hierarchy. The traditional humanities tend to be Eurocentric and text based (e.g., literature), focus on pre-twentieth-century history and ideas (e.g., classics and ancient, medieval and Renaissance history) and often stress argumentation (e.g., extended argumentative essays as the dominant form of assessment). These subjects also emphasise theory (e.g., ideologies) more than action and applied knowledge, a high level of abstractness and remoteness from concrete experience (e.g., a lack of obvious vocational, practical value) and 'old', more established and certain knowledge (Teese and Polesel 2003, 24).

As we move down the curriculum hierarchy we find the modern humanities and social sciences, such as economics, geography, social studies and modern history, including Australian History (Teese and Polesel 2003, 24–25). The content of these subjects is not so easily severed from concrete experience—for example, the more obvious application of mathematics in geography and economics, or the focus on recent events in modern history and on contemporary social issues in social studies. Their content and methods are also less established and, thus, seemingly less stable and certain. The more seemingly concrete, practical, bodily a subject is, the further down the curriculum hierarchy it tends to be. Hence, the very bottom of the hierarchy is occupied by physical education, health, outdoor education and vocational subjects. These are subjects whose undeniable focus on practicality and physicality ensures their low academic and social status. Vocational subjects generally occupy the lowest position on the curriculum hierarchy, with their enrolments dominated by the most disadvantaged and marginalised students (Polesel 2008). The arts are scattered throughout the curriculum hierarchy, depending on how theoretical, abstract, established and structured their content is made to appear. More contemporary, practical, bodily art subjects tend to have a low status (e.g., drama, media arts). While music is often situated at the top of the hierarchy because it too can emphasise abstractness, theory and established, formal rules and knowledge. Thus, even the most seemingly imaginative, emotive and practical subjects are frequently taught in a way that emphasises theory, abstractness and formality.[4] This is presumably motivated by a desire to raise the status of these subjects and attract more 'academically' inclined students.

This curriculum hierarchy is associated with many educational and social problems, including some of those described earlier. One significant problem is that this hierarchy reinforces and perpetuates social hierarchies. Polesel and Teese argue that the curriculum hierarchy helps to perpetuate class and gender inequalities because the most privileged subjects are those associated with traditionally male, middle-class values (i.e., those attributes on the left of the list of dualisms), while lower status subjects are associated with traditional notions of 'femininity' and marginalised groups, including the working class and students from low socio-economic backgrounds (regardless of their gender) (Teese et al. 1995; Teese and Polesel 2003; Polesel 2008). The curriculum hierarchy also perpetuates problematic notions of knowing and thinking, and problematic ideals of the self, autonomy and society, all of which undermine the potential for truly educational schooling, meaningfulness and democracy. This is because the dualism inherent in the curriculum hierarchy means that it supports the separating of attributes and faculties that are actually interdependent and operationally co-dependent (e.g., Reason/imagination, theory/practice, abstract/concrete). Consequently, the curriculum hierarchy actually helps render all these attributes and faculties defective. Both these problems will be examined in more detail in following chapters.

Dualism is also reflected in dominant pedagogies, including the traditional teacher-centred, knowledge-transmission pedagogy. This pedagogy largely conceives of teaching as a process of depositing large quantities of discrete facts into the heads of passive students, whose main task is to uncritically accept these facts and store them away so that they can be regurgitated for assessment tasks and, possibly, used at some time in the future when the student becomes an autonomous adult. This pedagogical structure posits the teacher as an authority figure who possesses knowledge while students are seen as ignorant and dependent on the teacher. This pedagogy reflects dualism in that it assumes real knowledge is established and certain and should simply be uncritically accepted and memorised by students. It also assumes a fixed and unchanging notion of reality that students are expected to passively accept and adapt to. As such, this pedagogy also privileges content and methods that can be made to appear abstract, theoretical, very structured, formal, rule governed, absolute and universal. Methods and content that are contextual, relativistic and concrete are unsuitable because they are complex, interdisciplinary, unstable, contingent and open to interpretation and critique. Such content is not so amendable to being broken up into discrete ready-made facts that can be uncritically accepted by students. As many educational theorists have pointed out, an incongruity of this pedagogical ideal is that it doesn't scaffold the development of Reason, which is at the centre of the epistemological ideal that it assumes. Students don't have to engage in any form of reasoning because the focus is on lower-order thinking skills, especially memorisation and basic comprehension. There are several explanations for this apparent paradox. One is that it is assumed that children and young people are not capable of Reasoning well, if at all. As such, schooling must focus on providing them with the products of other people's Reasoning until they become fully rational, autonomous adults. This belief is often held in conjunction with the idea that in order to Reason well one first needs something to Reason about and, thus, students need to have their heads full of an abundance of solid facts so that when the capacity for Reason does kick in, students will be able to put it to good use (see Quirk 2005, Hirsch 1996, 1988). The criticisms of this pedagogical idea are vast, going back at least as far as Plato. Many of these criticisms will be explored in following chapters.

Some will argue that this traditional pedagogical ideal is old-fashioned and no longer widely practiced as it has been superseded by 'progressive' educational ideas, such as the ideas of Dewey and Freire. Thus, criticising traditional pedagogical ideas merely amounts to attacking a straw man. However, the influence of theorists like Dewey and Freire on classroom practice is largely overstated. Such ideas are certainly popular with educational theorists, and they are frequently paid lip service to in educational policies and curriculum documents. Yet, as many educationalists argue, they have had little impact on mainstream teaching practices or curriculum design (Yates 2011, 34; Reid 2005; Lagemann 2000; Buras 1999; Tanner 1997, 11). Such educational ideas are also widely misunderstood, including by many of the educators who claim to practice them. The detailed account of Dewey's educational ideas that will be given throughout the following chapters should make it abundantly clear that his ideas have not been widely implemented in mainstream or alternative schools.

Not only are traditional educational approaches still widespread, but they actually appear to be increasing in popularity. For example, they are reflected in 'the return to basics' and 'core knowledge' ideologies, which are popular amongst the general public, if not education academics. These ideologies emphasise all students learning the same content and skills, with a focus on students accumulating large quantities of 'facts' (e.g., Quirk 2005; Hirsch 1996, 1988).[5] Traditional educational ideas are also reflected in what McNeil (2009) calls 'the systematic approach to curriculum'. This approach stresses efficiency and accountability through prescriptive, government-mandated curricula; the rigid alignment of stated learning outcomes with curriculum content, pedagogy and assessment; an emphasis on 'basic' skills and knowledge (e.g., literacy and numeracy); and high-stakes testing. The systematic approach is currently dominating educational policies and practices in Australia, the United States and England. There is an increasingly large body of literature and research criticising this ideology (e.g., Ravitch 2010; Nussbaum 2010; McNeil 2009; Lingard 2009; Berliner 2009; Kelly 2009). This approach promotes schooling that is teacher-centred, content heavy and predictable, with many teachers simply 'teaching to the test'. Complex capacities like critical thinking, imagination and active citizenship are sidelined as the curriculum is narrowed to focus on skills and content that can be easily assessed in standardised tests, such as basic literacy and numeracy skills, the recall of facts and basic comprehension. The most efficient way to prepare students for such tests is through rote learning and drill.

Greene provides one explanation for the increasing popularity of traditional notions of schooling, arguing that they are seen as antidotes to the seemingly unstable and unpredictable nature of modern life, which is characterised by rapid technological advancements, easy access to masses of often contradictory information and increasingly globalised and multicultural communities (1995, 18). The stability of basic, core knowledge and skills is seen as more desirable than fostering critical and creative thinking and constructivist notions of knowledge, which only seem to encourage the problematisation of experience and existing knowledge, leading to further instability and complexity. Likewise, Kennedy criticises traditional schooling's "induced lack of interest in the novel, aversion to progress, and dread of the uncertain and the unknown" (2006, 18). Thus, the increasing complexity and instability of modern life strengthens the desire for certainty and the dualistic epistemological and educational ideas that accompany this desire.

It isn't just traditional pedagogy that embraces dualism. Dualism is also reflected in many so-called 'progressive' educational practices—that is, pedagogy that aims to promote learning that is more student-centred, creative, applied, collaborative, active and experiential. Even though Dewey and Freire are considered key figures in the progressive education movement, many of the teaching practices that are commonly labelled progressive bear little to no resemblance to the work of Dewey or Freire. This is because, as already mentioned, the ideas of theorists like Freire and Dewey are widely misunderstood by educators and are largely applied in a very superficial fashion. One common pedagogical practice that is commonly identified as progressive is project-based learning. In most classrooms, project-based learning involves students being given some topic or question to investigate. They are then sent to the library for a week or more worth of classes to find out as much information as they can about this topic from library books and the Internet. The information they find is then presented as an essay, report, poster or PowerPoint presentation. This is thought to be 'progressive' (i.e., student-centred) because rather than the teacher simply telling students the information, the students have to go and find the answers themselves. However, such teaching is not student-centred at all, nor does it overcome dualistic ideas of knowing and learning. Students are still just passively taking in established knowledge except that rather than getting the knowledge from the teacher they get it from another authority—books and websites. I recently heard an academic aptly refer to such activities as "hunter and gatherer missions". This is really just a more laborious, time-consuming and less effective means of depositing facts into students' heads. It is less effective because it seems to increase the likelihood that some students (e.g., those with better research, organisation and literacy skills) will acquire more knowledge than other students, whereas at least with the traditional teacher-centred approach, all students are presented with the same information. This is why many students seem to resent such teaching methods and perceive teachers who frequently use them to be lazy. Such activities don't provoke the type of critical and creative thinking, problem solving, active and authentic learning promoted by Dewey and Freire. Nonetheless, as Tanner points out, it is a common misconception that Dewey promoted, if not created, this type of project-based learning (1997, 64). Project-based curriculum was promoted by William Kilpatrick, another progressive educator from the same era as Dewey. However, even Kilpatrick's notion of project-based learning differed from the way projects are commonly used in schools today.

Other common 'progressive' practices do clearly reject traditional pedagogies and curricula. However, they don't really overcome dualism either. This is because they simply valorise or emphasise the attributes of the right-hand side of the list of dualisms, thus accepting the structure of dualism. That is, they celebrate emotionality, the imagination, the body and a relativistic, constructivist notion of knowledge. This is evident in the ideas and methods of many alternative schools, especially very liberal one's like A. S. Neil's famous Summerhill School, where classes are optional and the traditional curriculum hierarchy is reversed. Some such educational ideas have also made their way into many mainstream teaching practices. For example, it is not uncommon to hear teachers claim that when they facilitate classroom discussions they treat all students' opinions as equally valuable and correct. Thus, they assume complete relativism because they believe it is the only alternative to transmitting absolute truths into students' heads. As we shall see in the following chapters, these pedagogical practices are not educational, and they certainly do not cohere with the non-dualistic pedagogies prescribed by either Dewey or Freire.

A RESPONSE TO DUALISM: 'FEMININE' EPISTEMOLOGIES

In response to the problems of dualism, standpoint feminists have identified alternative epistemologies based on women's experiences. The term 'standpoint feminism' refers to the fact that these theorists suggest that women have some common position or standpoint, upon which a 'feminine' epistemology can be based. These epistemologies emphasise the connectedness, personal relationships, emotionality, corporeality and concreteness that is thought to characterise the feminine self.

For example, Keller draws on the methodology of geneticist Barbara McClintock in order to identify an alternative scientific method that involves the knower connecting to the known in an empathetic manner in order to let the object reveal itself in all its complexity. The relationality and empathy that characterises this scientific method gives rise to feelings of respect, responsibility and care for what is to be known, which counteract any attempts to manipulate, dominate and master the known (Keller 1985, 158–176; 1983).

Psychologist Carol Gilligan (1982) draws on Chodorow's object-relations psychoanalysis in order to explicate a distinctly feminine moral perspective, which she calls the 'care perspective'. Gilligan argues that dominant theories of moral development, particularly Kholberg's, only describe a male moral perspective, and this is why women are less likely than men to meet the highest levels of moral reasoning described by such theories. The masculine moral perspective, which Gilligan calls the 'justice perspective', emphasises abstract and universal moral principles and involves emotional and personal detachment. In contrast, the care perspective focuses on concrete relationships, care, responsibility and the particularities of moral situations. It involves an individual who empathises with others, is guided by their emotions and care for others and whose primary concern is to create and maintain open lines of communication between individuals.

Belenky et al. (1986) also draw on Chodorow to distinguish between what they call 'masculine' separate knowing and 'feminine' connected knowing. Like the justice perspective, separate knowing emphasises Reason and notions of objectivity and autonomy that involve radically distancing oneself from the objects of knowledge. Belenky et al. associate separate knowing with the doubting game where one evaluates beliefs and theories by aggressively looking for faults in them. Beliefs which withstand such attacks may qualify as knowledge. This contrasts connected knowing, which also aims at objective knowledge, but through empathising with what is to be known and letting it reveal itself as it is. Belenky et al. associate connected knowing with the believing game, where the knower tries to understand why another would hold a certain belief or opinion or why certain ideas may be correct or useful.

Such epistemologies have been widely criticised, particularly by those who adopt a postmodernist stance. Postmodernists, such as Lyotard aim to deconstruct 'grand narratives' or 'metanarratives', which are doctrines or modes of thoughts that claim to transcend personal, historical and cultural specificities and act as the foundations of other theories and beliefs (Fraser and Nicholson 1990). Dualism with its ideal of Reason, is one such grand narrative. Reason is claimed to be a universal human faculty that legiti-mises all other knowledge claims. However, as feminists and postmodern-ists have argued, it reflects the interests and experiences of a particular group of individuals, namely, white, Western, heterosexual, middle-class men. Standpoint epistemologies respond to this grand narrative by identi-fying a specifically feminine epistemology; however, Fraser and Nicholson argue that they too end up creating a type of 'quasi-metanarrative'. Such epistemologies suggest a universal and essential category of woman based on what are actually the experiences of mostly white, Anglo, middle-class, heterosexual women (1990, 26–27). Fraser and Nicholson specifically criticise those theorists who utilise Chodorow's psychoanalysis because her theory of gender development is based on the activity of mothering, which is too culturally, socially and historically specific to be the basis of a universal category of woman. Thus, notions of femininity derived from mothering will suppress differences between women (Fraser and Nicholson 1990, 28–29). Epistemologies based on these notions of femininity have the potential to marginalise women who do not adhere to them. This problem was made explicit by Lorde (1984) and Hooks (1981), who claimed that much Anglo-American feminism was racist because it claimed to speak on behalf of all women when it really reflected only the experiences of white, middle-class, heterosexual women, who ignored their own situatedness and the fundamental differences between women.

Not only may such feminine epistemologies be essentialist and exclusive, as Alcoff points out, they also legitimise ideals of femininity that are associ-ated with women's oppression (1995, 439). These feminine epistemologies are correct in their refusal to accept the illegitimate exclusion of valuable attributes like empathy and connectedness. However, an uncritical accep-tance and valorisation of such attributes as essentially feminine is equally problematic. The relegation of women to the private, domestic sphere has been justified by claims that women have a natural propensity for caring, sustaining interpersonal relationships and manual labour. Arguing that women's thinking emphasises care, connectiveness, practicality and the concrete could simply reinforce the assumption that childcare and house-work are women's work. It must be remembered that the dominant ideal of femininity is as much a patriarchal construction as hegemonic masculinity and it has obvious negative connotations (Code 1991, 17).

Finally, such feminine epistemologies also deny women access to poten-tially valuable epistemic tools, such as formal logic, abstract concepts, gen-eral principles and reasoning. These epistemologies are thought to entail opposing, incompatible epistemologies for men and women, forcing indi-viduals to choose between one side or the other of the dualistic table. By not questioning the division of different epistemological attributes along gender lines, the notion of a distinct feminine epistemology perpetuates the radical polarisation and hyperseparation that characterises dualism. This is problematic because dualism is itself patriarchal. Couldn't reconstructed, non-patriarchal versions of reason, objectivity, abstractness, the emotions, imagination, relationally, connectedness and the concrete have epistemological value for all people? As Hass and Falmagne argue, "the traditional dichotomy between the man of reason and the emotional woman would need to be rethought in terms of a more complex single human subject, able to reason *and* feel, to exist independently *and* in relation" (2002, 2).

A RESPONSE TO DUALISM: OPERATIONAL CO-DEPENDENCY

While I agree with the above criticisms made of the notion of a specifically feminine epistemology, I'm not convinced that such criticisms actually apply to many of the scholars they have been directed towards Keller, Gilligan and Belenky et al. actually appear to be recommending alternative epistemologies that do indeed aim to dismantle dualism and traditional gender stereotypes. For example, while Gilligan and Belenky et al. claim to have identified specifically 'feminine' ways of thinking and knowing, they do not actually prescribe these as ideals that should be celebrated and perpetuated by women or anyone else. Rather, they prescribe alternative perspectives that emphasise how traditionally denigrated feminine epistemological traits are actually interconnected with aspects of traditional, masculine epistemological ideals. For example, Gilligan's care and justice perspectives are only intended to be descriptions of what she sees as differences within men's and women's moral reasoning. Contrary to some criticisms of her work, she doesn't prescribe either one as an ideal of moral reasoning but rather argues that effective moral reasoning involves an integration of aspects of both the care and justice perspectives. By themselves both perspectives are inadequate and problematic. Similarly Belenky et al. are critical of both 'feminine' connected knowing and 'masculine' separational knowing, which they state are both types of procedural knowing. Procedural knowing aims at a problematic and undesirable notion of objectivity. The epistemology they prescribe is constructed knowing, which aims to integrate aspects of both these methods of knowing. Keller also states that the dynamic notions of autonomy and objectivity exemplified by McClintock are not intended to be specifically feminine ideals.

Thus, these feminist epistemologies actually aim to dismantle dualisms and gendered forms of knowing. As we shall see, such integrated, non-dualistic epistemologies are superior because they include all that is epistemologically valuable, regardless of what gender and epistemic status it has traditionally been assigned. Since dominant epistemological ideals and the pedagogies based on them incorporate dualism, they are impoverished and are actually counterproductive to the acquisition of knowledge and learning. In the following chapters, Dewey and various feminist theories will be drawn on in order to outline, in more detail, the epistemological, educational and social problems to which these dualisms give rise and to describe a more comprehensive, non-dualistic epistemology and pedagogy. It will be shown that P4C largely incorporates these non-dualistic ideals and, as a consequence, facilitates optimal and more inclusive ideals of thinking, subjectivity, autonomy, citizenship and learning. However, first we must have a general understanding of the many interrelated aspects of Dewey's philosophy upon which P4C is based.

2 Dewey's Community of Inquiry
A Response to Dualism

Even though Dewey's notion of communal inquiry is highly influenced by scientific methods of inquiry, it is not subject to the criticisms that Keller and other feminist epistemologists have made of dominant scientific ideals and traditional empiricism. Dewey himself was critical of traditional empiricism's inherent dualism. In this chapter, an overview of Dewey's interrelated theories of knowledge, meaning, democracy, community, autonomy, dialogue, experience, imagination, emotion, thinking and education is provided. The psychological theory of Lev Vygotsky will also be drawn on in order to extend and develop Dewey's notions of thinking, community and the self. These Deweyan ideals will be further elaborated on in later chapters, particularly as they have been taken up and developed by Philosophy for Children (P4C). Dewey's notion of experience is central to his notion of communal inquiry, which is central to his entire philosophy. Thus, Dewey's theory of experience is a good place to begin. This will provide the basis for analysing other aspects of Dewey's theory of inquiry, including the non-dualistic ideals of community, self, philosophy and education that this notion of inquiry entails.

REFLECTIVE EXPERIENCE

Dewey accepts the basic empiricist doctrine that all thinking is necessarily dependent on having experiences. However, he rejects the passive, dualistic notion of experience implied by traditional empiricism. As we have seen, this notion of experience describes a passive mind receiving random, fragmented sense stimuli caused by the external world. Rather, Dewey argues that experience involves an embodied and intentional mind consciously interacting with its environment. Not just any action upon the world constitutes an experience. For Dewey, an experience is an activity which has consequences that affect us in such a way that we *learn* something from it. Dewey uses the example of a child who puts his finger into a flame and burns it. This action itself is not an experience. Rather, the act combined with the realisation that this action causes pain or burning is the experience

(2004a, 133–134). Thus, an experience involves something *we do* as well as something that we *undergo*. It is both *active* and *passive*. We may be able distinguish between the active and passive dimensions of experience upon reflection for the sake of analysing the experience. However, in actuality, the active and passive dimensions of experience are entirely interdependent and interconnected.

This type of experience necessarily involves thinking or reflection. In order to render an action meaningful and respond to it appropriately, one must make a connection between the act itself and the consequences that flow from it. The very recognition that there is a connection requires some degree of *thought*. This is why Dewey states, "No experience having a meaning is possible without some element of thought" (2004a, 139). Experience that involves not only the recognition of a relationship between an action and its consequences, but also a detailed understanding of the nature of that relationship is more meaningful and intelligent. Dewey contrasts such experience to the method of trial and error where we do something and, if our action fails, we simply try something else until we find something that works. Such action is less controlled, less purposeful and less valuable than action that involves an understanding of the relationship between the action and its consequences. In fact, such action can even be dangerous because any of the actions we thoughtlessly try may have very negative consequences. In contrast, the type of experience Dewey describes may involve predicting and expecting that particular consequences will follow from particular actions. As Dewey states, such experience involves judgment because it involves taking some things as evidence that other things will follow (2004a, 140). This makes it possible for us to have purposes, aims or what Dewey calls "ends in view". When we understand why certain consequences follow from particular actions, we may be able to cultivate the conditions necessary for bringing about desired consequences and eliminate those conditions that make our actions ineffective (2004a, 139–140). Dewey calls such experience "reflective experience" in order to distinguish it from the less thoughtful method of trial and error (2004a, 139). In reflective experience, we are able to interact with our environment in a more purposeful, intelligent and meaningful manner. For Dewey, this notion of reflective experience is synonymous with thinking or inquiry (2004a, 145).

Thus, Dewey rejects the Reason/experience and mind/body dualisms implied by traditional empiricism, arguing that thinking is an essential part of experience as it unfolds. It is not some distinct process that follows the experience and renders it meaningful. This account of experience also overcomes mind/world and subject/object dualism and the focus on separation between the knower and known that characterises dominant epistemic ideals. In reflective experience, the subject doesn't separate themselves from the world in order to avoid affecting, or being affected by, an 'external' world. Rather, subject and object, knower and known, mind and world interact in such a way that mutual transformation takes place. The subject acts upon the world and undergoes the consequences of this action and, as a result, learns how to further interact with the world. By looking at the different aspects of the inquiry (i.e., thinking) process in more detail, we can more fully appreciate how Dewey's notion of reflective experience overcomes these dualisms.

REFLECTIVE EXPERIENCE AS INQUIRY

Selecting a Problematic Situation for Inquiry

Dewey believes that inquiry is initiated when we are exposed to a situation that we find confusing, conflicting, obscure or indeterminate in some way. Part of what makes a situation problematic is that some of its constituents are missing, unclear or the connections between its parts are obscure (1938, 105–107). Such situations interrupt our habitual interaction with the world, disrupting our established beliefs. They are, at least momentarily, meaningless to us, and we cannot automatically respond to them in a purposeful, intelligent manner. Consequently, we judge such situations to be problematic and inquiry is initiated as the means by which we reconstruct "an indeterminate situation into one that is so determinate in its constituent distinctions and relations as to convert the elements of the original situation into a unified whole" (1938, 104–105).

However, mere exposure to an indeterminate situation doesn't necessarily initiate reflective thinking. One may simply ignore the situation or be unmoved by it. In order for us to want to reconstruct a situation through inquiry, we must actually judge the situation to be problematic for us. A situation will be problematic for us is if it stands in the way of our achieving something we desire, are interested in or need (Dewey 2004a, 142). Thus, Dewey rejects traditional empiricism's claim that experience is random sense stimuli imposing itself upon the sensory organs of a disinterested spectator. He argues that experience is intentional and selective. We assess the ability of certain situations to provide us with experiences that are useful or desirable. Perception is an aspect of agency rather than the passive acquisition of sense data. It involves an agent with interests and needs moving out towards the world in an intentional manner. The selective nature of experience is most conspicuous in the well-known notion of selective hearing. We may be within close proximity to another and speak directly to the person, but if the intended recipient of the communication is not interested in what we have to say because they are absorbed in some other activity then they will literally not hear us. This doesn't apply just to hearing but to all the senses, including vision.[1] The selective nature of reflective experience also draws attention to the role that thinking, specifically judgment, plays in experience. As Dewey explains, "Judgment is employed in perception; otherwise the perception is mere sensory excitation or else a recognition of the result of a prior judgment, as in the case of familiar objects" (2004a, 138).

If reflective experience is selective, then it follows that one's emotions and physical needs also play an important role in thinking. Our emotional and physical responses to situations indicate to us which situations may be useful, valuable and problematic to us. They help us formulate judgments about which experiences are worthy of our attention. Thus, Dewey also rejects the Reason/emotion dualism. His account of the emotions is strikingly similar to the account given by many feminist epistemologists, such as that given by Jaggar:

> Just as observation directs, shapes, and partially defines emotion, so too emotion directs, shapes and even partially defines observation. Observation is not simply a passive process of absorbing impressions or recording stimuli; instead, it is an activity of selection and interpretation. What is selected and how it is interpreted is influenced by emotional attitude. (1989, 154)

The relationship between the emotions and inquiry is also one of interdependency. Like Jaggar, Dewey adopts what is often referred to as a cognitivist theory of emotion. According to cognitivist theories, having an emotional response to a situation involves the capacity to evaluate the situation or make a reasoned judgment about it. As Jaggar explains, in order to feel pride about some action, I must judge the relevant experience to be one worthy of pride. If I feel pride in a situation that is not worthy of pride, my emotional response is unreasonable and ineffective. It is ineffective because it may result in me believing I have done something well when I have not, and this mistaken belief will likely result in me interacting with world in an unproductive manner—for example, I may fail to adjust my behaviour and attitude so as to improve myself in the way that I probably would have if I had realised that my original action was actually not very successful and not worthy of pride. Thus, the emotions contain thought, especially judgment, which enables intelligent emotions that are relevant, meaningful and useful for guiding action. In turn, the emotions enable individuals to select problematic experiences to be reconstructed through inquiry. In Chapter 4, we will look at Dewey's theory of emotion in detail and at the role that the emotions play in communal inquiry and education.

Setting the Agenda for Inquiry

Once an experience has been selected for inquiry, there must be a careful articulation of the problem. This includes a clarification of the desired consequences that the indeterminate situation is stopping one from achieving. We can then formulate the problem as a series of questions that will need to be answered in order to bring about the desired consequences. This enables us to set the agenda for the inquiry and give it a clear direction and purpose. Setting the agenda should also suggest some possible solutions or means of bringing about the desired consequences (2004a, 145). The importance of agenda setting is nicely articulated by Dewey:

> To find out *what* the problem and problems are which a problematic situation presents to be inquired into, is to be well along in inquiry. To mistake the problem involved is to cause subsequent inquiry to be irrelevant or go astray. Without a problem, there is blind groping in the dark. The way in which the problem is conceived decides what specific suggestions are entertained and which are dismissed; what data are selected and which rejected; it is the criterion for relevancy and irrelevancy of hypotheses and conceptual structures. (1938, 108)

Since our emotions influence the selection of problematic situations to be reconstructed through inquiry, they also influence the desired outcome of inquiry and the possible means for bringing about this outcome. Thus, the emotions play an important role in setting the agenda for inquiry and in creating a problem solution. This role of the emotions is also implied by Jaggar's comment that "feminist emotions provide a political motivation for investigation and so help to determine the selection of problems as well as the method by which they are investigated" (1989, 161).

Formulating a Problem Solution

The articulation of the problem enables the formulation of a problem-solution. As mentioned, what makes the situation problematic is that some of its constituents or the relationships between them are unsettled, missing or obscure. However, some of them must be settled and observable for one to even select the situation as relevant. Thus, the first step towards developing a problem-solution is identifying and making sense of the constituents that are observable. These constituents are what Dewey calls the "facts of the case" (1938, 109). They suggest possible solutions by indicating what constituents are missing or unsettled and need to be reorganised. They also restrict the possible solutions for the problem, as any solution must take account of these facts.

However, since a solution must fill in what is missing or obscure in the problematic situation, it must go beyond the facts of the case. The solution aims to bring about a desired situation that does not yet exist: a situation in which the incomplete, problematic situation is a reconstructed, unified whole (Dewey 1938, 109). Thus, the imagination plays an important role in the inquiry process. The imagination enables us to go beyond what is given in actual experience and imagine alternative possibilities and means for realising them. Hence, Dewey's account of thinking overcomes the Reason/

imagination dualism inherent in dominant epistemological constructs. Dewey rejects the common belief that imagination is an obstacle to thinking, pointing out that if we merely observed the given facts of the case without imagining some alternative possibility, we would not actually be able to reconstruct the problem:

> Careful observation and recollection determine what is given, what is already there, and hence assured. They cannot furnish what is lacking. They define, clarify and locate the question; they cannot supply its answer. Projection, invention, ingenuity, devising come in for that purpose. The data *arouse* suggestions, and only by reference to the specific data can we pass upon the appropriateness of the suggestions. But the suggestions run beyond what is as yet, actually *given* in experience. They forecast possible results, things to do, not facts (things already done). Inference is always invasion of the of the unknown, a leap from the known. (2004a, 152)

Evaluating Tentative Solutions Through Reasoning

However, the reflective thinker cannot immediately and uncritically accept any idea suggested by the facts of the case. The solutions that are most obvious or immediately suggested may be inadequate, problematic or inferior to other possible solutions. Thus, the immediate suggestions aroused by the data need to be critically evaluated. Although he often appears to use the terms interchangeably, Dewey distinguishes between *suggestions* and *conjectures*, on the one hand, and *ideas*, on the other. While suggestions are more immediate and vague, ideas are suggestions that have been developed and subject to critical analysis. As Dewey explains, "Every idea originates as a suggestion, but not every suggestion is an idea. The suggestion becomes an idea when it is examined with reference to its functional fitness; its capacity as a means of resolving the given situation" (1938, 110).

In order to develop conjectures into workable ideas, the reflective thinker must "cultivate a variety of alternative suggestions", which need to be critically compared and evaluated (Dewey 1997, 75). This ensures the suspension of judgment and the further investigation and development of competing suggestions. This involves a search for further facts or reasons to reinforce or eliminate a suggestion until it can be confirmed through testing and application. In particular, we critically assess different suggestions by considering what consequences would follow from them if they were applied. Dewey reserves the term 'reasoning' specifically for the inferences we make in order to trace out the implications of a suggestion (1997, 75–76; 1938, 110–112). Tracing out the implications of a suggestion enables us to make other observations or look for facts that lend support to this suggestion or eliminate it as a possibility. A useful example of this reasoning process is provided by Dewey. A man returns home to find his house ransacked, and two possible explanations are immediately suggested: either he has been burgled, or his children have made a mess, as they often do. He considers the implications of being burgled as opposed to the children having made a mess. One implication is that certain valuable items will probably be missing. This possibility suggests further observations to be made, namely, that he check to see if the items are in fact missing. From the fact that they are missing, combined with previously observed facts (the state of the room), the man infers that his original idea that he has been burgled is the more warranted belief (1997, 82–83). Hence, the originally very tentative suggestion that he has been burgled has been reworked into a more definitive and justified idea.

Thus, developing a problem solution involves observing the facts of the case to see what possible solutions they suggest, considering what the implications of these immediate suggestions would be if they were applied to the problem, making further observations to search for evidence of these implications and connecting these observations back to previously made observations. Through this process, immediate suggestions are affirmed, eliminated or modified until a judgment can be made about which one best unifies and organises the facts of the case into a coherent whole. If a suggestion can't account for the facts of the case, it should be transformed or rejected and an alternative considered. If a suggestion has some ability to clarify and unify the fragmented constituents of the situation, then it will enable us to have a new perception of the situation and for the inquiry to progress until an idea emerges that will enable the problematic situation to be reconstructed into a coherent whole (Dewey 1938, 113).

Thus, creating a problem solution involves creating abstract ideas or theories that go beyond the concrete facts of the case. However, the observable facts of the case also act as provocations, criteria and justifications for these ideas (Dewey 1938, 112–114). This counters the abstract/concrete dualism that characterises dominant Western epistemology. As we have seen in Chapter 1, thinking is traditionally conceived of as a purely abstract process. However, in this Deweyian account of the inquiry process, abstract ideas and the concrete facts of the case interact, informing one and other of a potential solution. Neither one would be fully functional in inquiry without the other. As Dewey states, "[P]erceptual and conceptual materials are instituted in functional correlativity with each other, in such a manner that the former locates and describes the problem while the later represents a possible method of solution" (1938, 111).

Testing Ideas and Making Judgments

The reasoning process enables us to make a judgment about the best idea or solution. However, this judgment is still only tentative. It enables us to formulate a plan to test the selected idea. By testing the idea out before applying it to the real situation, we can reduce the possibility of failure or of any unforeseen negative consequences that the idea may produce. Testing the idea also enables us to improve good ideas prior to applying them. Once the idea has been successfully tested, it must actually be applied or used as intended. Dewey argues that it is really only once an idea has been enacted that we can make a final judgment about its ability to reconstruct the problematic situation into a unified whole. Thus, inquiry is not complete until we have actually observed the idea working as intended. Prior to this, the assumed or expected facts are merely "trial facts" (Dewey 1938, 114). Possible solutions remain merely ideas until they have been successfully used to bring about the expected consequences. Once ideas have successfully been applied, they can be called 'knowledge' or 'warranted belief'.

It follows that all inquiry is *practical*, in that it involves the testing of ideas and their application to concrete situations. Thus, Dewey also rejects the theory/practice dualism that characterises dominant Western epistemology. As we have seen in Chapter 1, practicality is associated with concrete particularities and physical activity and consequently is considered incompatible with the idea of absolute and universal knowledge. In contrast, Dewey argues that all thinking involves a reciprocal interaction with one's environment. The inquirers adapt the environment to suit their needs and purposes. However, they simultaneously adapt their own habits, beliefs, actions and interests in order to respond to the situation appropriately. Thus, all thinking is simultaneously practical, theoretical, concrete, abstract, emotional, imaginative, cognitive and corporeal.

MEANING AND KNOWLEDGE

It is through this process of inquiry that meaning and knowledge are acquired. The meaning of an idea is its use or purpose in bringing about intended consequences. As we have seen, in inquiry, ideas are created and used to reconstruct problematic situations. If experimentation and application of an idea reveal that it does indeed reconstruct a problem as intended, then we have ascertained the meaning of the idea. Dewey argues that knowledge is synonymous with establishing the meaning of something, stating that "a known object, a thing understood, a thing with a meaning—all three being synonymous expressions" (1997, 137). Thus, to know something is to understand how to use it to bring about certain consequences. Knowledge is the outcome and goal of inquiry. This pragmatist definition of knowledge is basically a tautology. As Dewey explains, "That which satisfactorily terminates inquiry is, by definition, knowledge; it is knowledge because it *is* the appropriate close of inquiry" (1938, 8).

Knowledge is not only the outcome of inquiry; it also enables future inquiry. The knowledge we posses is a kind of meaning store which we draw on in order to reconstruct problematic situations into meaningful wholes (Dewey 1997, 118). As we have seen, some parts of a problematic situation must be settled and understood in order for us to reconstruct the situation. The reason some things are immediately understood is because we are familiar with them from our past experience, that is, we have prior knowledge of them (1997, 119). Thus, we draw on our knowledge store to select and interpret experiences, imagine ends in view and create possible means for bringing them about. As Dewey states, inquiry involves "the ability to bring the subject matter of prior experience to bear to perceive the subject matter of a new experience" (2004a, 329). The greater our meaning store, the more alert we are to other problems in our environment. Thus, knowledge provokes further inquiry, which gives rise to a constantly expanding meaning store. This continuous building of knowledge and meaning is what Dewey means by the "the constant spiral movement of knowledge" (1997, 120).

In contrast to dominant epistemological ideals, Dewey believes that knowledge is acquired through a process of inquiry that is practical, concrete, corporeal and emotional. However, this doesn't render knowledge subjective. Inquiry is a process of reconstructing concrete experiences, and these experiences have subjective and objective elements. As we have seen, a problematic experience is judged to be problematic because it stands in the way of some needs or interests that the individual has. Thus, an idea that works must work to satisfy the needs and interests of the inquirer. This suggests that knowledge is merely relative or, more specifically, subjective. However, since a problematic situation is one that has some of constituents missing, obscured or fragmented, there are also objective conditions that ideas must take account of in order to be effective and, thus, counted as knowledge. One's emotions and interests should also be responses to the objective facts of situations, otherwise they are pathological and useless for reconstructing experience (see Chapter 5). Thus, the problematic situation is subjective-objective, and an effective idea or knowledge is also subjective-objective because it must reorganise this subjective-objective situation in order to work and bring about desired results. A more detailed account of Dewey's rejection of both subjectivism and objectivism will be given in Chapter 3.

While Dewey's epistemology doesn't amount to subjectivism, it does entail the rejection of the notion of absolute, universal and certain knowledge assumed by dominant Western epistemology. Dewey, along with the other pragmatists, accepts a type of fallibilism. This is because to know something is to know what use or purpose it has in a particular concrete situation. However, an idea that is effective and meaningful in one particular situation may fail to be so in some future situation or in a different context. It is always possible that future experience may problematise previous knowledge claims, forcing us to revise them. Dewey argues that inquiry is continuous because nothing is ever so settled and certain that it may not be subject to future revision and nor is such settlement necessary for knowledge claims to be valuable:

The "settlement" of a particular situation by a particular inquiry is no guarantee that *that* settled conclusion will always remain settled. The attainment of settled beliefs is a progressive matter; there is no belief so settled as not to be exposed to further inquiry. It is the convergent and cumulative effect of continued inquiry that defines knowledge in its general meaning. In scientific inquiry, the criterion of what is taken to be settled, or to be knowledge, is being so settled that it is available as a resource in future inquiry; not being settled in such a way as not to be subject to revision in further inquiry. (Dewey 1938, 8–9)

While inquiry doesn't provide us with absolute knowledge and certainty, it can provide us with understandings that are settled enough to enable meaningful interaction with our environment. The traditional association between knowledge and absolute certainty is one of the reasons Dewey actually preferred the term "warranted assertibility" to the term "knowledge" (1938, 8–9).

While Dewey rejects absolutism, he recognises the value of general and objective knowledge. In order for knowledge to be transferable, we must be able to abstract it, to some degree, from particular, concrete experiences. This is not a regress to traditional epistemology which devalues the concrete, subjective and particular. For Dewey, ultimately knowledge is that which works to reconstruct concrete experiences as intended. By rendering knowledge more objective and general, we render it more useful to more people in more diverse concrete situations. Any abstracted, generalised knowledge must always be brought back down to earth and applied to concrete problems to be of any value. The process of abstraction and generalisation must not aim to transcend the concrete particularities of embodied experience, as this would render the ideas useless as guides to effectively interacting with our environment, which is the whole point of inquiry and knowledge in the first place.

COMMUNITY, CULTURE AND OBJECTIVITY

Knowledge is rendered more abstract, objective and general when it is made more common or intersubjective. Common meanings result from the fact that our environment is a social one that requires us to co-ordinate our actions with others. Through conjoint activity, which necessitates communication, things acquire common, more objective meanings. A conjoint activity is an activity in which there is a common problem, the desired consequences are shared by all involved, and the best means to attaining these consequences are co-operatively performed and reflected upon (Dewey 1958b, 177–179). Through repeated conjoint use of a thing we achieve, what Dewey calls, "agreement in action" (1938, 46). Conjoint activity requires that individuals communicate their aims, beliefs and understandings in order to co-ordinate their actions. Communicating an experience, aim or idea involves describing it in a way that explicates its functional value for us as well as for others. Thus, through communication, objects and events take on new properties and meanings. They are transformed into something more general and objective because their meaning is common to at least two people. As Dewey explains,

> [Language] compels one individual to take the standpoint of other individuals and to see and inquire from a standpoint that is not strictly personal but is common to them as participants or "parties" in a conjoint undertaking. It may be directed by and towards some physical existence. But it first has reference to some other person or persons with whom it institutes *communication*—the making of something common. Hence, to that extent its reference becomes general and "objective". (1938, 46)

It is through the making of common meanings that culture is created. Culture is the pooling of a society's common knowledge, beliefs and practices. Thus, culture includes science, art, religion, technology, schooling, public institutions, law, political systems, social values, family structures, domestic practices, industry and, most importantly, language (1939, 6). Culture sets humans apart from other species. It crosses times and spaces, allowing societies to build on and reconstruct the knowledge of past generations, rather than having to start again when each generation dies out (2004a, 3; 1938, 43). Understandably, Dewey argues that language is the most fundamental cultural product(1938, 45).[2] This is because it is not only a product of culture but is also the means for producing culture because it enables the communication needed for conjoint activity.

Since communication renders knowledge more common and objective, communal inquiry is the most ideal form of inquiry. In communal inquiry, we collaboratively investigate a shared problem, test out ideas and co-operatively reconstruct experience. We can make suggestions, which others may support, develop or counter, causing us to reflect on our own position and either support it with evidence, provide further explanations or revise it. We must empathise with others in order to understand their point of view and adjust ours accordingly. Ideas that are not acceptable to the community are developed, revised or even rejected and replaced until some agreement is reached. Thus, knowledge that results from such communal inquiry is more general and objective because it has been tried and tested in a wider, more diverse field of experience. As such, it is more reliable in the sense that it is more likely to work and be meaningful for different people and in different situations. Thus, communal inquiry reduces the chances of our generalising and imposing beliefs and ideas on others that are actually only useful to ourselves.

It should be evident that these Deweyan notions of objectivity, abstractness and generality bear little resemblance to the dualistic notions inherent in the dominant epistemological ideal. First, as we have seen, the notion of pure objectivity, completely devoid of subjectivity, is rejected. Second, objectivity, abstractness and generality are matters of degree. They are not absolutes. Knowledge that is the outcome of a diverse, intercultural inquiry is *more* objective and general in that it is more likely to integrate diverse cultural experiences (Dewey 1938, 45–46). However, even this more objective knowledge maintains the subjective attributes and cultural backgrounds of those who participated in the inquiry and of the subjective attributes inherent in any existing knowledge and cultural tools used in the inquiry. Thus, this notion of objectivity does not involve the transcendence of subjectivities; rather, it is the integration, transformation and broadening of subjectivities. It is the result of subjectivities interacting in a transformative manner that gives rise to new meanings that go beyond anyone individual but are still reflective of all the individuals who participated in the community of inquiry. Thus, objectivity is intersubjectivity. As we shall see in Chapter 3, this notion of objectivity as intersubjectivity is strikingly similar to the ideal of objectivity described by many feminist epistemologists, notably Code's notion of "mitigated relativism" (1991, 320) and Harding's ideal of "strong objectivity" (1991, 149). Like Dewey, these feminist epistemologies reject the dominant assumption that the situatedness and subjectivity of concrete experience are obstacles to objectivity, arguing instead that ideas are made more objective by being exposed to more diverse concrete experiences.

DIALOGUE AND THE DEVELOPMENT
OF THINKING AND THE SELF

Not only is communal inquiry superior to private thought; it is a precondition of it. Dewey argues that all thinking has its origins in social interaction, particularly dialogue. However, he doesn't fully explain how dialogue gives rise to thinking. His account of the social origins of thinking is highly compatible with Vygotsky's influential theory of self-development. Vygotsky argues that thinking has its basis in biology, as it requires basic physiological abilities like sensory motor skills. He adds that higher-order mental functions, including reflective thinking, develop as a result of social interaction. Thus, thinking is cultural, as well as biological.

Vygotsky rejects traditional psychological theories that take individual psychological processes, what he refers to as *intrapsychological* functions, as basic. He emphasises the importance of *interpsychological* functions, which occur when individuals engage in social interaction. Vygotsky rejects the theory of individual psychological reductionism, which asserts that the processes that characterise social interaction can be reduced to, and explained in terms of, individual psychological processes. For Vygotsky, interpsychological functions have properties that exist independently of, and prior to, intrapsychological functions.

Vygotsky also argues that intrapsychological and interpsychological functions are interrelated. He believes that participants in social interaction internalise processes of the interaction. These internalised social processes become psychological functions. For example, Vygotsky noticed that when trying to solve problems, young children talk to themselves in the same way that individuals talk to each other in conjoint activity so as to give each other directions, encouragement, discouragement and co-ordinate their actions. By talking to themselves in this manner, children are able to more intelligently control and guide their action. Hence, this egocentric speech is children thinking aloud. Eventually we cease to verbalise these thoughts, but our thinking maintains a like structure and purpose. According to Vygotsky, egocentric speech, like all thinking, is the internalisation of communication with others. By engaging in activities with others that they could not perform by themselves, children internalise the habits and dispositions necessary to perform these tasks independently. Vygotsky refers to the space between what children can do with others and what they can do by themselves as the "zone of proximal development". This is the space in which children learn to act and think independently by being "scaffolded" or supported by others (1978, 104). The process of internalisation is not merely a process of transferring the social to the psychological. Through internalisation, interpsychological functions are transformed, taking on new properties (1978, 27). This is why social functions and psychological functions are not identical or reducible to one and other. Vygotsky argues that psychological functions maintain a "quasi-social" structure due to their origins in social interaction (Wertsch 1985, 66).

The quasi-social nature of thought is apparent if we consider the nature of reasoning. As Vygotsky explains, "[I]t is the collision of our thought with the thought of others that engenders doubt and calls for verification" (1978, 47–48). When we encounter others with differing perspectives, we are provoked to critically reflect on our own beliefs, compare alternatives and search for reasons to justify our beliefs to others, or we self-correct in light of criticism or better alternatives provided by others. The internalisation of this process gives rise to independent thinking, which has a similar structure. This idea is suggested by Dewey's pragmatist colleague Charles Sanders Peirce, who argues that private thought involves us providing reasons and explanations to convince our critical self that we should accept a particular belief or idea:

> [A] person is not absolutely an individual. His thoughts are what he is saying to himself, that is, is saying to that other self that is just coming into life in the flow of time. When one reasons, it is that critical self that one is trying to persuade. (quoted in Sharp 1993, 4)

Influenced by Peirce, Dewey develops this account of thinking further when he argues that *logical* principles and forms originate in dia*logue* or communal inquiry. As will be explained in more detail in Chapter 3, Dewey rejects the notion that logical principles are absolute "*a priori* principles fixed antecedently to inquiry and conditioning it *ab extra*" (1938, 12). He argues that logical forms accrue to subject matter in communal inquiry and are disclosed to us when we reflect upon the process of inquiry itself (1938, 4). While logical principles are not absolute and a priori ideals, they have an objectifying affect on inquiry. Communal inquiry is not possible unless there is some agreement about acceptable methods of inquiry. The inquirers must agree that certain thinking moves are acceptable and useful, while others are not. As such, logic provides common criteria that inquirers can use to compare and evaluate each other's ideas and reasoning. Thus, it's not just the diversity of experiences in communal inquiry that renders knowledge more objective and general but also the dia*logical* nature of communal inquiries.

Thus, like Vygotsky, Dewey argues that the capacity to think for oneself is the result of our internalising the logical moves and processes which characterise dialogue. He describes thinking as a type of internal dialogue, arising from communication with others:

> [S]oliloquy is the product and reflex of converse with others; social communication not an effect of soliloquy. If we had not talked with others and they with us, we should never talk to and with ourselves . . . Thus mind emerges. (1958b, 170)

However, he maintains that "soliloquy is but broken and imperfect thought", reiterating that communal inquiry is not only the original mode of thought, but the superior mode (1927, 218). Something of the communal inquiry process is lost when it is transformed through the process of internalisation into private thought. As both Dewey and Peirce argue, dialogue or communal inquiry is superior to private inquiry because it integrates multiple perspectives and, consequently, leads to knowledge that is more objective, reliable and useful.

It is through the process of internalisation and the development of thought that the self grows and becomes increasingly autonomous. Dewey's notion of experience has its basis in Darwin's idea of an organism adapting itself and its environment in order to flourish and survive. When an individual is unable to respond to a situation in such a way as to have their needs or desires met, they not only transform their environment but also adapt their impulses, dispositions, beliefs and actions so that they will co-operate with the environment and produce desired ends. Those actions, ideas, beliefs and dispositions, which the individual finds useful for reconstructing experience, are internalised or incorporated into the self. The individual will also try to transform or eliminate from the self those actions and beliefs that are unsuccessful for achieving its ends. Through this process of internalisation, individuals develop habits, which enable them to interact with the world more effectively, efficiently and meaningfully. As Dewey explains, habits constitute the self and guide our further selection and reconstruction of experience:

> All habits are demands for certain kinds of activity; and they constitute the self. In any intelligible sense of the word will, they are the will. They form our effective desires and they furnish us with working capacities. They rule our thoughts, determining which shall appear strong and which shall pass from light into obscurity. (1930a, 25)

Growth is the constant development and transformation of habits (2004a, 47). Growth is continuous because with every experience, the individual and their environment are changed, which in turn causes the individual to interact with the world differently. Consequently, the individual then encounters more unfamiliar situations needing reconstruction, leading to further experience and growth.

If the self develops through the constant reconstruction of experience then the capacity for thought is essential to self-development. As we have seen, it is thought or inquiry that enables us to meaningfully reconstruct experience. The capacity for reflective thinking enables us to have greater self-control and control over our environment. It enables us to transform our habits and our environment in a more effective and purposeful manner. Since thinking has its origins in social interaction, self-development and autonomy is dependent on community.

Dewey rejects the notion of self assumed in dominant Western epistemological ideals, which emphasises rugged individualism and separation from others (see Chapter 1). He describes a communal ideal of self that is interdependent and interconnected with others. This notion of self incorporates many of the attributes of the connected self described by some feminist philosophers and psychologists (see Chapter 1). Dewey rejects the assumption that connectedness and interdependency are obstacles to autonomy and independence, arguing instead that they are actually preconditions of it. This communal notion self and autonomy is developed in more detail in Chapter 6.

DEMOCRACY AND EDUCATION

Communal notions of self and knowing can be problematic. As many philosophers have pointed out, notably Young (1986), communities can also be sites of oppression. This is because communities often require the suppression and exclusion of difference. Dewey also recognised the oppressive potential of communities, arguing that only democratic communities facilitate growth and intersubjective meanings (2004a, 78). He describes a democracy as a community that has "more numerous and more varied points of shared common interest" as well as "greater reliance upon the recognition of mutual interests as a factor in social control" (2004a, 82). For example, democracies have shared interests that are moral, aesthetic, economic, epistemic and political, and so on. A community that shared only a few common interests, say economic interests, must rely upon some external means of forcing community members to co-operate in regards to non-economic matters. Thus, there would be less need for communal inquiry, which leads to growth. For there to be a large number of diverse, common interests, there "must be a large variety of shared undertakings and experiences", which give rise to intersubjective meanings (2004a, 80).

Another attribute of democratic communities is that they have a "freer interaction between social groups" which leads to "continuous readjustment through meeting the new situations produced by varied intercourse" (Dewey 2004a, 82–83). Thus, the members of democratic communities not only engage in communal inquiry with each other, but they also purposefully engage in inquiry with other communities. Such interaction gives rise to new situations, which lead to reconstruction and growth. This enables the community itself to grow and become more inclusive of differences. As Dewey explains, communities that shut themselves off from other communities aim to protect their past customs and traditions, which can mean that they are often oppressive, exclusive and unable to adequately respond to change (2004a, 76, 82). Thus, Dewey argues that divisions along class, race, cultural and gender lines are obstacles to inquiry, growth and knowledge (2004a, 82). Normally, when Dewey uses the term 'community', it is in this honorific sense. That is, he treats 'community' and 'democracy' as synonymous terms and excludes despotic or segregated societies from the category of community altogether.

It is important to note that these criteria for democracy are not essentialist, a priori ideals. Dewey developed them by extracting the desirable attributes of existing communities (2004a, 79). He believes that these criteria are general and objective because they have been tried and proven successful in many diverse contexts. However, since they are derived from, and applied to, concrete experience, they are not static and absolute but rather subject to ongoing reflection, adjustment and improvement. Social and moral values, laws, institutions, political systems and so on should not be imposed on individuals from above. They should grow out of individual's common experiences. Consequently, community members will find such ideals more achievable, meaningful and useful and will have an interest in the implementation and development of them.

The development of democratic communities requires the "deliberate and systematic education" of all individuals (Dewey 2004a, 83). Since democracies are opposed to control through external coercion and authority, they must facilitate the types of attitudes, skills and understandings that members of democratic communities exhibit. That is, they must facilitate the development of individuals who are willing and able to engage in varied communal inquiries with diverse others. It is in schools that such dispositions can deliberately be facilitated.

Not only is democracy dependent on education; education is mutually dependent on Dewey's conception of democracy. A democratic community is the mode of associated living most facilitative of inquiry and growth. The fundamental goal of education is to facilitate the continuous reconstruction of experience. This is because the capacity to effectively interact with our ever-changing environment is essential for living a meaningful and happy life and for growth. Growth is not just an aim of education but also the means to education, because it is through the reconstruction of experience (inquiry) that we acquire the habits, knowledge and skills, especially communal inquiry skills, required for the continuous reconstruction of experience. This is why Dewey states that growth is both the means and goal of education (2004a, 48). Since a democratic community is most facilitative of growth, it is also the most educative form of social life.

It is because Dewey believed that philosophy has this same goal as education—to promote a democratic way of life—that education was central to Dewey's entire philosophy. Dewey argues that "philosophic problems arise because of widespread and widely felt difficulties in social practice" (2004a, 314–315). The problems of philosophy result from our concrete interactions with our socio-cultural environment. Thus, like education, the aims of philosophy should be to describe and facilitate the most intelligent forms of conduct or ways of interacting with one's environment, and it is in schools that moral and mental attitudes can best be transformed and developed. The relationship between education and philosophy is eloquently expressed by Dewey in *Democracy in Education*:

> If we are willing to conceive of education as the process of forming fundamental dispositions, intellectual and emotional, toward nature and fellow man, philosophy may even be defined as *the general theory of education*. Unless a philosophy is to remain symbolic—or verbal— or a sentimental indulgence for a few, or else mere arbitrary dogma, its auditing of past experience and its program of values must take effect in conduct. Public agitation, propaganda, legislative and administrative action are effective in producing the change of disposition which a philosophy indicates as desirable, but only in the degree in which they are educative—that is to say in the degree in which they modify mental and moral attitudes. And at best, such methods are compromised by the fact that they are used with those whose habits are already set, while education of youth has a fairer and freer field of operation. (2004a, 315)

This is why Dewey thought of schools as laboratories for testing and implementing philosophical ideals (2004a, 316). Hence, the name of the experimental school he founded at the University of Chicago: the Laboratory

School. Since Dewey argues that the most intelligent and efficient way of interacting with one's environment is through the type of diverse, communal inquiry that characterises democracy, he outlines a pedagogy and curriculum that promotes this ideal.

If schooling is to facilitate this Deweyian ideal of communal inquiry, it cannot merely involve the transference of established facts and information from teacher or textbook to student. In fact, the still dominant knowledge transmission model of schooling effectively blocks student inquiry because it doesn't provide students with problems to reconstruct through inquiry. As Dewey explains,

> This static, cold-storage ideal of knowledge is inimical to educative development. It not only lets occasions for thinking go unused, but *it swamps thinking*. No one could construct a house on a ground cluttered with miscellaneous junk. Pupils who have stored their "minds" with all kinds of material which they have never put to intellectual uses are sure to be hampered when they try to think. They have no practice in selecting what is appropriate, and no criterion to go by; everything is on the same static level. (2004a, 152, italics added)

Since thinking begins with concrete experiences that are unsettled, fragmented, doubtful or problematic in some way, at least some curriculum content must be presented as if it is open, unsettled and contentious (2004a, 148). This will enable students to undertake their own inquiry and create their own ideas, even if they only rediscover knowledge and methods that are already well known by others (2004a, 153).

However, it is not enough to simply provide students with random problems to be worked through purely for the purpose of acquiring some particular skills or knowledge. Dewey makes a distinction between genuine problems and the mock problems that characterise traditional schooling. Genuine problems are the type of problems that would arise in real situations or personal experiences, and consequently they will give rise to knowledge and skills that can be transferred to situations beyond the school. Most importantly, a genuine problem is the pupil's own problem. It is not a problem for the student because they must solve it in order to pass an assessment or gain teacher approval. A genuine problem is one that the student desires to work through in order to gain meaning and make sense of their own experiences (Dewey 2004a, 149–150). In order for students to find some subject matter problematic and worthy of inquiry, it must be connected to the students' current experiences, needs and interests. Furthermore, if the subject matter is not connected to a students' current and past experiences, they will have no understandings, tools, resources, or suggested ideas that will enable them to reconstruct it (2004a, 157).

If the meaning of an idea is its use, then students must literally use ideas to reconstruct their experiences in order to fully understand and appreciate the ideas. Thus, Dewey also rejects the passivity of traditional education. He argues that practical activity is a necessary part of all learning, not a hindrance to it, as traditional pedagogies would have us believe. This is the other sense in which Dewey saw schools as types of laboratories, because students should test out and apply ideas. This is not equivalent to saying that applying knowledge helps students make use of already acquired knowledge. As we have seen, without the ability to physically alter the environment and control one's behaviour, one cannot be said to have knowledge at all. To know a thing is to have tried and tested it in concrete experience.

These ideas were effectively implemented at the Laboratory School, where the curriculum was famously organised around the theme of social occupations (Tanner 1997, 60–62). Students at the school learnt through participating in practical, everyday activities, such as sewing, gardening, cooking, carpentry, running a shop, mapping activities, science experiments, art activities, photography and so on. The aim was to promote the collaborative working through of real-life, everyday problems. This curriculum enabled students to develop manual skills, communication and social skills, and inquiry skills in a manner that emphasised the interrelatedness and interdependency of such skills in the process of reconstructing experience.

The emphasis on skills doesn't mean that students at the Laboratory School didn't also learn the knowledge encapsulated in the traditional academic disciplines. It is a popular misconception that Dewey and the laboratory school didn't value the acquisition of knowledge from the traditional academic disciplines. For example, Hirsch (1996) mistakenly attributes such a view to Dewey. Neither Dewey's theoretical ideas nor the Laboratory School's curriculum and pedagogy privileged the concrete, practical and physical over the abstract, theoretical and cognitive. As we have seen, Dewey rejects such dualisms. At the Laboratory School, theory and knowledge were integrated with the practical activities, enabling students to fully perform all the aspects of inquiry. Teachers first identified concepts, information and skills they wanted students to learn, and then identified concrete experiences and activities that would require students to learn such concepts, information and skills. They then carefully constructed the conditions that would facilitate such learning activities. Thus, as Tanner states, contrary to popular belief, "Dewey's curriculum was a structured curriculum" (1997, 26). Furthermore, inquiry-based activities were not the only pedagogical techniques used in the school. When necessary, the teachers utilised a wide range of pedagogies to compliment the practical tasks, including discussion, research, writing, fieldtrips, teacher explanation and demonstration and even, in some cases, plain old-fashioned drill (see Tanner 1997, 48, 64, 77, 87–88). This is explained by one of the Laboratory School teachers in relation to a task where students were building a spinning wheel:

> In connection with Miss Harmer's work they needed to know the ratio of revolution of the small to the large wheel in spinning. They got the

diameter of the large wheel and worked out the circumference and divided it by that of the small wheel, using the rule that the circumference is approximately 3 and 1–7 times the diameter, which they had used in finding the contents of a globe last fall. The numerical work involved division of fractions, and as they were rusty in this, an hour was spent in practice. (Georgia Bacon, 1898–1899, quoted in Tanner 1997, 77)

One of the reasons social occupations were chosen as the unifying curriculum theme was that it enabled students to learn important historical, scientific, geographical, social, mathematical and cultural facts and information at the same time that they were learning to engage in collaborative inquiries to solve authentic problems (Tanner 1997, 60). Rather than rote learning traditional subject knowledge in the traditional, teacher-centred manner, students learnt disciplinary knowledge in a concrete, contextualised way. They would learn about how such inventions, knowledge and facts were created or discovered so as to solve social problems and satisfy human interests and needs. As Dewey explains,

> In educational terms, this means that these occupations in the school shall not be mere practical devices or modes of routine employment, the gaining of better technical skill as cooks, seamstresses, or carpenters, but active centres of scientific insight into natural materials and processes, points of departure whence children shall be led out into a historical realisation of the development of man. (1990, 19)

For example, students at the laboratory school learnt the progress of the textile industry from primitive societies to their modern industrialised society (Tanner 1997, 60–62; Dewey 1990, 19–23). Students carried out the different tasks and activities associated with textile manufacturing during different stages of history. This enabled them to develop practical skills, such as weaving and sewing, farming and even how to build a spindle and loom. However, students also acquired important historical and geographical knowledge, such as understanding how people moved from farms and into towns and eventually big cities as the development of machines meant that textile manufacturing moved out of the private, domestic sphere into village spinning mills and eventually into big city factories. They also learnt about economics and industry, such as how society has moved from individuals producing whole garments to the division of labour that characterises factory work, as well as the transition from homemade garments to localised industry and then international trade. Tasks like building, sewing and weaving, and buying and selling textiles also required students to learn various mathematical skills and knowledge, such as measurement and arithmetic. Through designing garments, students also developed various artistic and design skills and knowledge. The preparation of raw materials (e.g., dying and steaming) enabled students to acquire scientific knowledge, such as knowledge of various chemical processes. Learning about and using various textile technologies, students also learnt about the physics involved in the machinery of production. One of the benefits of this type of curriculum is that it inevitably leads to a synthesising of the academic disciplines because real world problems and experiences require individuals to draw on knowledge and methods from diverse fields (Tanner 1997, 50, 82).

Such learning renders the content learnt more meaningful and valuable. Students come to understand the value and application that different knowledge and methods have in different social contexts. Such learning is also more likely to be engaging for students because it creates a need to know. At the Laboratory School, students acquired knowledge and skills because they *needed* them in order solve authentic problems and effectively interact with their environment. As Dewey explains, "[T]he occupation supplies the child with a genuine motive; it gives him experience at first hand; it brings him into contact with realities" (1990, 22). This is not the case with traditional teacher-centred pedagogies, where students are required to memorise fragmented and abstract ideas and processes. This is why such teaching depends on extrinsic motivations, such as grades, teacher approval, fear of punishment and various disciplinary measures.

While inquiry, the creation of meaning and growth can result through reconstructing individual experiences, the co-operative reconstruction of shared experiences is fundamental if students are to develop inquiry skills and common meanings, and thus grow. As we have seen, social interaction gives rise to dialogue, which in turn gives rise to thinking through the process of internalisation. In conjoint activities students are less likely to accept the first ideas or understandings that come to mind. This is because there is more likely to be several alternative responses given by different students. Students will be forced to critically evaluate these alternatives, leading to reasoning and the development of ideas that are more thoughtful and objective. In collaborating to solve a common problem, students practice and develop the communication skills, attitudes and values associated with the democratic way of life. This is why Dewey states,

> The educator is responsible for a knowledge of individuals and for a knowledge of subject-matter that will enable activities to be selected which lend themselves to social organization, an organization in which all individuals have an opportunity to contribute something, and in which the activities in which all participate are the chief carrier of control. (1963, 56)

Dewey adds that the teacher must also be a member of classroom communities, as opposed to an outsider who disseminates facts and regulates and controls student behaviour: "It is absurd to exclude the teacher from membership in the group. As the most mature member of the group he has a peculiar responsibility for the conduct of the interactions and intercommunications which are the very life of the group as a community" (1963, 58). As a more mature, skilled and knowledgeable community member, the teacher is needed to model desirable skills and behaviours, make thought provoking suggestions, ask important questions that provoke inquiry, help keep the activity on track and contribute a different perspective to the articulation of the problem and the search for solutions.

Dewey's educational ideas are not perfect. I don't believe that he fully realised his own philosophical and political ideas through his theories of curriculum and pedagogy or through his work at the Laboratory School. This is because he didn't fully allow students to engage in the type of social reconstruction that he prescribed as essential for both individual growth and democracy. Through re-enacting various social situations and performing various social occupations, one would expect students to become aware of, and concerned about, existing social problems and injustices. For example, the textile industry lessons may provoke a consideration of problems, such as: the division of labour in modern factories and the sense of meaningless this can produce for workers; the potential exploitation of workers by business owners; overcrowding in cities as a result of industrialisation; the demise of small villages; the exploitation of Third World nations; overproduction, waste and environmental degradation; materialism in modern life; and so on. There is evidence that students did consider some such problems at the Laboratory School. However, what opportunity was there for students to engage in an in-depth critical examination of such contemporary social problems and undertake some kind of transformative action in response to them? By enabling students to experience and re-enact the conditions and situations that gave rise to such problems, such a curriculum is likely to provoke students to genuinely care about these issues. It seems problematic to then deny students any opportunity to undertake some kind of transformative action in response to them. Even if this transformative action were restricted to the embryonic school community itself (e.g., taking action to create a more environmentally sustainable school), this would be an empowering experience for students and a more accurate enactment of Dewey's notion of inquiry as social reconstruction. Perhaps the Laboratory School did allow for some such action, but there certainly doesn't appear to have been a deliberate effort to foster such learning experiences, and this is incongruent with some of Dewey's own educational and philosophical ideas. It suggests that students are still only future citizens or citizens in the making not yet ready to participate in, and shape, their social cultural environment. It also weakens the connection between the school and the wider community, as students have little opportunity to respond to some of the real, contemporary social problems that exist beyond the school.

Such learning experiences are particularly important to secondary school students. While the Laboratory School was also attended by secondary school students, a lot of the curriculum, especially the projects and activities, seem more appropriate for younger students. While some of the practical activities were suited to secondary students, one suspects that many older students would be unenthusiastic about running a kitchen garden or a shop, building a club house or re-enacting primitive civilisations. Older students maybe more intrinsically motivated and capable of engaging with purely theoretical or text-based learning. However, Dewey's theory of inquiry means that individuals of all ages ought to be engaged in practical activities because all inquiry involves action. Dewey did not believe that practicality and hands-on learning was only for young students because they are more concrete thinkers. It seems that older students should be inquiring into more complex, authentic social problems and engaging with communities that are more complex and diverse than the embryonic school community. Yet there are few examples of this happening at Dewey's Laboratory School.

Some form of service learning would have been a valuable addition to the Laboratory School. It would have enabled students to participate in collaborative inquiries as a means to transforming current social problems, as opposed to students just re-enacting inquiries already performed by others and re-discovering, for themselves, existing knowledge. The later certainly has a place in the curriculum too and is necessary if students are to learn important knowledge and skills in a meaningful manner. Service learning would extend on such learning, leading to curriculum and pedagogy that more fully realises Dewey's educational ideas. Such learning would particularly benefit secondary school students (those aged 12 and above). Just as school content and skills should get more sophisticated and complex as students progress through their schooling, so should the practical activities and the communal inquiries that students participate in. This could be supported by allowing older students to extend their activities beyond the embryonic community of the school into the larger, more complex community outside of the school.

Another weakness with Dewey's theory of education is that although he placed communal inquiry at the centre of his ideas of curriculum and pedagogy, he never considered the potential benefits of adding philosophy to the school curriculum. Surely, the teaching of philosophy would have something to contribute to schooling focused on the development of effective thinking? Perhaps he thought thinking skills would naturally develop as a result of students being given problematic situations to collaboratively reconstruct. However, as we have seen, teachers at the Laboratory Schools still needed to explain and demonstrate maths and language skills as they were needed by students to solve problems. It wasn't just assumed that students would automatically learn to read and write well because a problematic situation necessitated such skills. Isn't there a similar need for the teaching of thinking skills or capabilities? Dewey himself recognised the importance of logic in developing the capacity for inquiry. Logic enables metacognition—thinking and talking about the process of thinking itself, which is essential for identifying and developing effective thinking moves, as well as for identifying and avoiding faulty thinking moves or procedures. Surely some study of logic could also benefit students' development of the capacity for inquiry. Other areas of philosophy, such as ethics, political philosophy, metaphysics, aesthetics and epistemology, also seem to contain invaluable knowledge and methods that one needs to effectively interact with their socio-cultural environment. It is for such reasons that Nussbaum argues that Dewey's ideas about teaching critical thinking "are in need of supplementation" and she suggests that P4C may be able to provide such supplementation (2010, 73).

Thus, Dewey's ideas may appear to be more fully realised in P4C than in his own pedagogy. Dewey's theory of communal inquiry is the basis of the P4C pedagogy: the Community of Inquiry. P4C involves transforming the classroom into a community of philosophical inquiry. Some of the benefits of philosophy as a subject matter include its highly contentious nature, which provokes inquiry, and its metacognitive aspect, which provides students with tools and a language for inquiring into the procedures of inquiry themselves. In the following chapters, it will be shown that P4C's classroom community of inquiry is a model of Dewey's ideal of democracy and it incorporates and promotes his anti-dualistic philosophy. P4C is a pedagogical ideal that Dewey himself would probably have approved of. However, in Chapter 8, it will be argued that P4C is also inadequate for realising Dewey's epistemological and political ideals because it fails to facilitate the practical aspect of thinking and learning that is so fundamental in Dewey's philosophy. P4C falls into the trap of emphasising the theoretical and dialogical at the expense of action and practicality. It will be shown that this problem can be overcome if P4C is integrated with a critical, social justice type of service learning. This reconstructed P4C curriculum and pedagogy should be better able to realise Dewey's desirable non-dualistic philosophy than can either Dewey's own educational ideas or traditional approaches to P4C.

3   A Response to Absolute/ Relative Dualism

Truth and Meaning in Dewey and Philosophy for Children

Different notions of truth and knowledge imply and encourage different ideals of thinking and learning. In this chapter, we will examine the notions of truth, knowledge and meaning assumed by Philosophy for Children (P4C) and the educational implications of these notions. There is considerable disagreement amongst P4C theorists and practitioners about whether the Community of Inquiry implies either relativism or absolutism. However, both relativism and absolutism are incompatible with P4C, as neither can facilitate the desirable Deweyan notions of *reflective thinking, community, care, open-mindedness, empathy* and *meaningfulness* that P4C aims to promote. It will be argued that relative/absolute dualism gives rise to classroom practices that are not educational, and P4C's rejection of this dualism is one of the reasons it is superior to many other pedagogies.

P4C adopts a middle-ground position between relativism and absolutism. This middle-ground theory of truth can be found in the work of Dewey and other pragmatists, as well as in the work of contemporary feminist epistemologists, notably Lorraine Code and Sandra Harding. A middle-ground theory incorporates the best aspects of both of these positions: relativism's emphasis on the constructed, subjective, cultural, social and historical nature of truth claims; and absolutism's emphasis on critical thinking, objectivity, general principles and the need to communicate across cultures, times and spaces. This middle-ground position rejects the dominant dualistic view that the attributes associated with relativism and absolutism are incompatible. Rather, it assumes that such attributes are operationally co-dependent in the process of acquiring knowledge and meaning. Before I outline the educational value of P4C's epistemological ideals, I will examine the educational problems that result from assuming either relativism or absolutism. This will enable an understanding of how P4C's middle-ground position overcomes these educational problems.

THE PROBLEM OF ABSOLUTISM IN EDUCATION

I will use the term 'absolutism' to refer to the view that there are truths that are eternal and universal. This position assumes that there is some fixed, objective reality and that truths are statements, propositions or beliefs that accurately represent or correspond to this reality. Consequently, truths are absolute and universal. Insofar as we have access to the truth, such an ideal of truth implies that we have some purely objective method of knowing, which allows us to know this reality as it 'really' is, independently of our own interests, needs and situatedness. In Chapter 1, it was explained that Reason has long been considered the only method by which individuals can transcend or suppress their situatedness so as to discover absolute truth. As previously explained, such ideals of truth, reality and reason have dominated Western epistemology and culture because they are thought to provide us with certainty.

Absolutism is associated with the traditional, teacher-centred, knowledge-transmission model of education, which emphasises the accumulation of facts. If truth or knowledge is absolute and universal, then it is also complete, settled and unproblematic; as such, once absolute truths have been discovered by one person, they can simply be transmitted to others (Dewey 2004a, 320). Inculcating students with these supposedly indubitable facts is thought to provide students with the cultural knowledge that they need in order to effectively participate in their society. It is also thought to benefit society by ensuring that our most important bodies of knowledge and cultural traditions are maintained and passed from one generation to the next. As we have seen, this educational ideal is most overtly promoted by those who argue for a 'return to basics' approach to schooling and those who defend the idea of core knowledge curricula, such as Quirk (2005) and Hirsch (1988, 1996). This educational ideal holds that a good education is one that deposits indubitable knowledge into students' heads in the "most direct and efficient manner" (Benjamin 1978, 311). As Golding explains, the most efficient and effective way of transferring such indubitable knowledge from one generation to the next is rote learning (2005b, 5). In the traditional classroom, it is assumed that absolute truths are known by the teacher and described in textbooks. Thus, all students must do is acquire them by listening, reading and memorising. Hence, Hirsch's frequent praise for student's memorising large quantities of content (e.g. 1989, 30)

Freire famously referred to this knowledge transmission model of education as "banking teaching" because teachers simply *deposit* ready-made truths into student's heads (1993, 53). Banking teaching discourages students from thinking for themselves because they are required to passively receive the products of someone else's thinking. Because such knowledge is supposedly complete and unproblematic, it is not open to criticism and reconstruction. There is simply no need for thinking if the truths are absolute and have already been discovered (Lipman 2003, 18). In this pedagogical framework, students who dare to question established facts or suggest alternative interpretations may be punished for disrupting the learning progress or penalised on assessment tasks that merely require them methodically memorise and recite absolute truths.

Not only does such schooling fail to facilitate thinking, it renders the material learnt meaningless for students. In order to appear absolute, universal and unproblematic, school subject matter must be abstracted from the contexts in which it originated. This enables it to be efficiently transferred to students as uncontentious, discrete facts. This is why the proponents of traditional educational ideas often display open hostility towards ideologies like feminism, pragmatism and postmodernism, which posit that truth and knowledge claims are concrete, contextual and constructed. If these ideologies are correct, knowledge cannot be decisively abstracted from the concrete experiences and contexts that it originated in, nor can it be entirely separated from the interests of those who constructed it. Thus, it could not be transmitted to students as discrete, simple, ready-made facts because this notion of knowledge entails there are multiple, complex, culturally relative bodies of knowledge that are contentious and open to criticism. This is reflected in Quirk's (2005) hostile attack on those he calls "education reformers" (i.e., anyone who opposes the knowledge transmission pedagogy he promotes):

> Over the last forty years they [reformers] have labored to undermine the concept of knowledge transmission, relentlessly promoting social changes that trash the very concept of a shared tradition of knowledge: They demand that we celebrate "diversity" and discard the "melting pot" . . . They endorse the anti-truth philosophies of "postmodernism", "deconstructionism", and "constructivism". All these reject the traditional belief that different people can come to the same shared understanding of subject matter. These theories say that all knowledge is inherently subjective, a matter of personal opinion, and impossible to share.

While abstracting knowledge from concrete experiences renders it easy to transmit to students, it also renders it irrelevant and meaningless by disconnecting it from the very contexts that give it meaning and value. This problem is explained by Freire:

> The teacher talks about reality as if it were motionless, static, compartmentalized, and predictable. Or else he expounds on a topic completely alien to the existential experience of the students. His task is to "fill" the students with the contents of his narration—contents which are detached from reality, disconnected from the totality that engendered them and could give them significance. Words are emptied of their concreteness and become a hollow, alienated and alienating verbosity. (1993, 52)

If truths are presented as abstract, fixed and universal, students will be unable to adapt and apply them to make sense of their own lived experiences. Student's own interests and unique experiences are considered irrelevant to learning because the truths acquired in school are supposed to apply equally to everyone, regardless of age, race, class, gender, culture and individual peculiarities. However, when students can't connect ideas and theories to their own experiences and understandings, they appear meaningless and unimportant (Splitter and Sharp 1995, 71–72).

Freire, Dewey and many others have argued that banking teaching is dehumanising and oppressive because it doesn't enable students to autonomously transform reality or construct their own meanings. They have no ability to shape their socio-cultural environment in accordance with their needs, interests and understandings. Rather, banking teaching is a form of external social control that supports cultural imperialism. With banking teaching, students learn to conform to dominant ideals and assumptions, even if these ideals are actually biased, problematic or meaningless. Their minds are moulded to fit the dominant culture's supposedly fixed, universal and unproblematic representation of reality. As Freire explains, "The more students work at storing the deposits entrusted to them, the less they develop the critical consciousness which would result from their intervention in the world as transformers of that world" (1993, 54).

The banking concept of schooling is clearly incompatible with P4C, which is specifically designed to encourage students to think for themselves by meaningfully reconstructing their experiences. P4C encourages students to problematise, question and critique ideas and situations, transforming and using them to fulfil their own needs and make sense of their own experiences. In banking classrooms, there are no problematic ideas and situations, only complete, ready-made truths, which someone else has already discovered.

It has been argued that absolutism can be compatible with teaching students to think for themselves because students can be made to discover absolute truths. Students may be presented with subject matter as if it is open-ended, problematic and contentious even when it is actually assumed to be settled. However, as Gardner argues, if students sense that inquiry is merely a process of rediscovering known, established truths, they may resent having to undertake an unnecessary inquiry (1995, 45). Thinking itself may seem unimportant if most of the truths appear to have already been discovered and are not subject to revision or transformation. Furthermore, students aren't likely to have much success at discovering absolute truths in response to highly contentious or problematic subject matter, such as the problems explored in philosophy and social studies. If students were expected to find absolute truths to the problems dealt with in philosophy, they would most likely come to see the inquiry process as ineffective and/or philosophy as meaningless. If absolute truth is what is ultimately valuable, and thinking is only a means to discovering absolute truths, students and teachers will probably prefer banking teaching, which is a far more efficient and effortless means of acquiring absolute truths (Golding 2005b, 5). In fact, this seems to be the very reason why many students do prefer banking teaching to the inauthentic problem solving tasks they are often given in school.

Even if students did discover absolute truths for themselves, their thinking would still be directed towards definite answers that remain immune from criticism and transformation. This is why the claim that students first need to memorise a lot of established knowledge before they can engage in critical thinking is nonsensical (e.g., Hirsch 1996, 142–143; Quirk 2005). If the memorised knowledge is so established and universal that it warrants being uncritically memorised by all students in the first place, why would students later feel the need to critically reflect on it? Surely, critical reflection is permanently discouraged by such an ideal of knowledge. This is particularly problematic given that what passes for absolute truth often reflects dominant values and interests. If the truths students are guided to discover have been pre-selected by the dominant culture and are considered exempt from criticism, learning remains a type of indoctrination and cultural imperialism. Furthermore, students are still not encouraged to transform these absolute truths in order to connect them to their own particular experiences and interests. Such a pedagogy still fails to promote P4C's aim of enabling students to actively shape and make sense of their world (Lipman, et al., 1980, 85).

Absolutism also undermines P4C's emphasis on fallibilism, self-correction and continuous inquiry. Absolute truths are true for all time and in all places. Thus, once one believes they have acquired the absolute truth about some issue, inquiry is complete and further reflection is unnecessary (M. Matthews 1980, 24–25). If students believe that absolute truth is the outcome of inquiry, they will seek out conclusions that appear to be perfect, fixed, universal and settled. Anything less will appear inadequate. The search for perfect solutions can discourage students from acknowledging problems, uncertainties or limitations with their own ideas and the ideas of others. This concern is raised by Golding, who uses the term 'truth' when he actually seems to be describing 'absolute truth':

> In a truth directed approach we lack the motivation to keep exploring the issue or question that is available in a meaning directed system. We seek final answers, truth and certainty. Once we have them, we stop. When confronted by a puzzle we either get an answer and then we can stop, or if there are no obvious answers, we may feel baffled or confused and so give up. Either way we have no motivation to keep learning. If what we value is truth, then questions and problems are to be avoided by finding the right answer, and failing that, by giving up. (2005b, 6)

Absolutism is also associated with authoritarianism, dogmatism and an aggressive argumentative style, which is inconsistent with the caring, open-minded, collaborative thinking of P4C's Community of Inquiry. If one believes that they know the absolute truth, they are justified in believing that this knowledge should be accepted by everyone. Thus, those who believe they know the absolute truth are more prone to defending and endorsing their beliefs in an aggressive and dogmatic manner. Michael Matthews raises this issue in his critique of Plato's absolutism, which he associates with dogmatism and authoritarianism because it implies that "those who have been up the mountain and have had insight can feel justified in legislating for the spread of their insight" (1980, 24).[1] As such, absolutism "might limit our abilities to listen and attend to the other" and be open to alternative opinions (Turgeon 1998, 20). This can counter the development of a caring, trusting community where students are open to, and respectful of, alternative perspectives, and where each student feels safe and free to participate.

Problematically, absolutism is also associated with an intolerance for cultural diversity. As we have seen, absolute truths are truths that supposedly transcend differences of class, race, gender, age, religion, time and place. The assumption of absolutism could make students insensitive to the way that truth claims, including their own, are influenced by subjective, cultural and historical conditions. Absolutism also entails that there is some universal, culturally neutral pedagogy and curriculum that is equally suitable for all students. In actuality, educational practices and standards usually reflect the interests and values of the dominant culture, while failing to account for various cultural, gender and racial differences in learning and thinking styles and values (see Buras's [1999] critique of Hirsch). This is one of the reasons why students from marginalised groups are often seriously disadvantaged in mainstream schooling (see Chapter 7). The ideal of a universal pedagogy is incompatible with P4C's emphasis on inclusiveness, diversity, and having procedures that are always open to criticism and reconstruction.

THE PROBLEM OF RELATIVISM IN EDUCATION

Because of the prevalence of dualistic thinking, relativism is often considered the only alternative to absolutism. Relativists deny that there is a knowable, static reality and, consequently, deny the possibility of absolute, universal truth. According to relativism, truth is constructed and relative to particular cultures, times, places or individuals. Subjectivism is the narrowest form of relativism. Subjectivists reject absolutism's notion of a disembodied, impartial and purely objective inquirer. They argue that we are entirely incapable of transcending or suppressing our own situatedness and interests. Thus, even if there is some ultimate, fixed reality, we are not able to know it as it 'really' is. Rather, all experience and inquiry is conducted through our personal interests, values and embodied situatedness. Consequently, truth claims reflect the individuals who *construct* them. It follows that there are no objective standards with which to compare different representations of reality and all opinions and beliefs are equally true.

Subjectivism is associated with student-centred and constructivist pedagogies, which come under the broad umbrella of progressive schooling. Subjectivism implies that the teacher's beliefs and opinions are no more truthful than those of students (Wilson 1986, 89). Consequently, subjectivist pedagogies don't exhibit the authoritarianism and indoctrination associated with absolutism. Subjectivism may also seem to necessitate independent thinking. If truth is constructed and relative to individuals, then students must construct their own truths. Furthermore, if all truth is subjective and constructed, then all truth is open to revision and further inquiry. Unlike absolutism, subjectivism implies that students can actively reconstruct their world in accordance with their own interests and understandings. It is for such reasons that many teachers, especially 'progressive' educators, claim to promote some form of subjectivism, particularly in relation to classroom discussions. That is, they believe that in classroom discussions there are no right or wrong answers, and students are freely able to express their own opinions and construct their own meanings.

Since P4C is a more student-centred pedagogy that emphasises students constructing meaning, there is a common misconception that P4C embraces subjectivism. While subjectivism enables students to construct their own truths, it doesn't necessitate the Deweyian notion of reflective thinking assumed by P4C. In fact, it doesn't actually necessitate any ideal of thinking. As Gardner points out, if all ideas are equally truthful, then there isn't any need, or objective basis, for critically evaluating the beliefs of others or critically comparing alternatives ideas. There is also no need for individuals to provide reasons or evidence for their own beliefs because others have no basis for doubting or criticising them in the first place (1995, 39; see also Laws 2006, 2009). This is clearly incompatible with P4C. In P4C's Community of Inquiry, students' beliefs are exposed to the differing views of others, which problematises them, and this is intended to provoke students to critically reflect on and justify their beliefs or self-correct. In the Community of Inquiry, reflective thinking emerges as a means of evaluating and comparing alternatives. Hence, Law's claim that philosophy in the classroom is actually well placed to combat subjectivism (2009, 47).

Subjectivism is also incompatible with fallibilism (Schleifer 1996–1997, 32). This also renders subjectivism incompatible with P4C, which embraces pragmatism's fallibilist epistemology. According to subjectivism, there aren't any false beliefs because what makes an idea true is simply that someone believes it. If every belief is as true as any other, then there is never any need to self-correct. Individuals may change their mind as often as they want, but this would be entirely up to them. This contrasts the P4C classroom, where it is expected that students will be *compelled* to self-correct when reasons or alternative ideas render a current belief false or inadequate.

Since subjective truths incorporate the needs and interests of students, they would presumably be more useful and meaningful to students than abstract, absolute truths. However, the ideas and beliefs that students formulate will only be useful and meaningful if students can use them to effectively interact with their environment. For a belief to enable a student to effectively interact with their environment, it must account for constraints and limitations that extend beyond the student's own mind, including other people, physical constraints, and cultural beliefs and values. There are obviously beliefs, values and worldviews that are unrealistic, unfruitful and consequently going to lead to problems, not just for the students themselves, but also for the other people and the environment that students interact with.

There are also certain facts, methods and values that students do need in order to live meaningful lives. As Gregory states, we cannot allow students to make their way through life "without learning, for example, norms we have constructed for hygiene, nutrition, literacy, justice, and art appreciation" (2002, 401–402). For example, P4C aims to provide students with the capacity for philosophical communal inquiry, which it deems necessary for students to intelligently interact with their socio-cultural environment. However, according to subjectivism, all pedagogical methods and subject matter merely reflect the interests and values of particular individuals and groups. Thus, there is no objective justification for schools endorsing any particular ideals, methods or subject matter over any other. According to subjectivist pedagogies, endorsing any particular methods or subject matter is just a form of indoctrination and cultural imperialism. While we do not want to indoctrinate students by depositing 'absolute' truths into their heads, we need to be able to provide them with a critical and fallible understanding of the practices and norms of their society, many of which are contained within the academic disciplines (Gregory 2002, 401; Wilson 1986, 94–95).

Subjectivism's emphasis on individual differences also conflicts with P4C's emphasis on community and common meaning. In a Community of Inquiry, there must be some common problems for the participants to jointly inquire into. There also needs to be some agreement on what is reasonable and ethical. However, subjectivism implies that individuals are trapped within their own minds or bodies and are disconnected from the world beyond them, including others, whom we really only perceive from our own situatedness. According to this view, schooling and inquiry would presumably only be a means of gaining a greater awareness of one's personal interests, experiences, values and ideas. Thus, subjectivism implies an individualism that is incompatible with P4C's focus on community.

Subjectivism is also incompatible with P4C's focus on the development of a caring, empathetic and open-minded attitude. Since subjectivism claims that every opinion is as valid as any other, it is thought to promote democracy, egalitarianism and tolerance and respect for differences (Wilson 1986, 93). However, simply tolerating and accepting different views and beliefs isn't the same as treating them with care and respect. Open-mindedness, care and respect for other's ideas is characterised by making a concerted effort to understand them and being willing to be transformed by them. If all opinions are equally true and valuable, then students have no compelling reason to listen to or empathise with others (Gardner 1995, 39). In fact, according to subjectivism, you could not really understand and empathise with others even if you wanted to because you can only perceive others from your own biased and tainted perspective. Thus, subjectivism doesn't necessitate that students develop caring, trusting and transformative relationships with others.

Perhaps the most serious problem with subjectivism is that it renders inquiry pointless and meaningless. A Community of Inquiry that assumed subjectivism wouldn't make any progress or produce anything of value, such as more common or objective truths. As Gardner states, "[I]f the discussion never goes anywhere, if it remains mere conversation that touches first on one topic and then another, the worthiness of the process will never be reinforced by the worthiness of the product" (1995, 38–39). It could be argued that the value of communal inquiry is just that it provides participants with greater self-awareness. However, as Gardner explains, such a claim still implies objective truth because "it implies a standard; it means that participants are in a *better* position than they were before the discussion began" (1998, 79). If the standards were subjective, too, we would have no grounds for encouraging students to inquire and learn once they decided that they were personally satisfied with their own level of understanding. Really, subjectivism legitimises delusional thinking, rather than genuine self-awareness. If subjectivism is true, I can believe whatever I like about myself and no one else would have any basis for questioning my perception of myself.

There are less extreme forms of relativism that might be considered more educational and compatible with P4C. Cultural relativists argue that truth is relative to whole cultures or communities as opposed to individuals. Since members of the same communities have common understandings and practices, especially language, they can have a common conception of reality. Thus, in contrast to subjectivism, cultural relativism allows that there are truths and standards that extend beyond individual beliefs. However, cultural relativism still denies the possibility of absolute truths because truth is relative to the culture in which it originated.

However, cultural relativism is also problematic because it implies that only members of the same culture can really understand each other. A classroom Community of Inquiry that embraced cultural relativism would have to be very homogenous, otherwise there would be no way for the participants to communicate and no common standards in regards to acceptable methods of inquiry. Thus, cultural relativism seems to make intercultural inquiry impossible. Intercultural inquiry presupposes the existence of knowledge and practices, especially linguistic and logical practices, that can, to some degree, transcend cultural differences (Slade 1997; Turgeon 1998; Schleifer 1996–1997). The homogenous and exclusive notion of community that cultural relativism implies conflicts with the Deweyian ideal of democracy that P4C assumes. As explained in Chapter 2, Dewey argues that homogenous, exclusive communities are not as facilitative of thinking and growth because the community members are less likely to have their ideas and methods problematised by differently situated others and it is such problematisation of experience that provokes self-reflection and inquiry. For the same reasons, P4C's ideal of community emphasises inclusivity of differences and interaction with other communities, and assumes the possibility of a global community (Splitter and Sharp 1995, 245; Lipman, et al., 1980, 22).

TRUTH AND MEANING AS THE GOALS OF INQUIRY

Thus, it seems that in order to facilitate inquiry, meaningfulness and democracy, P4C must assume a somewhat objective, although not absolutist, notion of truth. However, this doesn't mean that such an ideal of truth must be the ultimate goal of inquiry. In rejecting relativism, Gardner argues that the Community of Inquiry's "value lies in the fact that it leads toward [objective] truth" (1995, 39). Yet, it is not obvious why truth of any sort is intrinsically valuable or that truth itself should be the ultimate goal of inquiry and learning. This point is made by Golding:

> [I]s it so important that acquiring 'truth' or learning to be truth-seekers should be the fundamental aim of education? Knowledge is important but if we can't use it to make sense of things it is of no use to us. Perhaps what is most important for us is to develop an understanding of ourselves and our world? Perhaps our education system should be set up for students to seek understanding and meaning? (2005b, 1)

What Golding seems to be hinting at is that truth really only has instrumental value. It's value is that it enables us to solve problems, interact with our environment in a purposeful and intelligent manner, understand ourselves and make sense of our world. False beliefs and ideas are problematic because they lead to experience that is confusing, chaotic and unfulfilling. In general, truths are valued because they enable us to acquire meaning. Meaningfulness involves having experiences that are coherent and lead to growth, as opposed to experiences that are fragmented and problematic. Meaningfulness involves living in harmony with one's environment, even if only intermittingly. The centrality of meaningfulness is reflected in the P4C literature, where communal inquiry is generally described as a means to achieving meaningfulness more so than as a means to acquiring truth (Lipman, et al., 1980, 8–13; Splitter and Sharp 1995, 64–83). However, truth is also an important ingredient in the construction of meaning. This is suggested by Lipman's claim that "above all, inquiry involves questioning, more narrowly a quest for truth, more broadly a quest for meaning" (2003, 94–95). What is missing in the P4C literature is a proper understanding of the relationship between truth and meaning and an understanding of which notion of truth enables us to meaningfully interact with our environment.

I contend that John Dewey's pragmatist theory of truth is the notion of truth most conducive of meaningfulness. This is primarily because Dewey's notion of truth incorporates the valuable aspects of both absolutism and relativism, while eliminating their negative aspects.[2] Meaningfulness can only be achieved in an inquiry that incorporates the fallibilism, open-mindedness, creativity, subjectiveness, respect for differences and sensitivity to context that relativism aims at but fails to produce. However, meaningfulness also requires the critical thinking, logical analysis, objectivity and intercultural inquiry that absolutism emphasises but also fails to produce. After an account of Dewey's notion of truth is given, we will be able to examine how P4C's adoption of this Deweyian ideal means that is better able than other dominant pedagogies to facilitate inquiry, meaningfulness and democracy.

DEWEY'S ACCOUNT OF TRUTH AND MEANING

According to Dewey, true ideas or beliefs are those that enable us to meaningfully reconstruct experience (1978, 13). As we have already seen, inquiry is initiated when we encounter situations that are fragmented or incomplete in some way and, consequently, we are unable to respond to them in a purposeful and intelligent manner. Through inquiry we construct, test and apply hypotheses (what Dewey calls 'ideas') that are intended to connect up the fragmented parts of the situation and transform it into a unified, coherent and determinate whole. Such situations are meaningful because they are situations in which we know how to act and know what consequences to expect from our actions. Thus, we can act in a purposeful, intentional way so as to satisfy needs, desires or interests. For Dewey, truth and meaning are properties of the hypotheses or ideas that we create so as to meaningfully reconstruct experience. While the meaning of an idea is its use—or, more specifically, the consequences which follow from it when it is applied to the situation for which it was intended—the truth value of an idea is determined by whether or not application of the idea brings about the intended consequences (1978, 4). If, when applied, an idea brings about its intended consequences, it is true. As such, a true idea is an idea that *works* to reconstruct the problematic situation for which it was intended. It works because it interacts with the situation in the right way so as to produce intended results. Thus, when applied to problematic experiences, true ideas are those that produce meaningfulness. In contrast, false ideas or hypothesis "fail to clear up confusion, to eliminate defects" and may "increase confusion, uncertainty and evil when they are acted upon" (2004b, 90). They don't effectively interact with the situation and, consequently, they perpetuate disharmony between an individual and their environment (1978, 5–6).

Dewey sometimes describes truth as involving a correspondence between existence and thought. However, this isn't the notion of 'correspondence' assumed by many correspondence theories of truth. Correspondence theorists believe that a true belief or proposition is one that accurately corresponds to an external, fixed reality. This theory is problematic because there seems to be no way of getting outside of our minds to check whether or not a belief does in fact correspond to an external reality. Thus, such a notion of truth is rather redundant. It also assumes the problematic subject/object, mind/world dualisms that Dewey rejects. In contrast, Dewey argues that thought and existence, knower and the known, idea and situation, belief and the world are interconnected in the process of constructing truth. The belief and the world are not two entirely distinct, pre-existing things. Through the process of inquiry, the situation and the idea interact and transform one and other so as to produce intended consequences. These consequences, which do not exist prior to inquiry, are what establish the truthfulness and meaning of the idea, not the correspondence of a complete idea to an antecedent reality.

This pragmatist notion of truth is often thought to entail subjectivism because it is mistakenly thought to imply that true ideas are those which bring about personal satisfaction. This subjectivist version of pragmatism was sometimes espoused by Dewey's colleague William James, especially in regard to his defence of religious beliefs. For example, James (1978) argues that belief in the existence of God coincides with belief in an afterlife, which makes for a more content and meaningful life. Thus, belief in the existence of God is a true belief because it is a more personally satisfying one.

However, this subjectivist position cannot be attributed to Dewey or the other classical pragmatists. Dewey himself was critical of such an account of truth (2004b, 90–91). According to Dewey, true ideas are intended to bring about ends that are desired or needed by us and, consequently, they may also bring about consequences that are personally satisfying. Yet, this doesn't mean that personal satisfaction *determines* the truth of an idea. The truth of an idea is determined by its ability to effectively reconstruct the problematic situation for which it is intended. The situation contains factors that go beyond the needs of the agent. It includes "extra-ideal, extra-mental things", which an idea must account for in order to be effective (1978, 3). For example, in a murder investigation, a murder hypothesis is true if it organises and accounts for forensic evidence, witness testimony, the suspect's motives and so on, all of which are what Dewey would call the known facts of the case. In order for a hypothesis to effectively reconstruct the problem it is intended for, it must account for these facts of the case, as well as explain any missing or unknown information, such as the time of death, the cause of death and the identity of the murderer.[3] Thus, the truth of an idea is constrained by a reality that extends beyond the personal interests and needs of anyone individual.

The intentions, desires, interests and needs of the inquirer(s) are also conditions that a hypothesis must account for in order to work and be true. As we have seen in Chapter 2, they are fundamental in the selection and articulation of problems, and in the creation and testing of hypotheses. However, the needs and interests of the inquirer(s) must also be formulated in response to the extra-mental conditions of the situation. Interests and needs that failed to take into account the facts of the case would be unrealistic and impossible to satisfy (Dewey 2004a, 120). Thus, the needs, interests and expectations involved in inquiry are not purely subjective either. They must also be provoked and limited by the situation.

In general, the need that ideas are intended to satisfy is the need for meaning or understanding. However, attaining meaning may not always be personally satisfying. To use one of Dewey's own examples, one suspects a drink of being poisoned, and in order to test this hypothesis, the person drinks it. As the person is dying a terrible death, she realises that her hypothesis was true. While she has attained meaning, she will briefly be very unsatisfied with this outcome. Thus, when Dewey talks of true ideas as those that bring about satisfactory conditions, he means that they are satisfactory in the sense that they eliminate perplexity and give rise to meaningfulness. As Dewey explains, "The satisfaction upon which the pragmatist dwells is just the better adjustment of living beings to their environment effected by transformations of the environment through forming and applying ideas" (1978, 4).

Even though Dewey claims that a true idea is one that effectively interacts with "extra-mental" conditions, this hasn't exempt him from the accusation that his theory of truth is merely a form of subjectivism. This is because the facts of the case are known by the subject through experience. Since experience is traditionally conceived of as purely subjective and cognitive, Dewey's critics argue that these extra-mental conditions are only ever known by us as subjective mental states or sense data. We have no unmediated access to this extra-mental reality. Hence, our ideas can only interact with other ideas, which means that the truth of an idea is a subjective matter after all (1978, 5).

However, this criticism presupposes a dualistic, purely subjective notion of experience, which is explicitly rejected by Dewey. Experience is often thought to be purely internal and subjective and is dualistically opposed to an external, objective reality (1978, 4). However, as we have seen, Dewey rejects subject/object dualism, arguing that experience is an interaction between an organism and their environment in which both are transformed. As Dewey states, "Experience is a matter of functions and habits, of active adjustments and readjustments, of coordinations and activities, rather than of states of consciousness" (1978, 5). Through experience, the individual incorporates extra-mental aspects of the situation and the extra-mental is in turn transformed and humanised by the individual (Gatens-Robinson 2002). The environment and the self are shaped and constituted through their interaction with each other (Dewey 2004a, 121). Thus, the conditions that true ideas must satisfy are not purely subjective, but are subjective-objective (1978, 5).[4]

Dewey's theory of truth explains how truth claims reflect the interests and understandings of the people who make them, without rendering truth purely subjective or culturally relative. It rejects the notion of pure objectivity, which allows groups and individuals to claim that their beliefs and values are absolutely true and universally applicable when, in actuality, they only represent the values and interests of particular individuals or groups. Since ideas are constructed and tested by individuals in response to particular situations, which are subjective-objective, all truth claims and meanings are relative to the particular people, times, places and cultures in which they are made. This is because an idea that works in one context, or for some people, may be problematic in other contexts or for other people. However, this contextual notion of truth doesn't eliminate the possibility of objectivity and generality. If the truth of an idea is relative to the particularities of the situation it was verified in, then we can make the idea more objective by testing it in many diverse contexts. This is why Dewey argues that social conditions have an objectifying and generalising affect.

COMMUNAL INQUIRY, OBJECTIVITY AND LOGIC

Dewey recognised that the beliefs and activities of other people, including past and future generations, can act as constraints upon, or as facilitators of, our own ideas and actions. Thus, a true idea is one that effectively interacts with socio-cultural conditions, not just objective-subjective conditions. This is why Dewey states that "telling a truth, telling a thing the way it is, means designating things in terms that observe the conventions of proper social intercourse" and "truth telling has always been a matter of adaptation to a social audience" (1978, 15). This doesn't mean that an idea is false simply because some people disagree with it. The actions and interests of others may be unreasonable, problematic and unable to account for the facts of the case, and, as such, we would be justified in criticising and rejecting them. Although Dewey frequently uses the term 'consensus', his ideal of truth doesn't require all participants in a society to agree on some idea. Not only may we reject, with reason, views and claims that are clearly unacceptable, but there may also be multiple, equally true solutions to any given problem. If true ideas are those that work as intended, it's possible, and probable, that there will be more than one idea that will work to solve any given problem. Different people may prefer different, equally acceptable means of achieving the same outcomes. So long as the different ideas don't undermine each other there is no reason why different people or groups cannot accept different beliefs or ideas. While such a notion of truth can account for cultural differences, it is not a form of cultural relativism. Rather, it is similar to Code's notion of "mitigated relativism", which "takes different perspectives into account" but is mitigated because it "affirms that there is something there, in the world, to know and act on—hence to constrain possibilities of knowledge and analysis" (1991, 320).

Since socio-cultural conditions are truth and meaning determining factors, inquiries should be communal. Dewey claims that "truth is having things in common" as the result of a communal inquiry into a socially important problem (1978, 67). As explained in Chapter 2, it is through making truths common that we render them more objective. Common truths integrate the understandings and interests of many different people, rather than transcend them as absolutism claims to do (1938, 8).

Communal inquiry also makes truths more objective by revealing the hidden assumptions, agendas, biases and cultural backgrounds of the inquirers and the situations inquired into. Dewey refers to these contextual factors as the "background" of the inquiry because while they are not the immediate, conscious objects of thought, they influence the selection and interpretation of the problem, the intended outcomes of inquiry and the construction, testing and acceptance of an idea (1977, 7–11). While background assumptions are essential in that they provide some knowledge, beliefs and interests which act as a basis for inquiry, they can also be problematic in that they often contain hidden biases. Thus, Dewey argues that objectivity requires that such background factors be revealed and their influence on inquiry recognised, even though they cannot be completely transcended:

> An empirical philosophy is in any case a kind of intellectual disrobing. We cannot permanently divest ourselves of the intellectual habits we take on and wear when we assimilate the culture of our time and place. But intelligent furthering of culture demands that we take some of them off, that we inspect them critically to see what they are made of and what wearing them does to us. We cannot achieve recovery of primitive naïveté. But there is attainable a cultivated naïveté of eye, ear and thought, one that can be acquired only through the discipline of severe thought. (1958b, 37–38)

Harding also recognises the role that such background factors play in scientific inquiry, stating that objectivity requires a "systematic examination of such powerful background beliefs" as part of the inquiry itself (1991, 149). Harding also rejects the absolutist's ideal of objectivity as requiring complete impartiality, disinterest and value neutrality. She argues that the assumption of this traditional notion of objectivity is the reason the backgrounds of inquirers often go unexamined. It is commonly believed that these background factors have been completely transcended (1993, 70–71). Harding contrasts the traditional notion of objectivity to her ideal of *strong* objectivity, which is actually more objective because it requires that the backgrounds of inquirers be revealed and subject to critical examination.

Communal inquiry reveals such background factors because when individuals are exposed to differently situated others, what is seen as normal or natural is made strange, problematic and conspicuous (Harding 1991, 50). It is the clash of different perspectives that renders such background factors problematic and exposes them to critical examination. As Dewey explains, it is only when some part of the background "exercises such a differential effect upon what is consciously thought of as to be responsible for some of the confusion and perplexity we are trying to clear up" that it becomes part of the "immediate matter of thinking'" (1978, 12). By making background factors conspicuous, communal inquiry forces individuals to recognise the extent to which their ideas are limited or relative and, if possible, to amend them so as they are more inclusive of differences. Dewey argues that a lack of such critical self-awareness is a problem with many philosophical theories (1978, 11).

This ideal of objectivity as commonality, intersubjectivity and background revealing, means that the more diverse, multicultural and inclusive a Community of Inquiry is, the more objective the truths verified in it will be. A culturally diverse community provides more diverse conditions for the construction and testing of ideas. Furthermore, the greater the number of differences between two individuals the more likely they are to recognise aspects of each other as strange and problematic. This is another reason why Dewey argues that communities should be inclusive of differences and should engage in inquiry with other communities. He doesn't perceive of our differences and situatedness as a barrier to objectivity, as relativists and absolutists do. Rather, objective truths come in to contact with concrete differences and contingencies as much as possible (1985, 21).

Harding also recognises the epistemic value of cultural diversity. However, she develops this idea even further by arguing that the perspectives and voices of marginalised individuals are more facilitative of objectivity because they occupy a position of otherness within mainstream society. The members of marginalised groups are more likely to see existing conditions and dominant ideologies as strange, problematic, inadequate and biased, whereas members of the dominant group are more likely to have a vested interest in maintaining the status quo, which has been shaped in accordance with their values and interests. Thus, as Harding argues, inquiries should start from the positions of marginalised people and communities if they are to aim at producing truths which are more inclusive and objective. An inquiry starts with the selection of a problem, not with a solution to one. Thus, problems must be selected and articulated in a manner that privileges the perspectives of those who are most marginalised (1993, 69–72).

While truths constructed in multicultural and cross-cultural inquiries are more objective, even truths that result from very diverse, communal inquiries are tentative and somewhat relative (Dewey 1938, 7). An absolute truth could only result from an inquiry that transcended all times and spaces and included all people (past, present and future). Only such an inquiry would enable us to verify the truth of an idea in every possible context. As such, we must always be open to the possibility that ideas currently held to be true may be falsified by some future situations or further inquiry and, as such, we should always be prepared and willing to self-correct and reconstruct our beliefs. Unlike absolutists, Dewey doesn't describe fallibilism as a problem, arguing that it reduces the possibility of static, inflexible, dogmatic and oppressive beliefs and practices, which fail to account for the contingent, diverse and transient nature of concrete experience (1978, 13–14; 2004b, 83).

While community gives rise to objective truths, objective truths enable community. All communal living requires that individuals have some common understandings, methods, values and standards, which they can use to communicate with each other. For Dewey, common or objective truths are synonymous with principles because all truths are "standards of valuation", which "regulate one's affairs" (1978, 16). Thus, common truths are principles, which guide the very social interaction that gave rise to them.

The principles of logic are particularly important types of common truths because they are the standards of good thinking that guide communal inquiry itself. However, as Christina Slade (1997) argues, the notion of a common logic is problematic because what counts as good thinking seems to differ between cultures. As such, the assumption of universal, a priori logic may ignore important cultural differences in thinking styles and lead to the exclusion and oppression of some individuals and communities. Yet, without some common logic, inter-cultural and multicultural inquiry appears impossible.

Dewey's theory of logic overcomes this dilemma. Dewey argues that logical forms originate in inquiry, denying that they are a priori principles applied to inquiry from without (1938, 11). When we reflect on the process of inquiry itself, the logical forms that characterise inquiry are disclosed to us (1938, 4). This is why Dewey describes logic as "inquiry into inquiry" or the "theory of inquiry" (1938, 20). By undertaking a metacognitive inquiry we identify the inferences and thinking moves that have been used to successfully reconstruct experience and acquire truth. We are also able to identify those thinking moves that led us astray, failed to produce clarity and were counterproductive in the acquisition of truth and meaning. Logical principles and fallacies are just the formalisation and generalisation of these thinking moves. The purpose of formulating logical principles is to enable future inquiry to go on more economically and efficiently. Such principles enable us to reproduce thinking that has been successful in past inquiries and eliminate fallacious thinking:

Logic is both a science and an art; a science so far as it gives an organized and tested descriptive account of the way in which thought actually goes on; an art, so far as on the basis of this description it projects methods by which future thinking shall take advantage of the operations that lead to success and avoid those which result in failure. (2004b, 77)

Since logical forms originate in particular inquiries, they are culturally and historically located (Dewey 1938, 20). Thus, like all common truths, logical principles are open to criticism and revision. If the procedures of inquiry appear problematic or culturally biased, inquirers can try to reconstruct them so that they are more inclusive and effective. The clash of different thinking styles in intercultural inquiry can actually lead to the development of more objective and effective methods of inquiry. However, if there is no agreement reached about inquiry procedures then further inquiry will be impossible. There need not be total consensus, but enough agreement for the inquiry to progress. If the problems inquired into are equally important to all participants then everyone will be motivated to reach some agreement about what inquiry procedures are acceptable.

TRUTH AND MEANING IN PHILOSOPHY FOR CHILDREN

Since the goal of P4C's Community of Inquiry is also to construct meaning, the inquiry begins with something problematic, because this is what provokes questioning, inquiry and the quest for meaning. As explained, one of the educational benefits of philosophy is the highly contentious nature of its subject matter. Since a problematic situation is one that stands in the way of something that the individual finds useful, necessary or interesting, curriculum content must not only be open and contentious; it must be relevant to the needs, interests and understandings of the students. As such, P4C is a student-centred pedagogy, in that the curriculum is connected to the experiences and interests of students (Splitter and Sharp 1995, 70; Thomas 1997, 44). Rather than simply depositing established knowledge into student's heads, P4C creates an environment which provokes students to reflect on their own experiences. For example, in Lipman's P4C program, the philosophical narratives are written in a language, and set in contexts, relevant to the everyday experiences of children (2003, 156). The intention is to provoke students to incorporate "the puzzling, the strange and the mysterious into [their] own network of personal experiences" (Splitter and Sharp 1995, 72). Students then formulate their problems as questions, which set the agenda for the inquiry (Lipman 2003, 98). Since the problems investigated incorporate the interests and experiences of students, the Community of Inquiry will involve the construction of ideas that must satisfy subjective conditions in order to work and be true. Thus, the community of inquiry is not purely objective in the sense implied by absolutism, where the inquirers are supposed to be disembodied, disinterested knowers. In accordance with Dewey, P4C accepts that the values and interests of the inquirers affect the way the problem is defined and the construction, testing, application and acceptance of ideas. As Splitter and Sharp explain, "[J]ust as in physics we learn that the things we observe are affected by our observations, so the person who thinks for herself understands that the subject matter of inquiry can never be completely severed from herself as inquirer" (1995, 16).

However, the fact that students construct ideas in response to their own interests and personal experiences doesn't mean that the Community of Inquiry is merely an opportunity for individual students to assert as true whatever beliefs satisfy their own needs and interests (Splitter and Sharp 1995, 69). True ideas are those that meaningfully transform the student's problematic experiences, which are not merely subjective (Splitter and Sharp 1995, 67). Like Dewey's notion of experience, P4C describes experience as an interaction between students and their world, in which both are transformed by each other. While students construct truths and shape their environment in accordance with their own interests and needs, they are limited and guided by the existence of a world that extends beyond their own minds; by conditions that are extra-mental and extra-subjective. Thus, as they reconstruct their environment, students must simultaneously adapt themselves, their interests and their beliefs in accordance with the facts of the case. This is why, echoing Dewey, Sharp describes inquiry as simultaneously a process of discovery and invention (Sharp 1987, 41).

Consequently, P4C explicitly rejects the subjectivist notion that all ideas and beliefs are equally true and valuable. Some contributions made in the classroom Community of Inquiry will be false, inadequate or problematic, while others may be true and valuable, depending on how well they reconstruct the subjective-objective situation for which they are intended:

> Communities of Inquiry give full reign to children's creative and imaginative impulses. But the participants in such communities must become aware that their own thoughts and world-views do not define the limits of human knowledge and understanding. Even as we want children to value themselves and to cherish their own thoughts and ideas, we also want them to appreciate that what they believe to be right and true may turn out to be neither. (Splitter and Sharp 1995, 69)

P4C also requires students to develop their interests, values and desires in relation to the facts of the situation. Lipman and Sharp reject the view that values are subjective and mental, while facts are purely objective and external to the self. This fact/value dualism leads to the dangerous view that one's values are not open to critical examination. If such a view were accepted in the Community of Inquiry, students would end up "talking about their feelings and wants rather than assessing the *objective worth* of what their feelings and wants are about" (Lipman and Sharp 1978, 349).

Thus, the construction of meaning in the P4C class requires that students articulate problems, formulate desired outcomes and construct ideas that will properly interact with all the conditions of the situation, which are objective-subjective. It is only because inquiry and the truths constructed in the Community of Inquiry are subjective-objective that they can lead to the construction of meaning. If the truths constructed didn't respond to the interests of students, they would not reconstruct their experiences and produce meaning for them. It is the failure of traditional schools to take into account the experiences and interests of students that renders learning meaningless because "without interest education becomes a matter of performing tasks with no inherent connection to the person" (Thomas 1997, 44). However, unless values, desires and ideas effectively interact with the extra-mental aspects of problematic situations, they will not lead to the meaningful reconstruction of experience either. This is the problem with student-centred pedagogies that embrace subjectivism. They recognise the importance of the student's own experiences and opinions but fail to prepare students properly for the limitations and constraints of the world. In contrast, P4C provides students with skills and ideas that will enable them to meaningfully reconstruct their environment because in P4C students construct ideas that respond to their own needs and interests as well as the extra-mental conditions of the situation.

As such, unlike schooling that incorporates absolutism and relativism, P4C fosters reflective thinking. Since there are objective standards and conditions, students must critically assess different ideas, values, interests and methods to see which ones are most effective and useful. They must construct criteria so as to critically compare alternative ideas and seek out reasons and evidence that support some ideas and methods over others. However, the subjective, personal aspect of the problematic situations necessitates that P4C students do the thinking for themselves (Splitter and Sharp 1995, 170; Lipman, Sharp and Oscanyan 1980, 85). The teacher plays an important role in assisting and guiding the students in the construction of ideas, as well as in the formulation of a manageable problem, but students articulate the problematic situation in accordance with their own worldviews. Consequently, only students can construct a solution that will satisfy their own needs and understandings. Thus, the subjective dimension of the Community of Inquiry effectively eliminates the possibility of banking teaching:

> [M]eanings, in terms of relations and connections which are grounded in one's own personal and interpersonal experience, cannot be handed down or dispensed from above. Even one's closest friends cannot provide them. They must be constructed for oneself, although not necessarily by oneself. (Splitter and Sharp 1995, 74)

The meanings [children] hunger for cannot be dispensed to them the way wafers are dealt out to communicants at a mass; they must seek them out for themselves, by their own involvement in dialogue and inquiry. (Lipman, et al.,1980, 7)

Thus, unlike subjectivist and absolutist pedagogies, P4C students are independent thinkers who actively create meaning, as opposed to being the recipients of 'absolute truths', 'discovered' by adults. P4C can only foster independent thinking because it rejects absolutism and relativism in favour of a middle-ground theory of truth. Thus, this idea of truth is an educationally and socially powerful one. It gives rise to the sort of person that Lipman's, Freire's and Dewey's pedagogies aim at: persons who can identify, reflect on and intelligently transform problematic aspects of their experience.

The communal nature of P4C also counters the egoism that is associated with subjectivism and many student-centred pedagogies. Communal inquiry requires that the problems inquired into be common problems that are of interest to all community members. As such, the Community of Inquiry should "result in a settlement that takes into account all the considerations and points of view, as well as the interests of everyone" (Lipman 2003, 96). However, as with Dewey's communal inquiry, this doesn't mean that consensus is required. Community members may agree to disagree. As Davey explains, "There may still be disagreement amongst the community members, but, if after reflection the group decides to accept the different opinions, they have come to this conclusion collectively" (2004, 27).

The communal structure of the Community of Inquiry also facilitates reflective thinking, which in turn leads to the construction of more objective truths. Communal inquiry requires students to critically assess different positions, and when their own views are challenged by others, they must produce reasons to support them or self-correct. In communicating their ideas and intentions to others, students are prompted to think more carefully about the appropriateness and social value of their ideas. The classroom Community of Inquiry also facilitates background revealing because it exposes one's ideas and thinking to differently situated others in the community. This provokes students to develop a critical self-awareness of how their own personal interests and cultural situatedness affect their thinking and understandings (Lipman 2003, 123). Hence, as with Dewey and Harding, in the P4C classroom, individual differences and situatedness are not considered obstacles to objectivity, but rather facilitators of it (Lipman 2003, 25). This is one of the reasons that many P4C theorists also promote the notions of intercultural inquiry and global community (Splitter and Sharp 1995, 246).

Thus, objectivity and generality are achievable in the P4C classroom, not through transcending the subjective and the particular, but through the convergence or fusion of multiple perspectives, subjectivities and concrete experiences. This is reflected in the common use of the term "inter-subjectivity" as an alternative to objectivity in the P4C literature (Thomas 1997; Lipman 2003; Splitter and Sharp 2005). As Sharp states, "When I use the term 'objectivity', I mean an inter-subjective truth arrived at by human beings through inquiry, experimentation, consideration of the evidence and dialogue" (1987, 40). Even though intersubjective truths may be generalised and common, they are never completely abstracted from the experiences of the individuals who created them, which would render them meaningless to those individuals. As Kennedy explains, in the Community of Inquiry, "knowledge is constructed through the interaction of individuals within the group, and so it is really group knowledge, but that knowledge is, in the very process of its emergence through individuals, internalised by each individual" (1995, 166). As we have seen, this notion of objectivity increases the usefulness of an idea by increasing the capacity for the idea to be transferred to different situations. Thus, the intersubjective ideas that emerge in communal inquiry are more valuable to students because students will be better able to use them in diverse situations they encounter beyond the classroom.

The assumption of intersubjective truths facilitates an "intense sensitivity to contextual individuality", which is an important aspect of reflective thinking (Lipman 2003, 208). Rather than ignore potential problems and contextual differences in the search for 'perfect solutions' or 'absolute truths', P4C students must be careful to identify the potential problems that may result from transferring an idea from one situation to another. They learn that an idea that works or is true in one context may not be in some other context. Intersubjective and contextual truths discourage individuals from making illicit generalisations, including stereotypical comments about other people, cultures and situations. Thus, P4C students learn to be sensitive to cultural and individual differences and to generalise with care (2003, 220). The construction of meaning requires students to try to predict changes in situations, imagine and assess important differences between contexts, pay attention to details and imagine potential problems (2003, 219). As such, intersubjective truths encourage students to be more imaginative, critical, careful, flexible, comprehensive and nuanced thinkers.

P4C's intersubjective notion of truth also facilitates a willingness to self-correct, which is also an important attribute of the reflective thinking P4C aims to foster. As Lipman states, the outcomes of the Community of Inquiry "provide us with grounds for assuming, warrants for asserting. They represent *provisional judgments* rather than firm bases for absolute convictions" (2003, 93). As such, in the Community of Inquiry, self-correction isn't perceived to be an embarrassing admission of failure. Since P4C accepts that all truths are contextual and have the potential to be falsified by future experience, self-correction is a *normal* and *indispensable* feature of all inquiry. Students know that revising their ideas and thinking methods in light of valid criticism helps progress the inquiry and leads to ideas that are more intersubjective, useful and meaningful:

The spirit of fallibilism that prevails in a community of inquiry is an invitation from all participants to have their errors pointed out to them, so that ways of correcting them might be sought. Such a spirit helps to defuse the contentiousness that absolutism and fanaticism inspire, and thereby it undercuts the violence to which such contentiousness often leads. The resolution to confront the problematic and deal with it in a spirit of reasonableness is a world apart from the inflexible insistence that education means the acquisition of knowledge that is authoritative and absolute. (Lipman 2003, 123)

DEWEY'S IDEAL OF LOGIC IN PHILOSOPHY FOR CHILDREN

Like Dewey, Lipman argues that logical principles originate in communal inquiry (2003, 92). Thus, as Slade (1997) argues, P4C recognises that like all knowledge, logical principles are shaped by social and cultural conditions. The constructed and situated nature of the Community of Inquiry procedures means that they are also fallible (Lipman 2003, 206). Students may find that a thinking style or method may be acceptable in one situation but not in another because of cultural differences in communication and thinking. P4C's incorporation of this Deweyian ideal of logic fosters procedural thinking, which is another essential attribute of reflective thinking. Procedural thinking is thinking about the procedures of inquiry itself. It is broader than metacognitive thinking. While metacognitive thinking is thinking that reflects upon the procedures of thinking, procedural thinking *critically* reflects upon those procedures and aims to improve them (Lipman 2003, 26). Procedural thinking aims to identify the strengths, weakness, fallacies and effectiveness of different thinking styles in order to make future inquiry more effective and efficient. Procedural thinking is how logic is created because it involves formalising and generalising thinking practices into principles and standards which can be transferred from one inquiry to another. P4C participants critically reflect upon the procedures of inquiry and abstract and formalise different types of thinking moves. The principles then act as objective criteria, which Community of Inquiry participants must utilise and uphold, not because they are absolute truths that students must uncritically accept, but because students themselves have identified them as valuable for the construction of meaning. In contrast, if the logical principles that guided the inquiry were considered to be a priori, absolute and ready-made, procedural inquiry would not really be necessary because students could just uncritically memorise them and submit to them. None of this means that the P4C procedures can simply be rejected or adapted at whim. If students wish to challenge a procedure, then they must be able to convince others that it is ineffective or inferior. If students fail to adhere to accepted procedures, without providing good reasons for doing so, they will be subject to criticism by others. As Lipman states, the Community of Inquiry's commitment to logic also helps counter subjectivism:

One of the merits of Logic is almost purely educational. To students eager to vaunt their newfound relativism, it provides a superb reminder that what may be true for one may not be true for all, that not everything follows from everything else, and that relativism does not necessarily exclude objectivity. What logic does beautifully is demonstrate to incredulous students that rationality is possible, that there is such a thing as logical connectedness or validity, and that some arguments are better than others. (2003, 179)

FALLIBILISM, OPEN-MINDEDNESS AND RESPECT IN PHILOSOPHY FOR CHILDREN

P4C's adoption of a Deweyian notion of truth also enables it to facilitate care, empathy, open-mindedness and respect. As we have seen, neither absolutism nor relativism facilitate such attitudes and skills. In the P4C classroom, students value the ideas and perspectives of others because they are essential for the acquisition of intersubjective truths and meanings. Individuals will only be willing to share their ideas with others if they believe they will be treated with care and respect. Thus, in order to build trust in the Community of Inquiry, students learn they must be respectful of, and caring towards, others and their ideas. Intersubjectivity also requires open-mindedness and empathy. Students must be open to other's opinions and ideas because the contributions of others lead to more objective, useful and meaningful ideas. This fosters the development of the capacity for reasonableness. Reasonableness is not just the ability to use reasons so as to convince others of one's own ideas, it includes the ability to change one's own mind when prompted to do so by reasons provided by others. Reasonableness involves attentive listening and empathy if students are to be moved by the reasons and ideas of others (Lipman 2003, 269).

This doesn't mean that P4C students must accept, or even tolerate, another's position. As Cam explains, in the Community of Inquiry, "[R]espect is shown when people are willing to consider other people's points of view or they acknowledge other people's contributions. Respect doesn't require agreement" (1995, 52). Respecting the ideas of others involves taking them seriously enough to critically evaluate them, accept them if they are useful, and revise or reject them when they are not. Empathy enables us to understand other's ideas, not so that we will accept them, but so that we can make a more informed judgment about their truthfulness and value (Lipman 2003, 270).

In this chapter, it has been argued that truth is a necessary instrument for the construction of meaning. True ideas are those that work to purposefully and meaningfully reconstruct problematic experiences. However, only a certain notion of truth can lead to meaningfulness. Neither an absolutist nor a relativist notion of truth is adequate. As Dewey argues, truths that produce meaning are subjective-objective, social-cultural and intersubjective. It is because P4C incorporates this Deweyian ideal of truth that it is able to overcome the educational problems associated with both absolutism and relativism. Dewey's notion of truth enables P4C to facilitate seemingly incompatible personal attributes, ideals of thinking and social practices, all of which are necessary for the construction of meaning. The Community of Inquiry participants are interested, culturally situated, goal-orientated individuals, who are critically aware of their own interests and situatedness, the facts of the case, the thinking process itself and the interests and values of others. It is because of this that the Community of Inquiry can produce independent thinkers and meaningfulness for its members.

4   A Response to Reason/
Imagination Dualism
The Imagination in Dewey
and Philosophy for Children

Egan states that the imagination "is a concept that has come down to us with a history of suspicion and mistrust" (2007, 4). Like experience and the emotions, the imagination is frequently thought to be an obstacle to Reason. While Reason is conceived of as an abstract, objective and rule-governed method of delivering absolute truths, the imagination is considered "unconstrained, arbitrary, and fanciful", as well as "particular, subjective, and idiosyncratic" (Jo 2002, 39). This negative view of the imagination can be traced back at least as far as Plato, and it is evident in contemporary educational ideas and practices. Dominant approaches to schooling emphasise the accumulation of indubitable facts rather than the development of imagination (Nussbaum 2010; Egan and Judson 2009; Egan 2007; Haralambous, et al.2007; Kennedy 2006; Greene 1995; Dewey 1997). Imaginativeness, which children are thought to be prone to, is associated with daydreaming, idleness, irrationality and absent-mindedness. At best, the imagination is seen as a valuable capacity that is entirely distinct from Reason and is primarily cultivated in 'the arts'.

In this chapter, I will draw on Dewey's theory of inquiry to argue that the imagination is not an obstacle to reason, nor merely a valuable and distinct capacity, but rather an integral element of all thinking. This Deweyian notion of imagination will be referred to as the 'intelligent imagination' to distinguish it from other accounts of the imagination, as well as from fantasy and reverie. All schooling must cultivate the intelligent imagination as a basic, interdisciplinary capability, and integrating philosophy, specifically Philosophy for Children (P4C), into the curriculum is one way that schools can make some progress towards achieving this. There is some concern that P4C's emphasis on logic and critical thinking may promote traditional notions of Reason and thinking that are defined in opposition to the imagination and emotion (Field 1997; Haynes 1994; Valentino 1998, 29). However, it will be shown that P4C rejects Reason/imagination dualism because it assumes Dewey's notion of communal inquiry which necessitates the development of the intelligent imagination.

THE PLATONIC NOTION OF IMAGINATION

Considering the significant influence Plato's ideas have had on Western notions of truth, knowledge, thinking, reality and education, it is not surprising that some of his negative comments about the imagination are reflected in contemporary approaches to schooling. For Plato, Reason and philosophy give us access to reality and absolute truth, while the imagination and art are associated with sense experience, the emotions and unreality. Plato conceives of reality as the nonphysical, transcendental realm of the forms, which are abstract entities. The physical world of sense experience is not reality, but merely a copy of reality. Images are copies of the physical world, filtered through the interests, emotions and restricted embodied perspectives of those who create them (Plato 1998, 598b). Thus, for Plato, what is imagined is three degrees away from reality. To illustrate this idea, Plato provides the example of a bed. There is the form of bed, which is an abstract idea or concept. This is the real bed. Then there are the physical beds that we sleep on, created by craftsman to resemble the form of bed. Thus, these concrete beds are only copies of the form of bed. Finally, there are images of beds. These images, such as paintings of beds, are mere copies of concrete beds. That is, they are copies of copies of reality (1998, 597b–597e). Plato believed this applied to the images in dreams, poetry, myths, music and rhetoric, as much as to the images created by painters and sculptors.

Plato's concern with the imagination is not just that images are unreal but that that we may mistake images for reality, like the prisoners in Plato's cave who believe the shadows on the wall are real and, consequently, never learn the truth about their world. Even when an escaped and enlightened prisoner returns to inform the other prisoners that reality is actually outside the cave, the prisoners are unable to accept that there could be anything more real than the shadows on the wall (1998, 514a–518b). This is particularly concerning given the imagination's capacity to construct very seductive images of reality, just as artists often represent the world in an idealised or beautified manner. This is why Plato associates painting, poetry, sculpture and music with the rhetoric practised by the sophists, an activity which he describes as immoral and aimed at deception. An individual who is deluded about their own nature and abilities and the world around them is unlikely to live a happy life or be a productive member of society. Such a person is likely to ignore 'real' problems and potential dangers and devote themselves to the pursuit of unachievable ends.

While Plato is more frequently associated with a purely negative view of the imagination (e.g., Egan 2007; Fesmire 2003), he does not entirely condemn the imagination or the arts (e.g., Bundy 1922; Thayer 1977). The imagination is included on Plato's divided line, which represents four stages of human understanding (Plato 1998, 509c–511e). The line is first divided into two parts, with one part representing the visible realm of material objects, and the other representing the intelligible realm of the forms. The visible realm is further divided into two parts, with one part representing opinion or belief and physical objects and the other representing imagination and conjecture. While the imagination is included in the stages of human understanding, it is still associated with the subjective senses, and relegated to a status lower than mere opinion. However, Bundy argues that the section of the line representing the intelligible realm also includes imagination (1922, 368–369). The intelligible realm is also divided into two parts, the first part is called 'understanding' while the other, superior part, is called 'dialectic'. In the stage called 'understanding', one uses images of physical objects in order to understand the form of the thing being contemplated. For example, a mathematician will use a mental image of a triangular shaped object in order to theorise about the form of triangularity. This stage seems to correspond to science in that it involves hypothesising, generalising and theorising about the material world. Thus, Plato may actually suggest two notions of the imagination, one perceptual and the other intelligible (Bundy 1922, 368–369). However, even on this reading, the imagination is still distinct from, and subordinate to, pure Reason or dialectic, which is not dependent on either perception or imagination. As such, imagination also remains a potential obstacle to Reason.

Since Plato believed the imagination could be a powerful force that could lead us astray, he also thought education should help individuals overcome or control their imaginations. However, in accordance with his divided line metaphor, Plato suggested that the imagination, controlled by Reason, had some educational value. For example, carefully created stories and music played an important role in Plato's theory of primary education (1998, 376e–392e, 401b–403c). However, the later years of schooling, which were to be limited to those who would perform the more important protective and leadership roles in society, were to be largely devoted to mathematics and philosophy in order to develop the faculty of Reason, which remained the ultimate goal of education.

While not all philosophers have put forward negative views of the imagination, they have largely tended to ignore, sideline or be weary of the imagination. As Egan explains, even those who suggest that the imagination plays some fundamental role in human understanding have expressed uncertainty about its nature and value (e.g., Hume and Kant). As such, the imagination is predominantly considered to be mysterious and potentially problematic, if not dangerous.

DEWEY'S THEORY OF IMAGINATION

Dewey is one of the few philosophers who unambiguously emphasises the fundamental interrelatedness of the imagination and thinking. However, as Fesmire points out, Dewey's account of the imagination has been largely ignored, even by Dewey scholars (2003, 64). This is probably because his comments on the imagination are scattered throughout his immense body of work rather than explained in one comprehensive piece of writing. Dewey describes several roles that the imagination plays in the process of inquiry: (1) conceiving of alternatives to problematic situations or ends-in-view; (2) suggesting means to reach those ends; (3) evaluating those means through considering their possible consequences if applied (what Dewey calls 'reasoning'); (5) making use of past experience; (6) constructing and applying general principles and abstract ideas and concepts; (7) moral imagination; and (8) enabling dialogue and communal inquiry. This section will provide an explanation of each of these functions of the intelligent imagination.

Dewey rejects the Platonic notion of an entirely non-physical, abstract realm of ideas. Thus, thinking is not conceived of as some disembodied, transcendental method of acquiring absolute truths. As we have seen, Dewey described thinking as synonymous with reflective experience. It is the reconstruction of problematic, unsettled or fragmented experiences into coherent, meaningful situations. Problematic experiences occur when our habitual way of interacting with our environment becomes ineffective for satisfying our needs and interests. Consequently, thinking emerges as the means to readjusting and coordinating ourselves and our environment so that we can survive and grow. The imagination plays a fundamental role because it enables us to go beyond actual experience and imagine situations as other than they are. Thus, we are able to imagine fragmented, incomplete situations as coherent, meaningful wholes. This notion of imagination need not literally involve having mental images at all. According to Dewey, the imagination is a means of creating and considering alternative possibilities that are not immediately present in concrete experiences. Without this capacity, we would simply have to accept the status quo and there would be no need for thinking. Although he is also referring to fancy and reverie, Dewey suggests the problem solving function of the imagination in the following passage:

> The things most emphasized in imagination as it reshapes experience are things which are absent in reality. In the degree in which life is placid and easy, imagination is sluggish and bovine. In the degree in which life is uneasy and troubled, fancy is stirred to frame pictures of a contrary state of things. By reading the characteristic features of any man's castles in the air you can make a shrewd guess as to his underlying desires which are frustrated. What is difficulty and disappointment in real life becomes conspicuous achievement and triumph in reverie; what is negative in fact will be positive in the image drawn by fancy; what is vexation in conduct will be compensated for in high relief in idealizing imagination. (2004b, 60)

The imagined possibilities for a problematic situation are the desired 'ends-in-view' that give inquiry a goal, purpose, framework and direction.

Through inquiry we consider means to actualise these imagined possibilities. These means are also imagined because they are yet to be actualised. They suggest future possible action. Until these means have actually reconstructed the problematic situation as intended, they are only tentative solutions, or what Dewey calls 'ideas' (2004a, 152; 1997, 75). 'Hypothesising', 'speculating', 'conjecturing' and 'suggesting' are all other words that Dewey uses to describe this imaginative process of creating possible means for reconstructing experience. When these ideas have been actualised, they are called 'facts', 'truths', 'knowledge' or 'warranted assertions'.

Ideas and suggestions are not imaginative just because they go beyond what is immediately given in experience. An imaginative idea is one that we expect to be realised (Dewey 1997, 7). Dewey distinguishes between imagination, on the one hand, and fancy or reverie, on the other. The latter are concerned with thoughts that have little or no possibility of realisation and, thus, are unlikely to reconstruct experience (1958a, 267–269, 273; 1967, 170–171). Unlike the imagination, the thoughts entertained in reverie do not "aim at knowledge, at belief about facts or in truths" (1997, 3). Barrow describes a similar notion of imagination, stating that imaginative ideas are not just original but also effective in that they are "conducive to a good solution to, or resolution of, the task or problem at hand" (1988, 85). When Plato talks about the imagination leading us away from reality and truth, he seems to have in mind what Dewey calls 'fancy' or 'reverie'. Dewey would agree that reverie has this potential but, unlike Plato, he clearly distinguishes between reverie and the imagination. The primary function of the latter is actually to help us understand and transform reality. Imagined possibilities and ideas must be realistic in order to be effective. Imaginative thinking requires us to carefully observe and assess the problematic situation and construct ideas that account for the facts of the case (Dewey 1958b, 62). As Dewey states, "[T]he data *arouse* suggestions, and only by reference to the specific data can we pass upon the appropriateness of the suggestions" (2004a, 152). Thus, the imagination does not completely transcend reality or distract us from attaining clarity and knowledge. It actually enables understanding of, and a more harmonious interaction with, reality. As Dewey states, "[T]he healthy imagination deals not with the unreal, but with the mental realization of what is suggested. Its exercise is not a flight into the purely fanciful and ideal, but a method of expanding and filling in what is real" (1997, 166; see also 224).

Dewey's notion of intelligent imagination bears some similarity to the capacity represented on the third section of Plato's divided line, which Plato calls 'understanding'. As we have seen, Plato's notion of understanding resembles scientific inquiry in that it involves *hypothesising* about the physical world. This is the other stage of Plato's epistemology that involves imagination. This suggests that Dewey and Plato had a similar understanding of at least one of the functions of imagination—conjecturing, hypothesising, making suggestions about the physical world. However, their different metaphysical and epistemological beliefs mean that they disagree about the value of this notion of imagination. Since he rejects the notion of a non-physical realm, Dewey also rejects the notion of pure Reason represented by the fourth section of Plato's divided line. For Dewey, there is no type of thinking or means of human understanding that supersedes the imagination and experience. For Dewey, the processes represented in the first, second and third sections of the divided line are the only possible means of human understanding (although Dewey would also disagree with the way Plato divides these processes up and defines them). Since Dewey believed that all modes of human understanding were experiential and imaginative, the imagination occupies a much more fundamental and less ambiguous position in his epistemology than it does in Plato's idealist theory.

While Dewey rejects Plato's notion of transcendental Reason, he believes that a different notion of reasoning plays an important role in inquiry. This notion of reason is also experiential and imaginative. Dewey specifically reserves the term 'reasoning' for the inferences we make in order to develop the suggestions that we immediately infer from our observations into workable ideas. As explained in Chapter 2, this is the difference between suggestions and conjectures, on the one hand, which are more immediate and vague, and ideas, on the other, which are more developed and have been subject to critical examination. The way in which we develop suggestions into ideas is by inferring what consequences would follow from them if they were actualised. This process of inference making is what Dewey means by 'reasoning'. Thus, reasoning enables us to consider if a suggestion will reconstruct the situation as intended or if it will result in undesirable consequences. This helps us form a judgment about the likely effectiveness and value of the suggestion for reconstructing the problematic experience. Reasoning is an imaginative process because it involves imagining the consequences of suggestions if they were applied. These consequences go beyond experience. This is why Dewey states that "inference is always an invasion of the unknown, a leap from the known" (2004a, 152). Even if we don't accept Dewey's stipulative definition of reasoning, it is clear that all reasoning is an imaginative activity because all reasoning involves going beyond immediate experience to make various connections.

The imagination doesn't just enable us to bring to mind future possibilities; it also enables us to make use of past experiences (Dewey 1967, 169; 1991, 106). Since past experiences go beyond what is immediately given there is a strong link between memory and imagination (1967, 169; 1991, 106; Russell 1998, 197). Our past experiences are also essential components of inquiry because they suggest alternative possibilities, as well as means for bringing about these possibilities. If a problematic situation is completely unfamiliar to us, if we have no relevant prior knowledge to help us make sense of it, we will be unable to meaningfully reconstruct it. This is why Dewey states that all conscious experience has of necessity some degree of imaginative quality. For while the roots of every experience are found in the inter-action of a live creature with its environment, that experience becomes conscious, a matter of perception, only when meanings enter it that are derived from prior experiences. Imagination is the only gateway through which these meanings can find their way into a present inter-action; or rather, as we have just seen, the conscious adjustment of the new and the old is imagination. Interaction of a living being with an environment is found in vegetative and animal life. But the experience enacted is human and conscious only as that which is given here and now is extended by meanings and values drawn from what is absent in fact and present only imaginatively. (1958a, 272)

The imagination is also necessary for creating and applying general prin-ciples and abstract concepts and ideas (Jo 2002, 40). Generalising involves abstracting from the particulars in immediate experience and creating something more common which will help reorganise and make sense of the experience and future experiences. This is exemplified by Dewey's under-standing of logical principles. As we have seen, Dewey believes that logi-cal principles are derived from abstracting the successful or unsuccessful thinking methods or inferences from particular inquiries and transforming them into general principles or rules that may be used for guiding future inquiry (Chapter 3). Thus, generalising involves imagining how a particu-lar instance of something may be transformed in such a way that it can be usefully applied in other contexts. Generalising also requires us to imag-ine how particular situations, objects and instances are connected or alike so as to group them together under a common idea, principle or concept. The application of such general principles back to concrete particulars also involves imagination.

The imagination also enables moral reasoning, which is an essential attribute of all thinking. Ethics is one area where the imagination has gained significant attention because of its obvious connection to empathy (e.g., Nussbaum 2010; Kirkman 2008; Glover 1999; Greene 1995; John-son, 1993). Empathy involves imagining alternative perspectives, how other people might feel and what their desires, needs and interests may be. The empathetic or moral imagination is particularly important for understanding and interacting with those most different to ourselves. This is why Harris (1997) argues that racist people are people who lack the imaginative capacity that would enable them to consider and appreciate alternative cultural perspectives. Imagination is essential for communal life because it enables an awareness of other individuals, including past and future individuals, even in their physical absence. Such awareness gives rise to thinking and conduct that promotes social, not just personal, freedom, growth and happiness. For Dewey, the empathetic imagination is actually necessary for all inquiry. There are two reasons for this. First, because our environment is necessarily social and cultural, Dewey believed that communal inquiry was always superior to individual inquiry (Chapter 2). Second, like Vygotsky, Dewey argued that all thinking has its origins in dia*logue* (Chapter 2). If communal inquiry is always the superior mode of thinking, and thinking itself originates in social interaction, the empathetic imagination is essential for all thinking. Without the empathetic imagination, communal inquiry would not be possible because individuals could not properly understand each other's ideas and needs and develop the sense of mutual trust that a functioning community requires.

Thus, unlike Plato, Dewey does not conceive of the imagination as something opposed to thinking, reasoning, knowledge or reality. According to Dewey, the imagination enables us to not only understand reality but also transform it so that it is more conducive to human flourishing. The imagination also enables us to imagine ourselves as other than we currently are and transform ourselves so that we can interact with our environment in a more harmonious manner. Thus, this notion of imagination is essential for autonomy and happiness.

THE IMAGINATION IN TRADITIONAL EDUCATION

Traditional schooling discourages the imagination by presenting students with facts as if they are settled, unproblematic and ready to be memorised. There is an underlying assumption that the aim of schooling is to help students adapt to a fixed environment. Yet, if everything appears certain, absolute, unproblematic and complete, then there is no reason for students to imagine things as other than they are. As Dewey explains, "The feeling that instruction in 'facts, facts' produces a narrow Gradgrind is justified not because facts in themselves are limiting, but because facts are dealt out as such hard and fast ready-made articles as to leave no room to imagination" (1997, 223–224).

While this type of schooling is old-fashioned and has been extensively criticised, I have argued that it is still widely adopted in various forms (Chapter 1). It is reflected in 'the return to basics' and 'core knowledge' ideologies, which emphasise all students learning the same prescribed content and skills, with a focus on students accumulating facts through memorisation and drill (e.g., Quirk 2005; Hirsch 1987). Such educational ideas are also reflected in what McNeil (2009) calls the "systematic curriculum", an educational ideal that stresses accountability and efficiency. It is currently the dominant educational ideal in Australia, the United States and England, where it has been widely criticised by educationalists (e.g., Ravitch 2010; McNeil 2009; Lingard 2009; Berliner 2009; Kelly 2009; Nussbaum 2010). As explained in Chapter 1, this ideology fosters a type of schooling where complex capacities like imagination are sidelined as the curriculum is narrowed to focus on easily testable skills and content, such as basic literacy and numeracy skills and the recall of facts. Egan identifies the prevalence of the systematic approach as a barrier to fostering the imagination:

> In general, imagination has not fared well as might have been expected in educational writings about the design of curricula, teaching methods, and studies of student's learning. It seems to have become sidelined by agendas that are more urgent, that seek specific social objectives from teaching, and that focus on efficiency and accountability. From the perspectives of those who have encouraged and directed this general movement in public education, imagination seems something of a frill; containing value, no doubt, but a value left to the "arts" rather than to the more central purposes of a public system that is paid for by people who often have objectives for their investment that are more specific. (2007, 3–4)

Not only is the imagination often "left to the arts", but the arts themselves are sidelined in the systemic approach to schooling. Berliner (2009) argues that many U.S. schools have decreased the amount of time devoted to the arts so that teachers can focus on teaching the skills and knowledge assessed on high stakes tests (see also Nussbaum 2010). The time demands of the systematic model also discourage the teacher's imagination, which, in turn, reduces the likelihood of students engaging in imaginative learning experiences. One teacher quoted by Apple stated, "I just want to get this done: I don't have time to be creative or imaginative" (2009, 206). As Apple explains, "[W]e should not blame the teacher here. In mathematics, for example, teachers typically had to spend half the allotted time correcting and recording the worksheets the students completed each day" (2009, 206).

When the imagination is identified as educationally valuable, it tends to be narrowly associated with specific subject areas, like the arts and creative writing. The inclusion of the arts on the core curriculum is often justified on the grounds that the arts have a unique ability to foster the imagination. For example, Greene argues that the arts have such a unique ability because artworks go beyond immediate experience and evoke alternative and multiple versions of reality:

> It is because I believe that encounters with the arts can awaken us to alternative possibilities of existing, of being human, of relating to— others, of being other, that I argue for their centrality in curriculum. I believe they can open new perspectives on what is assumed to be "reality," that they can defamiliarize what has become so familiar it has stopped us from asking questions or protesting or taking action to repair. (1993, 214)

While I agree that the arts do foster the imagination and should occupy a central place in the curriculum, the problem with focusing narrowly on the arts as a means to fostering the imagination, is that this can reinforce the view that the imagination is distinct from reason and that it is not relevant to subjects like maths and science. We don't want the imagination to be seen as something peculiar to the arts. Nor do we want the arts to be seen as opposed to reason because they emphasise the imagination. As Nussbaum argues, "[Students] need to see an imaginative dimension in all their interactions, and to see works of art as just one domain in which imagination is cultivated" (2010, 103). This echoes Dewey's claim that all academic disciplines "are full of matters that must be imaginatively realized if they are realized at all" (1997, 223–224). Schools must help students see that all good thinking, whether it is in science, art or physical education, is imaginative. Philosophy may assist schools in achieving this goal.

FOSTERING THE IMAGINATION THROUGH PHILOSOPHY

Philosophy problematises the taken-for-granted aspects of everyday experience and, as such, provokes the consideration of alternative possible ways of being in the world. Philosophy involves questioning, wondering, criticising and going beneath the surface of what is immediately given. Unlike the closed questioning that characterises traditional schooling, philosophical questions don't presuppose one correct, fixed answer. Philosophical questions are often open-ended and may have many answers which are likely to be contentious, be open to criticism and lead to further questions. Thus, philosophical questions open up a space for the imaginative consideration of alternative possibilities. Philosophy is also unique in that it draws out the problematic, contentious and, thus, imaginative aspects of other disciplines. Other school subjects often take it for granted that truth, freewill, justice, democracy and beauty exist, and they even make uncritical assumptions about what such concepts mean. In contrast, philosophy assumes that such concepts are contentious and much philosophical inquiry is devoted to exploring them. Because such concepts are so fundamental to all our experiences and understandings, philosophical inquiry can provoke us to imaginatively reflect on every aspect of our lives. As a high school philosophy teacher, teachers of other subjects frequently told me that my philosophy students were constantly bringing up philosophical issues in their classes. While some teachers appreciated the depth of understanding and critical attitude that these students were displaying, others seemed to find it frustrating because they wanted the students to stop complicating the content so that they could move through the curriculum more efficiently. Philosophy's introduction into the curriculum may help foster the imagination in all subject areas and disrupt schooling narrowly focused on the efficient acquisition of content.

The seemingly abstract and often idealistic nature of much philosophical subject matter may also excite the imagination. Philosophers have heavily

relied upon imaginative devices like metaphors, similes, analogies, allego-
ries, hypotheticals, thought experiments and fictional narratives as means
of exploring and clarifying philosophical problems and ideas. Such devices
are useful for clarifying and reinforcing the relationship between the seemingly abstract problems and ideas of philosophy and our concrete experiences. One well-known example of this is Parfit's teletransporter. Parfit
asks us to imagine using a teletransporter to travel to Mars at the speed of
light as a way of getting us to think about personal identity:

> When I press the button, I shall lose consciousness, and then wake up
> at what seems a moment later. In fact I shall have been unconscious for
> what seems like about an hour. The scanner here on earth will destroy
> my brain and body, while recording the exact states of all my cells. It will
> then transmit the information by radio. Travelling at the speed of light,
> the message will take three minutes to reach the Replicator on Mars.
> This will then create, out of new matter, a brain and body exactly like
> mine. It will be in this body that I shall wake up. (1984, 199)

This scenario prompts us to consider if the replica would be identical to the
person who got in the teletransporter or if it would be a new person. Such
fictional scenarios can help us draw out the implications and significance
of complex metaphysical problems and theories for our everyday life. Metaphorical thinking plays an equally important role in philosophy. As we
have seen, Plato himself famously utilised metaphorical thinking. Plato's
most famous metaphor, the Allegory of the Cave, explicates his complex
idealist theory of reality and knowledge, while emphasising the fundamental implications of this theory for our everyday experiences. Furthermore,
many philosophical theories are normative rather than descriptive. As such,
they outline ideals that may not currently exist. When there are no concrete examples of normative ideas, philosophers often rely on metaphorical
thinking, stories or hypotheticals to explain and evaluate such ideas (e.g.,
Williams 1973). It is for such reasons that Parfit states that these imagi-
nary devices help us clarify and develop our understanding of reality (1984,
200). As we have seen, Lipman's P4C curriculum also relies upon fictional
narratives to embed philosophical ideas in stories relevant to the lives of
young people. These stories prompt philosophical inquiry that involves students unpacking and creating fictional scenarios, hypotheticals and metaphors as a means of clarifying perplexities and making sense of their world
(see Hamrick 1989).

The close relationship between philosophy and the imagination is also
implied by the claim that children, who are thought to be naturally imaginative, have a natural propensity for philosophy. It is argued that children
wonder about the seemingly mundane, ask questions of a philosophical
nature and are constantly searching for meaningfulness (Matthews 1980).
The child's tendency for wonderment and curiosity results from the fact that

they are constantly having new experiences but lack the concepts that would help them make sense of that experience. Furthermore, their thinking has not been so moulded by dominant cultural beliefs and values. The constant stream of new and confusing experiences provokes philosophical wonderment, as well as the search for alternative possibilities and explanations. It is not surprising that Splitter and Sharp believe their imaginative tendency may give children an advantage when it comes to philosophical thinking:

> When it comes to that aspect of thinking, which is concerned with meaning and understanding—with making sense of something which presents itself as puzzling or intriguing—the young child's ability to imagine new possibilities and think creatively may be even more valuable than her mature counterpart's greater experience and linguistic sophistication. (1995, 97)

FOSTERING THE IMAGINATION THROUGH PHILOSOPHY FOR CHILDREN

Since the aim of a P4C class is to meaningfully reconstruct philosophically puzzling experiences, imaginative thinking is of fundamental importance. While children may have a natural propensity for imaginativeness, their thinking may also be more fanciful than imaginative at times. Students need to be scaffolded to develop the capacity for imagining possibilities and creating ideas that have the potential to be realised. This means that students must learn that even the imagination is governed by logic (Sigurdardóttir 2002, 38). An idea or method that assumes that 1+1=3 or 'if A then B, not A, therefore not B' is unlikely to be effective at meaningfully reconstructing experience. Since P4C is specifically aimed at facilitating reasonableness and incorporates the philosophical sub-discipline of logic, it is well equipped to help children create ideas that are imaginative rather than just fanciful. In the P4C classroom, children are encouraged, through teacher questioning and specially designed activities, to seek and give reasons for ideas, search for evidence, consider alternatives, construct criteria to evaluate ideas, consider the implications of different ideas, look for examples, construct analogies, make generalisations and so on. As we have seen, logic provides children with a language and tools to discuss good and bad inferences (Chapter 3).

The communal inquiry structure of the P4C classroom also scaffolds the intelligent imagination because it encourages children to consider alternative perspectives. When our ideas are made problematic by the differing or critical views of others, we must look beyond what is familiar and search for alternative meanings. Furthermore, the corrective potential of others can help us avoid thinking that is unrealistic and fanciful as opposed to imaginative. This is why Sigurdardóttir states that "four eyes are better than two, and communication with other people—listening to different perspectives—seems to be the best way to avoid imagination's dead ends" (2002, 34). Imagining with others helps us imagine alternative possibilities and ideas that are more objective because they take into account the needs and interests of others. This limits the possibility of students imagining and desiring ends that are unlikely to be successfully realised in a social environment. The communal nature of the P4C classroom may help facilitate the empathetic imagination, which can enable students to imagine socially reconstructive ideas.

P4C's emphasis on fallibilism, self-correction and open-mindedness also fosters the development of imagination because these capacities are dependent on the intelligent imagination. The greater one's capacity for imagination, the less likely they are to fear changes, difference or problems. This is because imaginative people know that if a new experience or idea problematises their beliefs, they will be able to respond by imaginatively creating new understandings. As such, imaginative people are less likely to feel despair or be defensive and dogmatic when their beliefs are challenged. Consequently, they are more likely to be open to alternative perspectives and new experiences and be more likely to self-correct. They are more likely to see problems and alternatives as opportunities for imaginatively recreating current beliefs and gaining new knowledge. This is suggested by Lipman's description of creative thinkers:

> The merely critical thinker is somehow conservative, in the sense that he or she is not content until finding a belief that dispenses with thinking. On the other hand, the creative thinker is essentially sceptical and radical. Creative thinkers are never so happy as when they have been let loose, like bulls in china shops, to smash to smithereens the bric-a-brac of the world. (2003, 254)

Thus, the open-minded, self-corrective and flexible thinking that P4C aims to facilitate is essentially imaginative thinking.

Another one of P4C's fundamental goals is to facilitate autonomy or the capacity to think for oneself (Lipman 2003; Splitter and Sharp 1995). Independent thinking and autonomy also involve the intelligent imagination, which enables individuals to imagine things differently to how other people perceive them, and to dominant social values and practices. It is also through the intelligent imagination that individuals transform and influence their social-cultural environment in accordance with their own ideals. Thus, without the imagination, one would simply have to follow the crowd and accept the status quo, even if one found it oppressive or undesirable. For marginalised groups, including children and young people, the imagination may be particularly important. Their interests and experiences may be those least reflected in dominant values and knowledge. The imagination enables young people to create and express ideas that are not entirely constrained by adult understandings. The intelligent imagination also enables us to transform ourselves in accordance with our personal goals or ideals. By helping students imagine reasonable ideas and possibilities, P4C can help students set realistic and attainable goals for themselves and construct effective means for attaining them. As Degenhardt and McKay explain, a lack of autonomy often results from individuals setting goals that are unrealistic or ill conceived:

> In envisaging future developments in our lives, in trying to foresee chosen activities and commitments, it is easy to focus on and exaggerate the rewards of a particular life-style. We may then become disillusioned and even bitter when we encounter the realities of such a life-style and our own aptitude for participating in it. This could have been avoided if our initial imaginings had been fuller, more disciplined, and better informed. (1988, 253)

Thus, P4C can enable schools to foster Dewey's desirable notion of intelligent imagination. This is because P4C emphasises the problematic, idealism, community, reasonableness, autonomy, open-mindedness, fallibilism and the search for meaningfulness. This contrasts traditional schooling which reflects Plato's concern that the imagination may lead us away from truth, understanding and happiness. Traditional schooling discourages the imagination by focusing on the accumulation of 'facts' and the mastery of basic skills. Very student-centred pedagogies can also discourage the development of intelligent imagination because they often assume relativism, which fails to provoke students to critically reflect on their imagined aims and desires and assess the likelihood of them being realised in concrete experience (see Chapter 3). If, as Dewey states, the aim and the means of education is growth, without the capacity for intelligent imagination, which is the ability to meaningfully transform oneself and one's world, one could not be educated. This is why Greene states that "a kindred imaginative ability is required if the becoming different that learning involves is actually to take place" (1995, 22). As such, philosophical Communities of Inquiry should be central to all learning.

5 A Response to Reason/
Emotion Dualism

The Emotions in Dewey
and Philosophy for Children

Since the emotions are associated with the body, the subjective, the private and the concrete experiences of everyday life, especially the experiences of women, they too have been conceived of as radically opposed to Reason, and as unable to provide us with knowledge. As such, schooling has also tended to exclude or devalue the emotions. The emotions have traditionally been thought to distract students from acquiring objective truths about the external world by focusing their attention on their own inner world and personal needs. The dominant assumption is that like the imagination, the emotions distract students from the cultivation of Reason, the acquisition of facts and development of autonomy. In fact, schooling is often conceived of as a means to helping children transcend their imaginative and emotional natures. The devaluing of both the imagination and the emotions is reflected in the traditional curriculum hierarchy, where subjects like maths and the physical sciences are generally considered more valuable and important than the arts, which are associated with both imagination and affectivity (see Chapter 1).

Goleman's (1996) writing about emotional intelligence instigated a reconsideration of the important role that the emotions play in our capacity to form good judgments and act intelligently. This provoked many schools to develop emotional literacy programs. However, as Boler (1999) explains, many of these programs emphasise controlling the emotions and encourage students to uncritically conform to dominant social ideals of good emotional behaviour. Such programs are also usually separated from the academic curriculum. For example, pastoral care programs which focus on student's emotional and social development are generally considered 'extra-curricular' and run during form periods, homeroom or some other non-academic timeslot. Thus, even when the emotions are considered to be valuable they are segregated from the 'real' educational activity of knowing.

Sometimes the emotions are considered to be a form of thinking, often referred to as 'caring thinking'. However, caring thinking is generally posited as a distinct form of thinking that compliments critical thinking. Even this notion of caring thinking underestimates the importance of the emotions, which are not merely an attribute of some distinct form of thinking but are integral to all thinking. Unless one has the capacity for emotional intelligence, one cannot think at all. In this chapter, Dewey's theory of emotion will be utilised to argue that, like the imagination, the emotions are central to all thinking and must be facilitated in all aspects of schooling. Since Philosophy for Children (P4C) incorporates Dewey's notion of communal inquiry, P4C has the potential to foster the emotional aspect of all good thinking.

DEWEY'S THEORY OF EMOTION

Dewey's theory of emotion integrates and builds on aspects of Darwin's account of the emotions and the James–Lange theory of emotion. Dewey's theory aims "to bring these two [theories] into some organic connection with each other, indicating the modifications of statement demanded by such connection" (Dewey 1971, 152). Thus, in order to understand Dewey's account of the emotions, we must first have some understanding of the strengths and weaknesses of these two theories of emotion.

Darwin believed that emotional behaviours are outward expressions of inner states. He described the entire emotional experience as consisting of three stages: 1) some object of perception exists (e.g., a bear); 2) this perception gives rise to some inner emotional state (e.g., fear); 3) this inner state results in emotional behaviours (e.g., rapid heartbeat, increased perspiration, trembling, yelling, running, etc.). The theory rests upon three basic principles. The first being that emotions are "serviceable associated habits" (Darwin 1979, 28). He argues that emotional behaviours are actions that have proven useful for expressing feelings, useful in the sense that they enable us to either satisfy desirable sensations or eradicate unpleasant ones. Eventually, such behaviours become habitual and are reproduced in associated situations even though they may no longer be of any use. They become automated responses to experiences that bear some resemblance to the sorts of experiences that gave rise to such behaviours in the first place. Darwin states that these habits are inheritable. Since habits lead to physiological changes in the nervous system, these emotional behaviours have been passed on from one generation to the next. For example, the behaviours associated with fear result from the fact that throughout numerous generations, individuals have tried to escape from dangerous situations through some type of exertion, which is typically accompanied by an increasingly rapid heartbeat, heavy breathing, dilated nostrils, pallor, perspiration, trembling of muscles and so on. As a consequence, now "whenever the emotion of fear is strongly felt, though it may not lead to any exertion, the same results tend to reappear, through the force of inheritance and association" (1979, 308).

Darwin's second principle is the principle of antithesis, which states that some emotional behaviours are not themselves serviceable associated habits but are merely the opposite of other emotional behaviours. According to Darwin, when a state of mind is induced that is the exact opposite of some other state of mind, "there is a strong and involuntary tendency" to perform movements that are the direct opposite of the movements accompanying the opposing state of mind (1979, 28). For example, if joy and anger are taken as opposite emotions, joy may be accompanied by certain expressive behaviour simply because that behaviour is the opposite of the behaviour associated with anger.

The third principle is that emotional behaviour may involve the direct action of the nervous system, "independently from the first of the Will, and independently to a certain extent of Habit" (1979, 28). Thus, emotions can involve automatic physiological responses or reflex actions, such as the increased heart rate that accompanies fear.

While Darwin's notion of the emotions as serviceable associated habits seems plausible, other aspects of the theory are less convincing. In particular, many have found the principle of antithesis quite unsatisfactory. One reason for this is that it isn't very Darwinian. This principle entails that some emotional behaviour is, and always was, entirely useless in that it was never a means to survival or growth. It seems as though Darwin developed the principle of antitheses as a last resort to explain particularly puzzling emotional behaviour—emotional behaviour that couldn't be explained as serviceable associated habits. However, some of the emotional behaviours that Darwin attributes to antithesis could actually be better explained as serviceable associated habits. For example, Darwin uses antithesis to explain the raising of the arms and the open hands associated with astonishment, stating that such behaviours are the opposite of a state of indifference or listlessness. Wallace understandably criticised this explanation, stating that the behaviours are "too definite, too uniform, and too widespread, to be derived from such a vague and variable cause as the opposite of a position of unconcernedness" (1873, 116). He goes on to offer a more plausible (and more Darwinian) explanation, stating that:

> astonishment, among our savage ancestors, would most frequently be excited by the sudden appearance of enemies or wild beasts, or by seeing a friend or a child in imminent danger. The appropriate movement, either to defend the observer's face or body, or to prepare to give assistance to the person in danger, is to raise the arms and open the hands, at the same time opening the mouth to utter a cry of alarm or encouragement. It is the protective attitude of an unarmed man. (1873, 116)

For the same reasons as Wallace, Dewey also rejects Darwin's principle of antithesis but he does adopt Darwin's notion of emotions as serviceable habits. In fact, the idea that emotional behaviours are, or once were, useful behaviours is even more prominent in Dewey's theory of emotions. However, Dewey rejects Darwin's suggestion that such behaviours are useful because they express emotional states. For Dewey, emotional behaviours are "acts originally useful not *qua* expressing emotion, but *qua* acts–as servicing life" (1971, 154). That is, such behaviours either are, or once were, intentional, goal-orientated actions directed towards objects in the world. They are actions that either are, or once were, useful for survival, growth or interacting with our environment in a meaningful manner. Dewey argues that we mistakenly believe such behaviours to be primarily expressive because this is how they appear from the standpoint of an observer, or upon reflection on one's own behaviour. However, to the individual performing such actions, they have a more practical and objective end. Hence, the reason Dewey rejects Darwin's principle of antithesis because such opposite behaviours have no intentionality (1971, 166). He accepts Darwin's third principle but emphasises that even automatic behaviours that result from direct action of the nervous system are, or once were, useful and intentional. For example, the rapid heartbeat associated with fear increases the circulation of blood throughout the body in preparation for rapid movement, such as running. Thus, as Cunningham notes, Dewey's theory is actually "more Darwinian than Darwin's" (1995, 866). Dewey also rejects Darwin's suggestion that the emotional state and feeling precede and provoke the emotional behaviour, partially adopting an alternative explanation provided by James.

James (1884) famously rejected the notion that emotional behaviours express feelings, arguing that feelings are actually a consequence of emotional behaviours. While Darwin suggests that feelings precede and give rise to emotional behaviour, James claims that it is the behaviour which comes first and gives rise to the feeling and emotional state. Thus, he reverses the last two stages of the emotional process, as described by Darwin. According to James, an emotional experience involves 1) some object of perception (e.g., a bear); 2) the stimulation of emotional behaviours by this object of perception (e.g., rapid heartbeat, trembling, yelling, etc.); and 3) an inner emotional state (e.g., fear) which is actually our awareness of the behavioural changes that take place in the second stage. Drawing on Darwin's third principle, James posits that emotional behaviours are directly and involuntarily stimulated by our perceptions. That is, we see something frightening, and this perception automatically triggers a rapid heartbeat, heavy breathing, perspiration and trembling of muscles. The feeling or emotional state is our conscious awareness of these physiological changes or behaviours. James' theory has been widely criticised because, as Solomon explains, it is thought to suggest "that putting on a happy face will indeed result in feeling happy" (2003, 145). That is, the theory seems counterintuitive. Commonsense suggests that we smile because we feel happy, clench our fists because we feel angry and cry because we feel sad.

Dewey accepts James's claim that the feel of emotional experience is our awareness of the physiological changes that accompany emotional behaviour. Thus, contra Darwin, Dewey believes that at least some of the emotional behaviour (what Darwin calls the 'expression') precedes and gives rise to the feeling (what Darwin calls the 'emotion'). However, Dewey states that James's theory of emotion is really only an account of feeling, which is but one aspect of the entire emotion experience. James is often misunderstood to be equating the feel with the entire emotion, and this misunderstanding is the main source of the criticism of his work. As Dewey points out, James doesn't say we *are* angry because we strike but rather that we *feel* angry because we strike. He never claims that the entire state of anger can be explained as merely the conscious awareness of physiological changes resulting from striking, which suggests that anger could simply be brought about by striking and that anger doesn't exist until after one strikes. James is merely talking about the feel of the angry state, not the entire experience of being angry. What James does is abstract the feel aspect of the emotion, which, as Dewey states, can only be done upon reflection because feeling certainly has no existence by itself (Dewey 1971, 171–172). Dewey states that this misinterpretation of James's theory results from James's failure to fully explain how the feeling aspect of experience is connected to other aspects of the emotion experience (1971, 172). Dewey's theory of emotion aims to rectify this oversight.

Dewey states that the emotion encompasses three phases: the *feel*, the *object or idea* (intellectual content), and the *action or behaviour* (1971, 172–173). In order to explain the connection between the three phases of emotion, Dewey begins with the notion that emotional behaviour begins as an "instinctive reaction, not a response to an idea as such" (1971, 174). Dewey states that this instinctive response results from our internalising actions that have previously proven useful for survival in associated experiences. Thus, they are habits and passed on from one generation to the next. However, with an emotional experience, the initial instinctive response is not a complete and purposeful action. It is a syncopated action. If the instinctive response automatically and completely leads into a totally coordinated and useful action, then there is no emotional seizure. Emotion results from some type of tension or conflict. It is when the instinctive or habitual response is inhibited because other conflicting actions are also suggested or because no complete, coordinated response is immediately suggested that emotion is experienced. It is only when the instinctive response is inhibited that we become conscious of it. This consciousness of an inhibited action is the feel of emotion. This is how emotional behaviours look from the point of view of an onlooker. They look like incomplete, rather useless actions (e.g., jumping when frightened, clenching one's fists in ager, throwing one's arms up with joy). At the same time that this instinctive behavioural response triggers feeling, it also triggers cognition as a means to understanding and more intelligently responding to the perception. Thus, the instinctive response simultaneously stimulates feeling and cognition and, in some cases, the enactment of a more complete, purposeful action. This means that the emotional idea or belief (intellectual content) is actually coloured with emotion. It doesn't precede or follow the feeling but emerges in conjunction with the feeling. Thus, as Dewey explains, our perception is not just an emotionless perception of a bear, but a perception of a fearful bear (1971, 175–181). Hence, for Dewey, the feeling, the object or idea and the developing behaviour inform and constitute one another, enabling the individual to intelligently respond to the situation. The feel, the object and the total behaviour do not exist, in their entirety, prior to the other or prior to the completed emotional experience. As Dewey explains, "[F]actors of a coordination (whether due to inherited instinct or to individually acquired habit) begin to operate and we run away; running away, we get the idea of 'running-away-from-bear', or of 'bear-as-thing-to-be-run-from'" (1971, 178).

Since Dewey describes emotions as involving intentional behaviours directed towards our environment, he rejects the dominant notion of the emotions as purely subjective and physiological. For Dewey, the emotions are objective-subjective because they respond to, and are directed towards, objects in the world and other people (1967, 239–240; 1971, 161, 173). Since the emotions are purposeful behaviours, they have an intellectual or rational aspect. Our emotions contain a judgment about the value, use or worth of the objects that they are directed towards:

> This immediate correlation of the emotion with an "object," and its immediate tendency to assume the "object" when it is not there, seem to me mere tautology for saying that the emotional attitude is normally rational in content (i.e., adjusted to some end). (Dewey 1971, 161–162)

As Solomon explains, such views of the emotions "break down the Cartesian barrier between experience and the world, between the 'inner' and the 'outer'" (2003, 149). The emotions, as purposeful behaviours, are not opposed to an external reality. They enable us to interact with our environment and other people in an intelligent and transformative manner. According to Dewey, it is when emotions do not have real objects that they are harmful because they don't enable purposeful interaction between an individual and their environment (1971, 161).

Thus, Dewey's account of the emotions is a cognitivist theory of emotion (Solomon 2003, 93; Cunningham 1995, 866). Like Aristotle's theory of emotion, Dewey's theory entails that there are such things as reasonable and useful emotions, as well as unreasonable and counterproductive emotions. Those emotions that don't enable meaningful, purposeful interactions with our environment, such as pathological emotions, are unreasonable. Thus, like other cognitivist theories of the emotions, Dewey's theory rejects Reason/emotion dualism. Jaggar argues that many cognitivist theories merely replace Reason/emotion dualism with an equally problematic Reason/feeling dualism because they describe emotion as a cognitive process that is distinct from feeling, which is described as a purely physiological, subjective and impulsive process. Alternatively, the emotions are thought to consist of both a physiological, feeling aspect and a superior, cognitive aspect. Thus, Reason/feeling, mind/body and subject/object dualisms remain intact (Jaggar 1989, 149–150). However, since Dewey argues that the objective (cognitive), behavioural and feeling aspects of emotion are all interdependent and constitutive of each other, his theory also rejects Reason/feeling dualism. These aspects of emotion are in no way distinct; it is only upon reflection that we describe them as separate aspects of emotion in order to analyse and theorise emotion. In actuality, they are inseparable elements of the entire emotional experience.

Cunningham points out that modern neuroscience provides empirical evidence to support Dewey's account of the emotions, at least in relation to fear. This research not only lends support to Dewey's theory, it also helps to clarify it. Cunningham draws on psychologist and neuroscientist Joseph LeDoux' research on the formation of emotional memories. LeDoux conducted experiments on rats that showed that when the cortex (the area of the human brain that enables fully conscious perception) was damaged or removed, the rats were still capable of generating fear memories, at least with simple perceptions. With more complex perceptions, the cortex was required because a more detailed interpretation of the stimulus was needed. Based on such experiments, LeDoux argues that emotional stimulations are initially processed in the thalamus rather than the cortex, which supports Dewey's claim that our initial responses are not conscious or cognitive but rather instinctive or habitual. LeDoux argues that the reason for this may be that pathways from the thalamus are shorter, involving only one neural link and, as such, they enable a faster, more rapid response, which is important for survival. In contrast, the pathways from the cortex involve several neural links and, thus, take a longer time to stimulate a response. However, the thalamus provides only a crude perception of the external world, whereas the cortex provides a more detailed and accurate perception. This is why the cortex is needed for more complex perceptions, as well as for the later refining and verification of initial responses once they are underway. Thus, LeDoux's research supports Dewey's claim that complete and purposeful emotional experiences involve an interaction of cognitive, feeling and behavioural processes. LeDoux argues that once the thalamus is activated, it then sends information to the cortex and the amygdala (part of the brain associated with feeling) at about the same time. However, "the reaction of the amygdala is more rapid than that of the cortex", which suggests that the further physiological changes the amygdala initiates trigger an awareness (the feeling) of those changes, "as well as the need for a more detailed interpretation of the stimuli" or perception (Cunningham 1995, 871). Thus, the amygdala seems to trigger the reaction from the cortex. Presumably, the more detailed perception would then inform, verify, reinforce or inhibit the feeling and the behaviour. Thus, as Cunningham states, this seems to support Dewey's description of the interrelatedness of the three phases of the emotional experience. It explains how the feeling, the idea or object and the completed behaviour are all constituted by one another through their interaction and coordination. As Cunningham explains,

> If subconscious processes activate the physiological responses of the organism at roughly the same time that the sensory data reaches the cortex, then the organism will normally be aware not only of the cognitive dimension (i.e. the sensory information) but also of its bodily reactions to the stimuli (manifestations of the physiological alterations). That is to say, the consciousness of the object will be permeated with both cognitive and emotive elements. And, as Dewey says, the perceived object will be a frightening bear. (1995, 872)

THE ROLE OF THE EMOTIONS IN INQUIRY

Dewey's detailed account of the emotions enables us to better understand the various roles that emotion plays in inquiry and the meaningful reconstruction of experience. The emotions enable us to select problematic experiences for reconstruction in the first place. Through emotional experience, objects, ideas and situations are seen as either valuable or as disagreeable. It is because we have emotions that certain situations, objects, ideas and aspects of experience appear salient and of interest to us, while others go unnoticed or receive little attention. As we have seen, Dewey rejects traditional ideals of experience, which tend to render the observer a passive, disinterested recipient of external stimuli (Chapter 2). For Dewey, experience involves an active, desiring, and interested individual, always moving out towards its environment in "one direction rather than another" (1972, 123). It is because we have desires and interests that we have problematic experiences, and inquiry as a means to reconstructing them. A problematic experience is one that obstructs or fails to satisfy our needs or desires in some way. We actively select such experiences for reconstruction because they disrupt our harmonious, habitual interaction with the world, leading to a "loss of integration with environment", a type of disequilibrium (1958a, 15). Such experiences are accompanied by emotions like agitation, frustration, tension, anxiety, perplexity, uncertainty, and even fear and anger. These emotions give rise to a "desire for restoration of the union" between the individual and their environment, which propels the individual to critically reflect upon the experience and reconstruct it through the process of inquiry (1958a, 15; 1967, 230–231). As Dewey states, "[E]motion is the conscious sign of a break, actual or impending. The discord is the occasion that gives rise to reflection" (1958a, 15). Thus, the aim of inquiry is to reinstate a harmonious coexistence between an organism and their environment and, in doing so, remove the frustration of desires, anxiety and perplexity (1991, 106). The restoration of the harmony between an individual and their environment after a process of inquiry is what Dewey calls the "reflective equilibrium", which is the aesthetic aspect of all reflective experience (1958a, 14). Not only do the emotions signal the need for inquiry, but they also signal its end or settlement because the reflective equilibrium should be accompanied by feelings of satisfaction, fulfilment, and possibly pleasure and contentment.[1]

This means that inquiry is controlled and guided by the emotions. It is because we have desires and emotions that inquiry has a purpose. Without the anxiety derived from the frustration of our needs and interests and the resulting desire for reintegration of the self and environment, there would be no need to imagine alternative possibilities or means for attaining them. As we have seen in the previous chapter, these imagined possibilities guide the inquiry because realising these possibilities is the aim of inquiry. This is why Dewey states that the failure to recognise the fundamental role of the emotions in thinking is "to neglect the function of needs in creating ends, or consequences to be attained" (1984a, 106). Thus, the imagination enables us to imagine situations not only as different to how they are, but as transformed in ways that are more compatible with our desires. As Dewey explains, "It has been noted that human experience is made human through the existence of associations and recollections, which are strained through the mesh of imagination so as to suit the demands of the emotions" (2004b, 59). The emotions not only initiate and guide the construction of alternative possibilities; they enable us to critically compare and select between alternative possibilities (Scheffler 1991, 9). The emotions provide us with preferences and, as such, criteria for choosing between competing possibilities.

Research in cognitive science also supports this hypothesis that the emotions play a central role in the formation of goals and the critical comparison of alternative possibilities. For example, Damasio (1996) argues that individuals with damage to the prefrontal cortex, which he associates with emotionality, show an inability to make rational decisions, especially in personal and social matters, often leading to self-destructive behaviour. While such individuals could make decisions in situations where the outcomes of those decisions could be calculated with certainty, in decisions that involved no such certainty, which would be most decisions, they displayed poor judgment. Such individuals had no damage to the regions of the brain associated with the intellect. However, Damasio argues that the regions of the brain that are damaged are those that enable individuals to make connections between emotions and relevant experiences. This is what he calls the "somatic marker hypothesis". This region of the brain enables certain experiences to be marked as likely to produce particular emotions. When this region of the brain is damaged, no such emotional marking occurs. Consequently, individuals suffering such damage are unable to have appropriate emotional responses to situations and are unable to make decisions that are in their own and others' best interests because they cannot connect the outcomes of such decisions to desirable or undesirable emotional states. In order to offer further support for this hypothesis, Damasio conducted controlled experiments where individuals were asked to participate in a gambling game, in which the aim was to maximise their profits. Those without damage to this region of the brain, including those with damage to other areas of the brain, were predominantly able to maximise their profits. In contrast, those with damage to the prefrontal cortex consistently made irrational choices that resulted in long-term losses. Such empirical research highlights the role that emotions plays in the selection of experiences, the critical comparison of alternatives and construction of ends, all of which are essential aspects of Dewey's account of inquiry.

The emotions also have a communicative and social function that plays a central role in communal inquiry, which, as we have seen, is the superior mode of inquiry. In the previous chapter, it was explained that empathy is essential for communal inquiry. Empathy is not only imaginative but also emotional because it involves imagining how another feels or would feel in certain situations. It involves being emotionally moved by the experiences, needs, interests and problems of others. Empathy enables us not only to understand others but also to communicate our ideas, feelings and perspectives. Through imagining what others think and feel we can communicate our own feelings and experiences in a way that the other is more likely to understand and appreciate.

While the communicative role of the emotions is not a focus of Dewey's work on the emotions, it was of particular interest to Dewey's colleague and fellow pragmatist George Herbert Mead. Mead's work draws on and develops Dewey's theory of emotion (see L. Ward 1989). Like Dewey, Mead argues that emotional behaviours are signs of impending action, which may be carried out or inhibited. As such, emotions communicate our feelings and intentions to others, who can modify their behaviour and prepare a response. In turn, the response of the other to our emotional behaviour signals to us whether they will assist us to attain our goal or act so as to inhibit our action. We can then modify our attitudes and behaviours accordingly and increase the likelihood of our own action being effective (i.e., not blocked by others). Thus, effective social interaction doesn't just involve dialogue but paying attention and responding to displays of emotion, which Mead describes as gestures. Mead argues that all gestures are pre-linguistic forms of communication that gave rise to language and thinking:

> Gesture . . . is primarily an expression of emotion. But the gesture itself is a syncopated act, one that has been cut short, a torso which conveys the emotional import of the act. Out of the emotional significance has grown the intellectual significance. It is evident but for the initial situation of social interaction the bodily and vocal gestures could never have attained their signification. Here is the birth of the symbol, and the possibility of thought. (quoted in L. Ward 1989, 470)

Dewey's own views on the social origins of thinking were partially derived from Mead's social psychology. Since the emotions and the imagination enable communication and social interaction, which give rise to language and thought, thinking, the imagination and the emotions are fundamentally intertwined.

CARING THINKING

Since Dewey's notion of thinking is communal, emotional and imaginative, it appears to have much in common with the notion of caring thinking popular with many feminist psychologists, epistemologists and ethicists. Psychologist Carol Gilligan (1982) argues that caring thinking is a method of moral reasoning associated with dominant ideals of femininity. She contrasts this care perspective with a 'masculine' moral perspective she calls the justice perspective. According to Gilligan, while the care perspective emphasises making moral judgments based on particular situations, concrete relationships and empathy; the justice perspective emphasises objective, dispassionate reasoning and universal moral rules. Caring thinking is also associated with connected knowing, while the justice perspective is associated with separate knowing. As explained in Chapter 1, connected knowers aim to understand others without imposing their own understandings on them. They utilise empathy and care as tools for connecting with others and building trusting relationships that allow the other to reveal themselves in their own terms. They want to understand why the other thinks what they do and how they came to their opinion. Connected knowers are more likely to accept that there may be many different, equally valuable perspectives. Separate knowers also aim to avoid imposing their own understandings and biases on others. However, they aim to do this through traditional notions of objectivity, which involve separating themselves from others so as not to influence or be influenced by others. Separate knowers aim to suppress their own feelings and personal preferences and rely upon general, abstract procedures and standards in order to understand and evaluate the opinions and actions of others.

Belenky et al. extend this notion of connected and separate knowing, arguing that these are not just methods of relating to other people but are also ways of knowing objects and ideas (1986, 102). They draw a connection between connected knowing and what Peter Elbow calls the "believing game" (in Belenky et al. 1986, 113). Connected knowers will try to be convinced by different ideas or perspectives in order to understand why another would accept them. They often find argumentation and critical thinking difficult. As one of the women in the Belenky et al. study explains,

> I'm not superanalytic. It's easy for me take other people's points of view. It's hard for me to argue, because I feel like I can understand the

other person's argument. It's easy for me to see a whole lot of different points of view on things and understand why people think those things. (1986, 113)

Elbow contrasts the believing game with what he calls the "doubting game", which Belenky et al. associate with separate knowing (1986, 104). The doubting game resembles methodological scepticism. The aim is to assume that an idea or argument is wrong or problematic in order to evaluate it. As Belenky et al. explain, "[P]resented with a proposition, separate knowers immediately look for something wrong—a loophole, a factual error, a logical contradiction, the emission of contrary evidence" (1986, 104). This is the type of thinking that Moultan (1983) argues is typical of traditional philosophical inquiry. She refers to it as the 'adversarial method', which is based on the assumption that if an argument has withstood rigorous and aggressive challenging, it can be accepted. Most of the women in the Belenky et al. study struggled to utilise the separate, doubting method of knowing, and responded badly when such methods were used against them, especially by authorities such as teachers.

The notion of caring, connected knowing bears many similarities to Dewey's notion of inquiry. Dewey uses words such as 'care', 'attentiveness' and 'interest' interchangeably (2004a, 120–121). To be interested in something is to judge it to have some value or importance. As such, "to take an interest is to be on the alert, to care about, to be attentive" to the object or person of interest (2004a, 121). Dewey also suggests that being interested or caring involves connectedness, stating that the "word interest suggests, etymologically, what is *between,*—that which connects two things otherwise distant" (2004a, 122). The interested knower is one who connects to the objects of knowledge, including other people.

However, Dewey's theory of inquiry is not synonymous with connected knowing. Belenky et al. argue that both separate and connected knowing are types of procedural knowledge, which aim to understand objects or people as they are, independently of the knower. In this epistemological relationship it is presumably only the knower who is transformed through their acquisition of purely objective, established facts. As Belenky et al. explain, "[P]rocedural knowledge is tilted toward 'accommodation' to the shape of the object rather than 'assimilation' of the object to the shape of the knower's mind" (1986, 123). This contrasts Dewey's epistemology where the relationship between knower and known is one of reciprocal, mutual adaptation (see Chapter 2). Dewey's epistemology is more like the notion of constructed knowing, prescribed by Belenky et al.

Constructivist knowers interact with the objects of knowledge in a mutually transformative manner and aim to integrate their own beliefs and perspectives with the beliefs and perspectives of others. Thus, constructivist knowing aims at intersubjectivity and depends on empathy. Constructivist knowers are passionate, interested, purposeful inquirers, who aim to shape and affect other people, objects and reality in accordance with their own interests, needs and desires. However, they are also critical of their own interests, needs and desires because they must adapt themselves to the world as they are transforming it. Since constructivist knowers don't merely want to understand others or objects as they are, but interact with them in a meaningful and transformative way, they must be critical and selective. However, like connected knowers, who play the believing game, constructed knowers must also try to see if problems or criticisms can be overcome. They are willing to be convinced of another's ideas but only if those ideas are accurate and valuable. Constructivist knowers also realise that they must refrain from acting in a way that will shut down the lines of communication, such as being overly aggressive, adversarial or dismissive. Thus, such thinking is critically self-aware, open-minded and empathetic; involves reasoning and criticism; but works to maintain open lines of communication through being considerate and respectful of other's ideas. For Belenky et al. and Dewey, care and connectedness aren't opposed to critical thinking or reason; they are intertwined and interdependent in the construction of meaning.

THE NEGATIVE EMOTIONS IN INQUIRY

Many of those who argue for the epistemological, ethical and political importance of the emotions have a tendency to emphasise the emotions associated with care, while ignoring or even condemning the 'negative emotions', such as anger, bitterness, contempt, jealousy and resentment. However, some feminist philosophers have recognised that the negative emotions can be epistemologically, politically and ethically valuable (Bell 2005; McFall 1991; Spelman 1989; Narayan 1988; Lorde 1984). For example, while anger is often counterproductive and harmful, when one is angry "in the right way, at the right time and with the right people", anger can be very valuable (Spelman 1989, 263). In fact, as Aristotle argued, it is unreasonable and immoral not to be angry in some situations, such as where some injustice has been committed. When one is angry about a situation, it is because they judge it to be unfair, unjust, wrong, immoral or bad. To be angry implies that one believes something of value is being denied or threatened in some way. As such, anger is not opposed to care because to be angry actually suggests that one cares about something that is being obstructed or threatened. As such, anger can help us identify and evaluate problematic situations and guide and motivate us to reconstruct them through inquiry. However, even displays of justified anger may not always support inquiry because sometimes reacting to others with justified anger can shut down lines of communication and be counterproductive. Thus, as Dewey explains, when anger has an appropriate object it can be effective for reconstructing experience (1972, 130).

THE FACILITATION OF THE EMOTIONS
IN PHILOSOPHY FOR CHILDREN

Since traditional classrooms are teacher-centred, they generally don't allow children to express their emotions, critically reflect on them, compare them to the emotional responses of others, or use them to guide their own thinking and decision-making. In contrast, the P4C classroom employs a more student-centred pedagogy, where the experiences, questions, problems and ideas of children are central in classroom inquiries. This is important for the development of emotional ability and understanding. Not only does P4C allow children to express their own emotions and experiences, but it actually depends on them doing so because it is these responses which initiate and guide inquiry. Thus, the P4C classroom values children's emotional responses and actively encourages children to reflect on and share them.

P4C deliberately provokes emotional responses through exposing students to philosophically problematic subject matter. Classroom philosophical inquiry can be initiated with various learning materials and experiences, including films, art works, contemporary issues and social problems, literature and any problematic experience. The important thing is that the material and experiences should provoke puzzlement, perplexity and wonderment, which will lead to questioning, inquiry and hopefully the construction of new meaning. Such puzzlement and perplexity is accompanied by emotional excitement of some type, which helps motivate, initiate and give direction to inquiry. Many of Matthews's examples of children's philosophical dialogue demonstrate how emotionally charged experiences can provoke philosophical reflection:

> John (7), thinking his father had hold of his cello, let go and the cello fell over and broke. Overcome with remorse (he was very fond of the cello), John went to his mother and hugged her quietly for a long time. Finally, he said, "I wish everything was on a film and you could rewind it and do everything over." A moment later he added "Of course then it would just happen again, cause there's only one film." (1979, 362)

Lipman's P4C learning materials are not likely to evoke such strong emotional responses as this. However, strong emotional responses are not necessary for the initiation of inquiry. Furthermore, puzzlement, confusion and wonderment need not necessarily be accompanied by negative emotions, such as discontent, frustration, anxiety, anger or distress. The philosophical puzzlement in the P4C classroom is probably more often associated with feelings of anticipation, surprise, enthusiasm, awe and excitement because it involves having experiences that are new, unfamiliar and strange, although not necessarily upsetting (Bitting and Southworth 1992). There is also excitement, delight and enjoyment because of the possibility of gaining new ideas and meanings, considering alternative possibilities, building relationships with others and growth. There is a place for the negative emotions, which many philosophical issues will give rise to because they challenge our most deeply held beliefs or provoke consideration of social justice issues and moral dilemmas. Such emotions were commonly displayed by my own philosophy students, especially when inquiring into ethical topics like animal rights and stem-cell research.

Students' initial emotional responses to philosophical problems need to be articulated as questions, problems or concerns that can be investigated through inquiry. In the P4C classroom, students reflect on why a certain story, idea, situation, event or opinion is exciting, unsettling, surprising, sad or frustrating. By considering what it is about the material or subject that causes them to feel the way they do, students can identify and articulate the problem, need, desire or interest that the emotion suggests. Students can then set about investigating this problem through inquiry and create ideas that aim to alleviate negative feelings and puzzlement and bring about the new understandings that are anticipated or desired. Whether an idea satisfies the emotional needs and desires that initiated the inquiry will be part of the criteria the idea must meet in order to be successful and bring about meaning for the students. Thus, students need to be encouraged to use their emotions as a guide for formulating problems and questions, constructing and critically comparing ideas and for making judgments about appropriate ideas and actions.

However, since emotions have an objective, cognitive element, students need to learn that not all emotional responses are equally valid, reasonable and conducive of meaningfulness. Some emotional responses can be counter-productive to inquiry, blinding students to alternative perspectives and counterarguments. The Community of Inquiry is dependent on students developing emotional intelligence. In the P4C classroom, any emotion that students have is not merely accepted and assumed as a legitimate basis for inquiry. Students are encouraged to critically reflect on their emotions and identify the beliefs, assumptions and values that underpin them. In order to judge the appropriateness of their emotions, students will need to critically compare these beliefs and assumptions to the facts of the situation and to other people's understandings and emotional responses. If students can see that the behavioural, feeling and intellectual aspects of their emotions aren't going to lead to intelligent, meaningful interaction with their social environment, then their emotions must be appropriately adjusted.

There are various ways that such emotional competency can be facilitated. Learning materials that provide examples of reasonable and unreasonable emotions provide students with an opportunity to name, describe and assess different emotional behaviours (Kristjansson 1981). Lipman (1995) offers an outline of how the P4C book *Harry Stottlemeier's Discovery* (Lipman 1992), which was designed to facilitate inquiry into formal logic, can be used for this purpose. For example, the Harry character is constructing a rule for conversion and asks another character, Lisa, to provide him with a sentence. Harry's intention is to show how his conversion rule applies to Lisa's sentence. However, the sentence Lisa gives him turns out to be a counter-example, and "with a flash of resentment, he wonders why Lisa has given him 'such a stupid sentence'" (1995, 6). Harry then realises that "if he had really figured out a rule, it should have worked on stupid sentences as well as on sentences that weren't stupid" (1995, 6). Thus, upon reflection, Harry concludes that his resentment towards Lisa is unwarranted and he adjusts his emotional response.

However, Lipman's P4C books are not really suited to this purpose. The facilitation of emotional intelligence really requires learning materials that contain salient, rich, complex, contentious and varied examples of emotions. Lipman's books contain a few, limited examples, but they weren't written specifically with the intention of provoking inquiry into the emotions. As Valentino argues, these books are focused on developing reasoning, which, although an important aspect of emotional intelligence, is inadequate for fostering emotional intelligence (1998, 29). The example from *Harry Stottlemeier's Discovery* may provoke critical reflection on the emotions, but it is not salient in the book and is more likely to be overshadowed by the logical themes. The example is also not complex and thought provoking. Harry's inappropriate resentment doesn't allow students to inquire into what emotions the characters might be having and why, whether such emotions are useful and justified and if alternative emotional responses are possible. This is because the situation is not open and contentious enough. Harry quickly and conclusively realises that his emotion is inappropriate and promptly adjusts his behaviour accordingly. The example models emotional intelligence rather than facilitating inquiry into the emotions.

As Valentino argues, fostering emotional intelligence requires learning materials that have been specifically designed so as to provoke inquiry into the emotions. Valentino states that facilitating emotional intelligence requires that "the same collection of descriptions and definitions already made for thinking skills should be made for feeling skills" (1998, 30). Students need flexible tools, methods and frameworks, including an emotional vocabulary, for analysing emotions. Some of the particular things students should do to develop such emotional tools and understandings include identifying and naming different emotions, as well as connecting different emotions to corresponding feelings, facial expressions, behaviours, objects, beliefs, values, personal characteristics and situations. This includes analysing subtle differences between emotions and being aware of their often-ambiguous nature (A. Johnson 1993). Valentino suggests that students construct scales of emotional intensity so as to identify and evaluate extreme and deficient emotions. Students also need to devise methods for controlling, adapting and transforming the emotions, such as being aware of impulses or habits, modifying one's behaviour and actions, and regulating one's physiological processes (e.g., breathing, heart rate, etc.).

In general, the P4C classroom needs to draw more specific attention to the emotions and the emotional aspect of all thinking.

Some P4C advocates have focused on the development of emotional intelligence. Schleifer et al. (2003) conducted research to ascertain if P4C had any effect on the ability of five-year-old children to recognise basic emotions (e.g., happiness, sadness, fear and anger).[2] The results showed that in two of the three schools involved, the P4C class showed greater improvements in their ability to recognise and define emotions.[3] Schleifer et al. attribute this to the fact that P4C students were "able to talk about fear, anger, and sadness, recurrent themes in the material used" which allows for "more clarity in identifying these emotions in others" (2003, 6). However, Schleifer et al. argue that the progress of the P4C students was limited, with many students still confusing even these basic emotions. Like Valentino, they believe that much more needs to be done in P4C classrooms to improve and assess emotional intelligence.

PHILOSOPHY AND THE EMOTIONS

Schleifer et al. did maintain that philosophical discussions played an important role in the improvements that were made in the P4C student's emotional abilities. The best explanation of this is that the discipline of philosophy already contains methods and subjects relevant to developing emotional intelligence. First, since emotions are types of judgments and all thinking involves the emotions, the study of logic is essential for the development of emotional intelligence. The emotions also have ethical, political, epistemological, metaphysical and aesthetic aspects. We have already considered some of the ethical and political dimensions of the emotions, including their potential for social reconstruction and ability to provoke responses to injustice. Students cannot assess the appropriateness of different emotions without a consideration of how different emotions affect others, what other people's emotional needs are and how emotions affect social harmony. Since emotions reflect the values, beliefs and interests of individuals, they are also related to issues of personhood and autonomy. P4C students should consider how expressing emotions is an important aspect of autonomy and how the denial of certain emotions to certain groups is a form of oppression. Aesthetics is also important for facilitating emotional intelligence. Emotional responses to art works are not just important for understanding and evaluating art but for understanding and evaluating emotions. Considering questions like, 'How do art works express emotions?' 'Is the spectator's emotional response relevant to an art work's value?' or 'Why do we experience sadness, fear, joy, etc., in response to fictional stories and films?' help us understand the nature and value of emotions. Finally, epistemological and metaphysical questions such as, 'What are emotions?' 'Are the emotions subjective, objective or both?' 'Can I really know what another person is feeling?' 'Can I have knowledge without emotions?' 'Would I be a person without emotions?' or 'Could I have a meaningful life without emotions?' are fundamental for understanding the nature and value of emotions. Satish (1981, 84–15) provides a transcript of a P4C class of fifth and sixth graders involved in such a philosophical inquiry into the emotions:

Paul: If man began without emotions then there would never have been any problems anyway.

Linda: I think there would be problems because if people have so much knowledge they will try to figure out why they don't have no emotions and try to figure out a way to get to them.

Danielle: Because they would know what emotions are and they they exist [sic].

Linda: Yes, Eric.

Eric: Without emotions people would become nothing more than animals because the only reason for us to live was to get food and do what was good for the species. Nothing else—after you have done with that you just sit around doing nothing.

Andrew: If you didn't have emotions you would be just by yourself. Your wouldn't like anybody else you just be with you. You would be your own nation because you wouldn't be doing anything to the other person—you just wouldn't know him all your life and everybody do it everybody else [sic].

Paul: There won't be no bombs dropped or no wars or anything else if there were no emotions . . .

Marcie: If there was no such thing as emotions we wouldn't be really here because God made everything because he cared and he wouldn't have cared if he had no emotions.

During this classroom dialogue, children considered the importance of the emotions for knowledge, learning, friendship and love, meaningfulness, happiness, personhood, community and existence. They also considered negative aspects of the emotions, such as conflict and war. Such philosophical dialogues can provide children with a deeper, broader and more critical appreciation and understanding of the emotions. P4C learning materials and facilitators need to conscientiously encourage inquiry into the emotions and all schools need to incorporate philosophy as an essential means of facilitating emotional intelligence.

THE COMMUNITY OF INQUIRY AND THE EMOTIONS

The P4C classroom also has an advantage over traditional pedagogies when it comes to emotional education because of its communal nature. The social nature of the emotions and their communicative function means that emotional intelligence can best be developed in a communal setting. The communal nature of the P4C classroom enables students to perceive other people's emotional behaviour and develop skills for interpreting and responding to facial expressions and body language (Valentino 1998). Participation in the Community of Inquiry enables students to understand how the emotions communicate ideas, values and interests. For example, they may perceive that anger can shut down inquiry, while at other times facilitate it. They may learn that displays of anxiety and frustration can communicate a need for assistance and compassion. They can recognise that emotional neutrality indicates a lack of interest or boredom. Such understandings enable children to use emotions to more effectively communicate and coordinate their activities with others, as well as to understand the motives, interests, needs and desires of others (A. Johnson 1993). All of which is necessary for a functioning Community of Inquiry.

Perceiving others' emotional responses can also cause one to critically reflect on one's own emotional responses or lack of emotional response. For example, a child who fails to respond to a sad situation with sadness may reflect on and transform her emotional response when perceiving that others respond with sadness. This can help reinforce appropriate emotional responses, as well as community. Furthermore, since our emotions incorporate our values, judgments, instincts, feelings, interests, intentions and perspectives, by reflecting on them, we gain a better understanding of ourselves, which is important for personhood, autonomy and mental health (A. Johnson 1993). By becoming more aware of our feelings, perspectives, beliefs and behaviour, and how they influence one another, we also gain greater objectivity. Thus, the Community of Inquiry can foster the type of emotional intelligence Mead described as essential to all communication, social action and thought.

The emphasis on procedural thinking in the P4C classroom also necessitates critical reflection upon the emotions experienced during communal inquiry. For example, if a student fails to respect another student, perhaps by ignoring them, ridiculing them or being dismissive and that student responds with anger, sadness or embarrassment, the Community of Inquiry must investigate this event. This is what a commitment to procedural inquiry entails—a critical examination of the procedures of inquiry, regardless of whether they are primarily logical, emotional or social because all these procedures determine the success of the inquiry.

The communal nature of the P4C classroom also facilitates empathy and care. However, as with Dewey, Belenky et al. and Gilligan, the idea of caring thinking required in the Community of Inquiry is not opposed to critical and creative thinking. Students must be open-minded, caring and empathetic. However, in order to progress the inquiry, solve problems and construct meaning, they must also critically compare different ideas and integrate different perspectives. The interconnectedness of creative, critical and caring thinking is most apparent in P4C's notion of reasonableness, which is a thoroughly social, emotional and imaginative concept. P4C's ideal of reasonableness involves not just the ability to provide reasons for one's ideas and actions, but also the ability to be moved by the reasons of others (Lipman 2003, 97). This involves the capacity for empathy, which, as we have seen, is emotional and imaginative.

THE EMOTIONS, IMAGINATION AND PRACTICALITY

Allowing students to engage with real social problems beyond the classroom is important for the development of emotional intelligence and imagination. If we encourage students to have emotional responses to philosophical problems, without providing them with any opportunity to act on those emotions, they may become frustrated and apathetic. Encouraging students to imagine things as different from how they are, without providing them with opportunities to enact such imagined possibilities, could counter efforts to promote active citizenship. Brunt makes a similar point in relation to gifted children. Drawing on Lipman, Brunt describes normative thinking as a type of caring thinking that involves imagining how people could or should be different to how they are. Brunt states, "Without active thinking being part of Normative Thinking, idealism can be stymied and cynicism result" (1996, 6). The importance of action for emotional development is supported by Dewey's emphasis on the behavioural aspect of emotions. As Dewey explains, it is instinctual or habitual behaviours that give rise to emotion. Thus, students cannot develop emotional competency without action:

> I believe that the emotions are the reflex of actions. *I believe that to endeavour to stimulate or arouse the emotions apart from their corresponding activities is to introduce an unhealthy and morbid state of mind.* I believe that if we can only secure right habits of action and thought, with reference to the good, the true, and the beautiful, the emotions will for the most take care of themselves. I believe that next to deadness and dullness, formalism and routine, our education is threatened with no greater evil than sentimentalism. *I believe that sentimentalism is the result of the attempt to divorce feeling from action.* (1972, 93, italics added)

Lipman also shows some recognition of the importance that action has for emotional development because he describes active thinking as an aspect of caring thinking (2003, 267–268). Active thinking involves taking action to create, preserve or develop what one cares about. However, the P4C literature tends to emphasise classroom dialogue, while saying little about students being engaged in purposeful activities beyond the classroom. In Chapter 8, I will outline how P4C can incorporate such activities by being integrated with a social justice approach to service learning. As we shall see, such a practical P4C pedagogy can better facilitate the emotional intelligence and imaginativeness required for reflective thinking and democratic citizenship. However, first we must have an understanding of the notion of democratic citizenship that P4C aims to foster. Thus, in the next chapter, I will examine the Deweyian notions of the self, autonomy, community, democracy and citizenship that P4C embraces.

6 A Response to Individual/ Community Dualism

Community, Autonomy and Democracy in Dewey and Philosophy for Children

In classical liberal theory, autonomy, self and citizenship have predominantly been conceived of in terms of rugged individualism, independency and self-sufficiency (e.g. Locke, J. S. Mill, Hobbes). Since community implies dependency and intersubjectivity, autonomy has also been defined in opposition to community. This individualistic notion of the self and autonomy has been very influential in shaping dominant social values, practices and institutions. In particular, it is reflected in the often individualistic and competitive nature of traditional schooling. Since children are typically considered to be dependent, they are largely excluded from the individualistic ideal of autonomy and citizenship. Thus, individualism is reflected in the dominant view that schooling is primarily preparation for future autonomy and citizenship. Schooling which assumes this individualistic notion of the self actually fails to facilitate the development of independent thinking, as well as a caring and altruistic disposition and collaboration. Consequently, it promotes undesirable notions of the self, society and citizenship. In response to the problems of individualism, some schools accept a notion of the self as socially and culturally embedded. Such schools emphasise the importance of community and shared cultural meanings. I will refer to these schools as 'communitarian schools'. However, communitarian schools have the potential to be homogenous, oppressive and exclusive and may also counter the development of independent thinking. In this chapter, it will be argued that both individualistic and communitarian schools are problematic because they accept an illegitimate community/individual dualism, which leads to impoverished and problematic notions of self, society and citizenship.

In contrast, Philosophy for Children (P4C) is able to overcome these problems because it incorporates Dewey's notion of a communal self and his ideal of democracy, which reject individual/community dualism. As we have seen, Dewey argues that thinking is the internalisation of social processes. Thus, in order to think for oneself, one must be a member of a community. However, for Dewey, only an open, pluralistic and inquiring community can facilitate autonomy and personal growth. Such communities are what Dewey calls 'democracies'. The P4C classroom is modelled on this type of democratic community. As such, it is well placed to facilitate the development of reflective, caring, reasonable and autonomous individuals who also recognise their interdependence and interconnectedness with others. In order to appreciate P4C's ideals of the self, autonomy and democratic citizenship, we must first consider the educational problems associated with individual/community dualism.

THE DUALISTIC CONCEPT OF THE INDIVIDUAL

Dewey argues that individualism developed as a response to authoritarian and totalitarian societies that force their citizens to adopt common values, practices and beliefs, while discouraging self-discovery, self-expression and individual freedom. In response, the autonomous individual was conceived of as one who is free to choose and act on his or her own ideal of the good. This notion of autonomy presupposes the existence of an ahistorical, pre-social human nature. When one acts in accordance with this original or authentic self, one acts autonomously. Other people, culture, as well as one's own physical and emotional needs, are seen as negative influences, which can interfere with one's ability to act in accordance with one's true self. This notion of autonomy is connected to the dominant ideal of rationality because it is thought that Reason is the only instrument that allows individuals to transcend these negative influences so as they can choose and act in accordance with their essential nature (Frazer and Lacey 1993, 48). Thus, autonomy is thought to involve freedom from the interference of others, culture, the concrete world and even one's own body. As Dewey argues, individualism supports, and is supported by, mind/body, mind/world, subject/object and self/other dualisms, which form the basis of traditional epistemological and metaphysical problems (2004a, 279–281).

This individualistic ideal of autonomy and selfhood is characterised by self-sufficiency and independence, which imply that one is free from the influence of others. Since self-sufficiency and independence are considered to be characteristics of autonomy; dependency, intersubjectivity and community are opposed to autonomy. While self-sufficiency and independence are seen as virtuous, dependency is considered a weaknesses. Fraser and Gordon (1997) describe some of the negative connotations that the concept 'dependency' has in dominant Western discourses, such as welfare dependency, drug dependency and co-dependency. They cite Senator Daniel P. Monihan's claim that dependency is "an incomplete state in life: normal in the child, abnormal in the adult", as an example of the dominant view that dependency in adults is a character flaw or even a personality disorder (1997, 25).

Considering the fact that the human environment is a social one, individual/community dualism is highly problematic. Since we share limited space and resources with others, we must act cooperatively in ways beneficial to society as a whole. However, if people are essentially independent, separate and self-sufficient, there is no motivation to act for the common good. Dewey describes this problem when he asks, "[G]iven feelings, ideas, desires, which have nothing to do with each other, how can actions proceeding from them be controlled in a social or public interest?" (2004a, 285). This is particularly problematic given that self-sufficiency and independence are often equated with material wealth (1930a, 249–250). Consequently, the individualistic concept of the self encourages fierce competition for limited resources, resulting in vast inequalities. Individualistic societies often encourage avarice and competitiveness so as to motivate individuals to contribute to the common good because it is believed they would have no incentive to do so otherwise. For these reasons, individualism is associated with a contractual notion of society and citizenship, where individuals surrender some of their liberties in exchange for protection, in the form of legal rights, from the interference of others. By entering into a social contract with the state, citizens are provided with the right and protection to choose and act in accordance with their own idea of the good so long as they don't interfere with the rights of others to do the same.

This contractual ideal of society has been widely criticised, particularly by feminists and communitarians, for normalising narrow and undesirable ideals of social relationships and citizenship. While the contractual model reflects the type of public, political and economic relationships that distinct and separate individuals voluntarily enter into for their own benefit, it bears little resemblance to the interconnected, caring and often self-sacrificing and non-voluntary relationships that characterise the private or domestic sphere (Held 1995, 210). The contractual model incorporates public/private and justice (rights)/care dualisms. This entails an undesirable ideal of citizenship characterised by self-interest and a notion of society based on conflict and competition, rather than interconnectedness, care and altruism. It also implies that citizens only have a negative responsibility not to interfere with others, and, as such, it doesn't require or encourage individuals to act altruistically or to care for those who are most dependent. As Elshtain points out, in the contractual model "children, old people, ill and dying people who need care are nowhere to be seen" (1995, 266). Others have criticised the contractual model for encouraging individuals to make dogmatic and aggressive demands based on their absolute rights. The apparent adversarial nature of rights may delimit the possibility of caring and altruistic relationships. For example, Sandel argues that justice is inappropriate and unnecessary in familial relationships because it can cause conflict and actually diminish feelings of love and altruism (1982, 28–35).

Many feminists have argued that this individualistic ideal of autonomy, society and citizenship normalises and universalises the experiences and values of white, middle-class males. Women and children are traditionally associated with the private sphere and considered to be emotional, concrete, subjective and, thus, incapable of performing the type of abstract reasoning that would allow them to be independent and autonomous. Fraser and Gordon's analysis of the different cultural-historical constructions of dependency reveals how the term has been associated with particular types of people, notably children and youth, the elderly, the disabled, the poor, migrants, refugees, blacks, women and other marginalised groups. They argue that "post-industrial culture has called up a new personification of dependency: the Black, unmarried, teenaged, welfare-dependent mother" (1997, 39). Thus, certain individuals are defined in opposition to the individualistic notion of autonomy and citizenship. For children, their dependent, irrational nature is considered acceptable and temporary (unless they are girls, black, poor, etc.). However, for women and other marginalised individuals, their dependency is seen as abnormal and permanent, meaning that they are perennially denied autonomy and citizenship.

THE DUALISTIC CONCEPT OF THE INDIVIDUAL IN EDUCATION

Education for Future Autonomy and Citizenship

Individualism is reflected in educational practices in various ways. The most conspicuous influence stems from the notion that children and young people cannot be autonomous citizens in virtue of their dependency. This position is supported by popular developmental theories, such as Piaget's, which suggest that children are egocentric and don't even begin to develop the capacity for objective and abstract reasoning until around puberty. Since rationality is necessary for autonomy, children are considered to be literally incapable of autonomy. Schooling which accepts these notions of childhood and autonomy won't provide students with opportunities to make autonomous decisions for themselves, construct their own meanings or participate in their communities as active citizens. An individualistic notion of the self and a traditional conception of childhood leads to the type of schooling described by White and Wyn, which is structured around the idea of 'futurity'. Such schooling aims to prepare students for the choices and civic responsibilities they will have in their future, adult lives (2004, 2–3). This still dominant educational idea was inherent in T. H. Marshall's foundational writings on citizenship:

> The right to education is a genuine social right of citizenship, because the aim of education during childhood is to shape the *future* adult. Fundamentally it should be regarded, not as the right of the child to go to school but as the right of the adult citizen to have been educated. (1950, 299, italics added)

As White and Wyn argue, schooling which is focused on preparing students for future adulthood is problematic because it ignores and devalues the current experiences, understandings and interests of students. Such schooling assumes adult/child dualism. As with other dualistic categories, child and adult are treated as static, ahistorical and radically polarised opposites. As 'child' is the subordinate category in the partnership, it is simply defined as 'non-adulthood', which means 'non-autonomy' and 'non-citizenship' and any similarities or continuity between these dualistic pairs is minimised or denied (Wyn 1995, 52). While the concepts of 'youth' and 'teenager' are clearly more ambiguous, in-between notions, they are often treated in much the same way as 'child', as simply meaning "'non-adults', a group who are deficit" (1995, 52). As such, many schools assume that the current experiences, interests and understandings of students are radically opposed to adulthood and citizenship. Student's aren't encouraged to express their own experiences and interests because they are actually seen as something to be transcended through schooling.

This ideal of schooling accepts that it's only when students finish school and become fully autonomous adults and citizens that they will find the knowledge acquired at school relevant, useful and meaningful. That is, it is expected that students will find schooling meaningless, boring and onerous. This is reflected in Quirk's (2005) suggestion that learning is work and students just need to do their work regardless of whether they find the work interesting or relevant:

> We need our kids to understand that everyone is expected to do a certain amount of work, and, as children, their business is learning. The rest of society is paying (over 600 billion dollars annually) for their period of study and preparation for life. If they refuse to do their "work" they are cheating society.

However, can we really blame students for being uncooperative and disruptive when they are forced to laboriously learn large amounts of content that appear to have no relevance to their lived experiences? This is one of the key reasons students lack intrinsic motivation to learn because they cannot see how the generally abstract, fragmented facts that constitute the curriculum are relevant to concrete experience. This is why so many teachers still depend on extrinsic rewards and punishments, including competition, to motivate learning.

The sense of meaninglessness associated with schooling based on futurity is exacerbated by the fact that even future citizenship and autonomy can appear elusive for many students because "not all adults have equal access to citizenship" (Wyn 1995, 49–50). As we have seen, women, migrants, racial or religious minorities, the disabled and those with low socio-economic status don't fit the individualistic ideal of autonomy and citizenship. For students who belong to these and other marginalised groups, the knowledge and skills learnt in schools can appear to be not only presently but also permanently irrelevant. In her research into young women's experiences of growing up, Buchanan asked one 18-year-old woman, "[W]hat does it take to be an adult woman?". The woman responded, "I don't know if it ever happens. Oh, it takes a lot (laughs). And it depends on whether you're a boy or a girl. For a woman to be considered a total adult I think she'd have to be near the end of her life" (1993, 62). For such students, schooling can appear to only benefit those privileged students for whom the dominant ideals of citizenship and adulthood are achievable in the first place. As such, schooling appears to perpetuate their oppression and exclusion, rather than provide them with greater freedom to exercise autonomy and political rights and responsibilities. It's not uncommon for marginalised students to make statements to the effect that school is a waste of time for them because they lack the personal attributes, finances, resources or contacts that would be necessary for them to attain further education, desirable lifestyles or even stable employment.

Education that is preparation for future autonomy and citizenship also supports the knowledge transmission model of schooling, which, as we have seen, actually mitigates the development of independent, reflective thinking. Since students are considered incapable of Reasoning and decision making, schools often seek to prepare students for future autonomy and citizenship by exposing them to as much different knowledge as possible. By filling student's heads with facts, it is intended that when students do become capable of making rational decisions, they will already possess an abundance of options to choose from. Thus, the more content that schools can get students to store away now, the more schools can maximise their future capacity for autonomy. As we have seen, the quickest most efficient way to get students to learn content is to systematically deposit facts into their heads and then examine them to make sure that they have remembered these facts.

However, far from teaching students to be autonomous agents, such schooling renders students perennially passive, uncritical, and uncreative, making them easy targets for manipulation and control by others (Freire 1993, 57). If we want students to be autonomous, independent thinkers, then we need to provide them with opportunities to critically reflect on their own interests and ideas, to solve problems, to create or transform knowledge, to shape their environment and to make decisions for themselves. As Bandman states, "The child cannot learn to make choices, even small or safe choices, without practice in choosing" (1993, 30). Independent thinking, autonomy and citizenship need to be actively facilitated and practiced in schools, but education focused on futurity assumes that children and adolescents are incapable of such practice.

Educating Autonomous Students

Since many schools that focus on preparing students for this individualistic notion of autonomy paradoxically seem to counter the development of autonomy, some educationalists and political theorists have argued that

children and youth should be treated and educated as fully autonomous citizens. For example, child liberationists reject adult/child dualism, arguing
that children should have the same freedoms and rights that adults have.
Those who take up this position don't critique the individualistic assumption that dependency is opposed to autonomy and citizenship. Rather, they
reject the assumption that children are essentially dependent, arguing that
children's dependency is primarily a result of adults not allowing them to
make decisions for themselves. The best-known defences of this position
are Farson's *Birthrights* and Holt's *Escape from Childhood*. Holt explains
the implications of this position for schooling:

> Young people should have the right to control and direct their own
> learning, that is, to decide what they want to learn, and when, where,
> how, how much, how fast, and with what help they want to learn it. To
> be still more specific, I want them to have the right to decide if, when,
> how much, and by whom they want to be *taught* and the right to decide
> whether they want to learn in a school and if so which one and for how
> much of the time. (1975, 59)

A. S. Neil's Summerhill School, founded in 1921, is the best-known
example of schooling that aims to provide students with just this sort of
freedom. Like Holt and Farson, Neil believed that if we want children to be
autonomous, independent citizens then we must treat them as such (1962,
24). He argues that all children are essentially good and that if left to
their own accord, children will develop in accordance with their own true
nature. His fundamental concern was to produce happy students, believing that happy people are those who are free to be themselves so long as
they don't interfere with the freedom of others (1962, 20). At Summerhill,
classes are not compulsory, and teachers have little more authority than
students. There are school rules and procedures. However, they are decided
at weekly school meetings, in which staff and students have one vote each
and students outnumber staff (1962, 53). In contrast to education based
on futurity, schools like Summerhill, which are often called 'democratic
schools', recognise that children have needs, interests, understandings and
experiences that should be treated with respect and care. By enabling students to make their own decisions, such schools can seem to be more facilitative of the reasoning skills, self-awareness, self-expression, independence
and self-confidence that is necessary for autonomy and citizenship.

However, such schooling is highly problematic. One concern is that it
provides students with a degree of freedom and responsibility for which
they are not cognitively, physically, emotionally and socially equipped to
deal with. Levinson argues that the denial of full rights to children is based
on paternalistic reasons. It is thought that if children were free to do as
they pleased, they would make choices that would reduce their long-term
capacity for autonomy and happiness (1999, 38). For example, if students

opted out of taking classes altogether, as many Summerhill students have for prolonged periods of time, they may not acquire knowledge and skills necessary for autonomy. The problem is that unless students request it, schools like Summerhill don't actively teach any skills and knowledge because this is seen as coercion, which fails to respect the student's current freedom. Thus, such schools also suggest that the capacity to think for oneself develops naturally. However, in order to acquire the multifaceted and complex thinking, social, affective and practical skills and knowledge that autonomy requires teachers need to actively facilitate and carefully guide students' learning (Meyers 1989, 193). Schools like Summerhill may actually be inimical to the development of autonomy because if students are simply able to do as they please, without ever being questioned, challenged or presented with alternative possibilities, they are unlikely to develop the capacity for reflective, critical, creative and self-corrective thinking. Such thinking is initiated when one has their beliefs and actions problematised and it is developed through participating in activities which require one to solve problems and inquire.

Individualism and Competitiveness in Education

Furthermore, even if schools like Summerhill grant students some degree of autonomy, so long as they embrace an individualistic notion of autonomy, they are still problematic. Schools are often criticised for their overt promotion of individualism, competitiveness and egoism, which counter the development of an altruistic and caring attitude, as well as the social skills normally considered necessary for democratic citizenship (Lipman 2003, 93–94; Johnson and Johnson 1991; Slavin 1985; Fielding 1976). For example, most schools still assume a notion of academic success that emphasises individual achievement, independent learning and self-sufficiency, as well as the ranking of students and even teachers and schools. This now operates on a global scale with the ranking of whole nations in international league tables based on the academic achievements of their students on standardised assessments (e.g., the Program for International Student Assessment [PISA]). Consequently, such schooling disparages dependency and collaboration. This issue is reflected in the current debate in Australia surrounding the introduction of performance based for teachers. Teachers' unions have argued that this initiative will provoke competition and discourage cooperation between teachers, including the sharing of resources and knowledge. An individualistic notion of academic success can discourage students from asking questions, seeking assistance, revealing confusion or emotional upset, as all of these are seen as indications of dependency and weakness. This is worrying, given that being perplexed, admitting uncertainty and asking questions is actually what initiates thinking, the construction of meaning and growth.

Thus, this individualistic, competitive school environment doesn't foster collaboration, communication, altruism and empathy. Consequently, individualistic schools impose rules on students so as to force them to cooperate with teachers and each other. This means that school rules are actually constructed as constraints upon students' natural inclinations to disregard or compete with each other. As such, it is not surprising that students generally find school rules and procedures oppressive. This could explain why even at Summerhill, where students are actively involved in constructing most school rules, the rules are frequently and deliberately broken (Neil 1962). While Summerhill students may have more regard for their rules because they aren't just imposed on them from above, the rules are still conceived of as constraints upon the student's natural inclinations, put in place for the sake of maintaining a harmonious school community.

THE DUALISTIC CONCEPT OF COMMUNITY

The dominant alternative to individualism is a communitarian perspective, which emphasises the socio-cultural nature of the self. Communitarians reject the notion of a pre-social, unencumbered self that is able to freely choose between various ideals of the good. This is because they argue that our identity, desires, interests and values are shaped by our environment, our relationships with others and the social roles and positions that we occupy. As such, the pre-social, unencumbered self of individualism would actually be an empty self because it wouldn't have any desires, interests, values and understandings on which to base autonomous decisions (Weiss 1995, 168). According to communitarianism, in order to be a self, one must be a member of a community. This means that individuals are interconnected and interdependent on each other for their own self-identity and autonomy. As such, maintaining social cohesiveness may outweigh individual rights and liberties because the community provides the very conditions that give rise to autonomous individuals in the first place.

However, it has also been argued that since community implies sameness and commonality, it is actually opposed to individuality and autonomy. Young argues that community is intended to eradicate the otherness and atomism of social life through the sharing of subjectivities. Through sharing subjectivities, it is hoped that individuals will become transparent to one and other, leading to a totalised, unified and harmonious society in which individual differences are transcended (1986, 10). Young denies the possibility of this ideal of intersubjectivity because in order to completely reveal oneself to others, the self would have to be a complete unity, with total self-knowledge. However, according to Young, subjects are not unified and complete, but heterogeneous, decentred and always in the process of becoming (1986, 11). Young argues that it is the desire for such a unified, transparent notion of the self that leads to the desire for membership in homogenous communities because only in communities with others very like me can I even come close to having such a notion of self and self-other relationships. Young argues that such commonality requires the denial of differences, via the exclusion and oppression of individuals who don't fit into, or won't adapt to, the dominant culture. Furthermore, in order to appear unified, the community must be defined in opposition to some excluded other. Those excluded are defined negatively by the fact that they lack the common, definitive attribute, which entitles membership in the group (1986, 13).

Communitarianism also suggests a problematic notion of citizenship. In order to develop into an autonomous self, we must be able to participate in a community, and in order for the community to flourish, it must have a constant stream of participants who contribute to the common good. Thus, communitarian citizenship emphasises community participation, maintaining relationships and promoting common values and practices (Waghid 2005, 325). Since individuals are necessarily interdependent and have common interests and values, communitarianism is sometimes thought to imply that legal rights and responsibilities are not fundamental, especially since they can be adversarial and diminish the caring, altruistic relationships needed for communal life. Overemphasising care, altruism and interdependency, while downplaying justice and independence, is just as problematic as individualism's reversed dualism. For example, some feminists have pointed out that the caring, trusting and interdependent nature of personal relationships is what enables them to become exploitative and oppressive (Elshtain 1995). This has been particularly the case for women. The ideal that women are naturally caring and altruistic has legitimised keeping women in the home to care for children and husbands, without pay and often while sacrificing their own needs for the good of the family and society. For women, putting oneself first or acting in one's own interests is often considered to be selfish, uncaring and unfeminine. I suspect this is just one of the many reasons for why men are still more likely to progress to leadership roles, even in female dominated industries or fields (e.g., education, schools). Females seem more willing to put aside things that would contribute to their own career progression (e.g., research) to devote more time to activities that support or assist others (e.g., teaching, administration), even though these activities are not considered as important when applying for promotion. Thus, many feminists are understandably reluctant to downplay the idea of legal rights, which women have used to gain emancipation, in favour of interdependence and care, which have actually been used to exploit and oppress women (Kiss 1997, 6–7).

THE DUALISTIC CONCEPT OF COMMUNITY IN EDUCATION

Many schools and educational theorists emphasise the importance of community and claim to promote the participatory, altruistic and caring attributes of communitarian citizenship. Etzioni proposes a type of communitarian schooling as a remedy to what he sees as the problematic atomism of modern society (1993, 114). Unfortunately, often the ideal of school community promoted, including that promoted by Etzioni, incorporates the homogeneity and exclusivity characteristic of the dualistic notion of community. This concerned is raised by Abowitz:

> 'School community' can signal escape from the public sphere to islands of like-minded (like-classed? like-raced?), ideological spheres of sameness and security. Community rhetoric can conceal erasure of differences in the narrowing and purifying of public domains. (1999, 143)

While communitarian schools may emphasise collaboration and care for others who are like oneself, they may also encourage intolerance for difference because students may feel that they have the right to force others to assimilate or to exclude them if they threaten social cohesiveness. Thus, communitarian ideals of schooling can encourage just as much aggressiveness, competitiveness and disregard for others as individualistic schools (Waghid 2005, 324).

The emphasis on social cohesion through creating a sense of tradition, communal values and common knowledge can also be seen to legitimise the inculcating of students with the dominant knowledge and values of their society. If autonomy requires being a member of a community with common beliefs and values, then education should simply transmit the dominant social values and beliefs to students. This belief is overt in the theories of many core knowledge curriculum theorists, especially Hirsch (1988, 1996) who emphasises the importance of transmitting mainstream culture to the next generation in order to maintain social cohesion. The communitarian ideal of the self as socially situated also suggests that students are not able to transcend their situatedness so as to critique or revise the ideas, interests and ends that they internalise from their society. Thus, communitarian ideals have the potential to be just as facilitative of rote learning as individualism.

Dialogue as a Pedagogical Tool

Rather than transmit dominant social values and knowledge to students, more progressive, communitarian-influenced pedagogies emphasise students' *discovering* or *constructing* common knowledge. Such pedagogies commonly utilise dialogue as the means through which individual students can communicate across differences and attain the intersubjectivity necessary for communal life. Ellsworth argues that educators utilise dialogue because they believe it is a "neutral vehicle that carries speaker's ideas and understandings back and forth" (1997, 49). Like Young, Ellsworth denies the possibility of such an ideal of communication and intersubjectivity because of our essential differences. She argues that dialogue cannot enable individuals to freely and completely transmit and receive each other's meanings because "the rugged terrain between speakers that it [dialogue] traverses makes for a constantly interrupted and never completed passage" (1997, 49). In order to reach agreement, in spite of differences between individuals, dialogue often involves aggressive argumentation as a means to persuading others to accept one's opinions. As such, classroom dialogue is frequently criticised for being just as aggressive and adversarial as individualistic learning practices.

Furthermore, Ellsworth argues that the procedures of dialogue are not neutral but socio-political constructs that aim to serve particular interests and purposes. The procedures of dialogue shape and influence the way meanings are received and communicated (Ellsworth 1997, 85). This implies that those who belong to the dominant culture will be better able to persuade others of their opinions because the methods of deliberative argumentation will reflect their values, interests and methods. The concern is that such pedagogy has the potential "to silence some students while giving advantage to those capable of eloquently and rationally articulating their points of view" (Waghid 2005, 328). Some students may either be unable to participate or will be forced to consent to the views of the dominant group. If they refuse to submit, they are likely to be seen as unreasonable and undemocratic.

Communitarian Citizenship and Service Learning

Since the communitarian notion of citizenship emphasises contributing to one's community, it also implies some type of service learning, which involves students doing community service or volunteer work, normally as a part of their civics education (Kymlicka 2002, 272). Etzioni argues that national service would be an essential part of a communitarian education because it would "provide a strong antidote to the ego-centred mentality" and it would also encourage and develop "the virtues of hard work, responsibility and cooperation to name a few" (1993, 114–115). As will be explained at length in Chapter 8, traditional service-learning programs promote an undesirable notion of citizenship as the uncritical and obedient performance of prearranged activities deemed to be valuable by the dominant culture. Such service learning doesn't actively facilitate the development of citizens, who are critical, reflective and creative transformers of their environment.[1]

Thus, communitarian educational ideals can be just as problematic as individualistic schooling. However, individuality and community are not essentially problematic ideas. Rather, it is the assumption that the individual and community are mutually exclusive that is problematic. While there are existing communities that fit Young's description of community, there are also communities that are supportive of individual growth, freedom and differences. What is needed is a reconstruction of these dualistic and essentialist conceptualisations of community, difference, the individual, autonomy and dependency, such as can be found in the writings of Dewey and in P4C. It is because P4C reformulates these dualisms that it can overcome the problems associated with individualism and communitarianism in schools and offer a pedagogy and ideal of school community that is better able to foster autonomy, as well as interconnectness and interdependency.

DEWEY'S REJECTION OF THE INDIVIDUAL/ COMMUNITY DUALISM

Dewey's Autonomous Self

As we have seen, Dewey argues that the self develops through reconstructing experience. When individuals are unable to respond to a situation in such a way as to have their needs or desires met, they reconstruct experience through simultaneously adapting themselves and their environment. Individuals internalise those actions, beliefs, attitudes and so on, which they find useful for meaningfully reconstructing experience and eliminate those that are detrimental to their own growth, survival and happiness. This process of internalisation is how individuals develop habits, which constitute the self and guide further experience (Dewey 1930a, 25). The self grows through the continuous development and transformation of habits (2004a, 47). Hence, like Young, Dewey believes that the self is never complete and static but is always in a process of transformation (2004a, 40).

This means that the self develops through an interaction of internal aspects of the self and external aspects of the environment:

> Honesty, chastity, malice, peevishness, courage, triviality, industry, irresponsibility, are not private possessions of a person. They are working adaptations of personal capacities with environing forces. All virtues and vices are habits which incorporate objective forces. They are interactions of elements contributed by the make-up of an individual with elements supplied by the out-door world. (1930a, 16)

The self is not entirely constituted by external forces, nor is it able to transcend its environment so as to choose and act in accordance with some essential self (1958b, 37–38). Since habits are the products of the self's interactions with its environment, a transcendental self would be an empty self. Yet, individuals still possess the capacity for self-determination. They just can't critically reflect on and revise all aspects of their self at the same time. In experience, individuals have *particular* habits and aspects of their environment problematised. Part of what renders them problematic is that they conflict with other stable features of the self and environment (1930a, 38). It is these unproblematic, stable aspects that guide our revision of problematic habits and situations. As such, all aspects of our character have the potential to be critiqued and revised. They just can't all be revised at once because the individual would have no habits to initiate and guide such revision.

If the reconstruction of experience is the means through which the self shapes itself and its environment, autonomy is the capacity to effectively reconstruct experience. As explained in Chapter 2, the capacity for meaningfully reconstructing experiences is the capacity for inquiry. Inquiry enables us to produce our own meanings, shape our own environment and control our own growth, rather than being entirely determined by others, our environment or natural impulses (Dewey 1930a, 304). This is why Dewey states that "if attention is centred upon the conditions which have to be met in order to secure a situation favourable to effective thinking, freedom will take care of itself" (2004a, 292).

For Dewey, freedom doesn't entail freedom from the influence of others. Since the human environment is a social one, in order for each individual self to act autonomously and grow, there must be a coordination of interests and actions through communal inquiry (2004a, 11–15). Since communal inquiry involves integrating multiple interests and perspectives, it is a more effective means of interacting with our socio-cultural environment. This means that the actions and beliefs that we internalise and which become our habits are necessarily mediated by, and inclusive of, others. Furthermore, as we have seen, communal inquiry is actually a pre-condition of private or individual inquiry because thinking is the internalisation of the processes that characterise communal inquiry or dialogue (see Chapter 2). Thus, Dewey rejects the individualist claim that socio-cultural influences are barriers to autonomy (2004a, 4). They actually enable us to think for ourselves and act autonomously in a social environment.

Dewey's notion of autonomy entails that we are necessarily dependent on each other for the capacity to inquire, autonomy and growth. Consequently, he also rejects individualism's negative notion of dependency. As Dewey explains, it is children's greater dependency, as well as their plasticity, which enables them to grow at such a rapid pace. While dependency denotes a lack of control or ability in some regard, this lack is compensated for by some other ability because if dependency were merely a sign of helplessness and impotency it would never be accommodated by "growth in ability, as it so often is" (2004a, 41). For example, one source of children's dependency is their lack of physical ability. However, they compensate for this with an impressive social capacity. As Dewey explains, "[C]hildren are themselves marvellously endowed with the power to enlist the cooperative attention of others" and "a flexible and sensitive ability to vibrate sympathetically with the attitudes and doings of those about them" (2004a, 42). Dependency is the chief influence in promoting the caring, empathetic and attentive dispositions that are essential for communal life and growth. This is why Dewey states that "the presence of dependent and learning beings is a stimulus to nurture and affection" (2004a, 44). Thus, dependency is not merely passive. It is interactive (Sprod 2001, 83). It plays a duel role in facilitating social interaction. It requires the dependent one to develop social and affective capacities so as to enlist the assistance of others, and it initiates the caring and altruistic dispositions of those who can assist. Since communal inquiry, which enables growth and autonomy, requires both these social capacities, Dewey rightfully describes dependency as a power and identifies the individualistic notion of the self as extremely problematic:

> From a social standpoint, dependence denotes a power rather than a weakness; it involves interdependence. There is always a danger that increased personal independence will decrease the social capacity of an individual. In making him more self-reliant; it may make him more self-sufficient; it may lead to aloofness and indifference. It often makes an individual so insensitive in his relations to others as to develop an illusion of being really able to stand and act alone—an unnamed form of insanity which is responsible for a large part of the remedial suffering of the world. (2004a, 42)

Dewey's Democratic Community of Inquiry

While the Deweyian notion of self is a communal self, his notion of community is not the homogenous, exclusive ideal of community described by Young. As we have seen, Dewey's notion of community necessitates individual differences (Chapter 2). It follows from the Deweyian notion of the self that every individual is unique because each experience that gives rise to the formation of the self is unique. No two selves can be identical. Furthermore, since the self is continuously growing, it can never have complete self-knowledge or make itself completely known to others. We are always somewhat unfamiliar and unknowable to each other, as well as to ourselves. However, in contrast to Young and Ellsworth, Dewey doesn't think that individual differences eliminate the possibility of communal inquiry and intersubjectivity. It is because we are unique that all interactions with others have the potential to be problematic experiences, which provoke critical self-reflection and growth (Dewey 1939, 109; Garrison 1996, 445). This is why "a progressive society counts individual variations as precious since it finds in them the means to its own growth" (Dewey 2004a, 294).

In contrast to Ellsworth's description of dialogue, the dialogue in a Deweyian communal inquiry does not have the primary aim of allowing individuals to deposit ideas into each other's heads. Communal inquiry is a creative process in which our ideas interact with the ideas of others so that they are all transformed into something new, intersubjective and inclusive of each individual's perspective (Garrison 1996, 446–445). It is only because common meanings incorporate the different perspectives of community members that individuals are able to use them to autonomously interact with their socio-cultural environment. If they reflected only the needs of one individual, they would be useless for reconstructing the socio-cultural environment. Thus, common meanings that are derived from very diverse communities will be more useful to individuals than those that are the products of homogenous communities because they incorporate more perspectives and, consequently, should have wider applicability.

This is why Dewey argues that democratic communities, those communities which are most facilitative of inquiry, autonomy and growth, are communities of radical inclusion (Sullivan 2002, 226). They are multicultural and global. By 'global community', Dewey doesn't mean a melting pot, where individuals surrender prior commitments to local and national communities. He states that individuals may be members of various communities but democratic communities are those that maintain open lines of communication with other communities, who can provoke them to constantly reconstruct themselves, progress and become more inclusive (2004a, 83).[2] For Dewey, anything that blocks communication and inquiry across communities and cultures is undemocratic because it impedes growth:

> Intolerance, abuse, calling of names because of differences of opinion about religion or politics or business, as well as because of differences of race, colour, wealth or degree of culture are treason to the democratic way of life. For everything which bars freedom and fullness of communication sets up barriers that divide human beings into sets and cliques, into antagonistic sects and fractions, and thereby undermines the democratic way of life. Merely legal guarantees of civil liberties of free belief, free expression, free assembly are of little avail if in daily life freedom of communication, the give and take of ideas, facts, experiences, is choked by mutual suspicion, by abuse, by fear and hatred. (1988, 227–228)

Young considers a similar ideal of community but rejects it because it's unclear to her how such communities would interact (1986, 19). Dewey intends for them to interact through the same type of inquiry or dialogue that characterises the social interaction within democratic communities. Thus, by 'democracy', Dewey doesn't mean merely a type of government but a whole way of life that supports each individual's ability to engage in continuous, collaborative inquiry with diverse others in and between all aspects of their life, including the political, educational, social, familial and cultural.

In contrast to Young's claims about community, Dewey's notion of community doesn't entail the exclusion of individuals who don't share our immediate temporal and spatial location. Even though Dewey does value face-to-face relations, he explicitly rejects the assumption that one's environment consists of their immediate physical space:

> Some things which are remote in space and time from a living creature, especially a human creature, may form his environment even more truly

than some of the things close to him. The things with which a man *var-ies* are his genuine environment. Thus the activities of an astronomer vary with the stars at which he gazes or about which he calculates . . . The environment of an antiquarian, as an antiquarian, consists of the remote epoch of human life with which he is concerned, and the relics, inscriptions, etc., by which he establishes connections with that period. (2004a, 11, italics added)

Not only is it in each individual's and community's best interests to engage with diverse individuals and communities located in different spaces and times; it is actually necessary. Since we share environments with them, we need to take them into consideration and engage with them—their ideas, needs and activities—if we are to act autonomously. This is why Dewey argues that the "the weal and woe of any modern state is bound up with that of others . . . internationalism is not an aspiration but a fact, not a sentimental ideal but a force" (2004b, 118). Dewey recognised that the development of "commerce, transportation, intercommunication, and immigration" during his lifetime increased the importance of communication between individuals living in different spaces (2004a, 21). Since Dewey's era, more sophisticated technology, especially the Internet, as well as mass media and an increasingly global economy have further highlighted the importance of effective intercultural inquiry for human and social flourishing.

Jane Addams, Hull House and Dewey's Democratic Citizen

Citizenship entails the right and responsibility to participate in democratic communities because such participation is the means to one's own freedom and growth, as well as human flourishing in general. Thus, a Deweyian citizen is an individual who engages in inquiry with others in order to meaningfully reconstruct their socio-cultural environment so that it is more facilitative of growth and freedom. The social work and philosophical writings of Dewey's friend and fellow pragmatist Jane Addams exemplifies this ideal of democratic citizenship. Addams argues that individuals have a responsibility and a right to interact with others, especially those outside their own immediate family and cultural community. Like Dewey, Addams emphasised international interdependence and participated in communities that crossed nations (Whips 2004, 130).[3] Addams believed that in interacting with those most different to ourselves, we could not only help others but broaden our own experiences and gain new understandings.

In 1889, Addams, along with Ellen Gates Starr and several other young women, created the Hull House settlement in the middle of Chicago's poorest, industrial area where new migrants made up 80% of the population. Addams saw that rapid industrialisation and immigration had lead to huge increases in poverty and inequality because society had not been reconstructed to accommodate these changes. Addams believed that in order to assist with such social reconstruction, she would need to position herself amongst those who were suffering the negative consequences of these socio-economic changes and engage with them in collaborative inquiries that would bring about necessary changes. Only then could she gain an understanding of the socio-cultural environment that she was trying to reconstruct and make sure that the needs and interests of those affected were incorporated in the solutions constructed. Thus, Addams, members of the neighbourhood, Hull House residents and individuals and groups from outside the immediate neighbourhood created the type of democratic community of inquiry prescribed by Dewey.

The results of this real life communal inquiry are impressive. The Hull House community was responsible for significant advances in juvenile law, industrial law, public education and health services, women's suffrage, civil rights and unionism. They were responsible for the creation of recreational spaces, services for working women and mother's pensions. As Addams had intended, they were also able to develop new skills, attitudes and knowledge which enabled themselves, as well as society as a whole, to more efficiently and meaningfully interact with their environment. Their research, writing and practice, as well as that of other scholars who were visitors at Hull House, including Dewey, contributed to new knowledge and, in some cases, even the development of whole academic fields. Significant contributions were made in fields like geography, education, medical science, philanthropy, the social sciences, philosophy, politics and law. Residents from Hull House went on to occupy many influential and important positions in diverse fields. Addams herself was the first woman to win the Nobel Prize for Peace in 1931 (Addams 1910; Seigfried in Addams 1964, xxxvi–xxxviii; Whips 2004).

In contrast to individualism's notion of citizenship, the notion of citizenship demonstrated at Hull House is not purely rationalistic, self-sufficient or disinterested in the welfare of others. The capacity and willingness to engage with different people in collaborative inquiries and transform one's environment requires a host of social, intellectual and affective abilities, including courage, open-mindedness, care, empathy, reasonableness and creativity. The neighbourhood people that Hull House residents visited were not always welcoming to the interferences of women whom they saw as representing a class of people responsible for, and who benefit from, their own oppression (Addams 1964, 17–18). Those members of the neighbourhood who let these strangers, potential oppressors, into their homes and lives also took an enormous risk. Thus, the ability to interact with others, especially very different others, requires courage. This is not only because the other may respond to us with hostility and aggression but because they have the potential to make us realise our own situatedness, biases, misconceptions and weaknesses, which can compel us to question things about ourselves that are so familiar and comforting. As Garrison explains in relation to Dewey's notion of self, "[S]uch openness [to different others] inevitably involves everything from mild discomfort, to unsettling awkwardness, to risking our very self-identity" (1996, 447).

The fear and risk-taking involved in communal inquiry can be decreased by engaging with others in a caring, open-minded, reasonable and empathetic manner, which builds trust and respect. Addams sometimes describes her social ethics as an extension of the feminine, caring, maternal role that women occupied within the domestic sphere. It was the loss of some of women's roles in the home due to industrialisation that led Addams to claim that women now had to apply their caring, altruistic capacities in the greater community (1964, 38–41). Like many contemporary feminists, Addams argued that democratic citizenship and inquiry must incorporate aspects of the caring relationships that characterise the feminine, private, sphere.[4] Addams also pre-empts contemporary feminists in that she doesn't set care up in opposition to rights but describes the two as operationally co-dependent.[5] In order to fulfil our right and responsibility to inquire with diverse others we must engage with them in a caring, sympathetic manner (1964, 8; Seigfried in Addams 1964, xxi).

PHILOSOPHY FOR CHILDREN'S REJECTION OF INDIVIDUAL/COMMUNITY DUALISM

Thinking for Oneself

Since the Deweyian ideal of autonomy is not opposed to dependency, it is not constructed in opposition to children, young people and other so-called dependents. Thus, P4C, which embraces this Deweyian ideal of the autonomous citizen, is not a pedagogy that focuses on preparing children and young people for future autonomy and citizenship. P4C assumes that children, regardless of their greater dependency, are capable of thinking for themselves and constructing their own meaning. However, unlike the Summerhill School, P4C doesn't assume that if children are left to their own accord, they will be entirely capable of making decisions that are in their best interests. Since it is through experience that the capacity for inquiry and autonomy develops, and children have less life experience than adults, children will normally be less autonomous than adults. Thus, there are differences between adults and children, but these differences are differences of degree. It's not the case that adults have full autonomy and children completely lack it. There is no such thing as absolute autonomy or maturity because growth is continuous (Dewey 2004a, 40). Autonomy and the capacity for citizenship develop gradually and constantly, as well as differently for different individuals. As such, P4C rejects adult/child dualism but not by denying that there are differences between children and adults. What P4C denies is the dualistic construction of these categories, which implies that they are polarised, essential and absolute.

Since children can have some degree of autonomy, they have a right to practice it. However, since this capacity is underdeveloped and can always be improved (even in adults), schools have a responsibility to actively facilitate the child's development of autonomy. Schools must provide students with both the opportunity to be autonomous, as well as with an environment and content that scaffolds autonomy. As we have seen, both the practice and the development of autonomy involves participating in communal inquiries. Thus, like all people, children have a right to inquire with others in order to both practice and develop their autonomy (Lipman 2003, 203; Bandman 1993). This right entails that society, particularly schools, have a responsibility to provide children with opportunities to inquire with others. P4C fulfils this responsibility by transforming the classroom into a Community of Inquiry as well as by providing students with philosophical content and tools to develop their capacity for communal inquiry (Splitter and Sharp 1995, 119).

Unlike learning based on futurity, in the P4C classroom, children's current experiences are educationally valuable because they are the "raw ingredients" of inquiry, rather than something to be overcome through education (Splitter and Sharp 1995, 169). As such, P4C requires students to develop self-awareness and the capacity for self-expression, which are necessary for autonomy. In order to act in accordance with their own needs and interests and to be able to shape their own character and environment, the student must have a good understanding of themself and some capacity to express themself to others. The communal nature of the P4C classroom facilitates self-awareness and self-expression better than individualistic schools because it requires students to both share their perspectives with others, as well as be exposed to the perspectives of others.

Contrary to schools like Summerhill, which suggest that self-awareness and self-expression are sufficient for autonomy, the P4C classroom conceives of autonomous thinkers as those who have a *critical* self-awareness and the ability and willingness to *reconstruct* themselves and their sociocultural environment. The purpose of reflecting on and expressing one's opinions in the Community of Inquiry is to critically evaluate how such opinions may be developed into possible means for reconstructing a problem common to all community members. However, the often-unreflective beliefs that children bring to the inquiry may be very subjective, ill founded and inflexible. As such, they are unlikely to produce autonomous interaction with a changing, multicultural, social environment. This is why Splitter and Sharp refer to children's initial opinions as the "*raw* ingredients" of inquiry because "the goal of inquiry is to help children transform these ingredients into a more comprehensive world-view, through reflective and self-correcting dialogue; that is, through the activity of the community of inquiry" (1995, 169). We have already seen that the P4C classroom's focus on logic, communal inquiry and a search for intersubjective meaning scaffolds students to transform their unreflective ideas into ideas that are more reasonable and objective (Chapter 3).

The Community of Inquiry

Thus, P4C rejects the individualistic notion that collaboration is an impediment to the development of independent thinking, adopting the Deweyian idea that community is a precondition of autonomy (Lipman 2003, 25; Splitter and Sharp 1995, 242; Cam 1997, 144; Sprod 2001, 148). As Lipman states,

> Unfortunately, autonomy has often been associated with a kind of rugged individualism: the independent critical thinker as a self-sufficient, cognitive macho type, protected by an umbrella of invincibly powerful arguments. In reality the reflective model is thoroughly social and communal. (2003, 25)

Consequently, P4C is able to do what both communitarian and individualistic schools struggle to, which is facilitate the development of autonomous, independent students who also recognise their interdependence and interconnectedness with others. Community of Inquiry participants realise that they are dependent on others for their capacity to think for themselves, as well as for their ability to construct justified, common meanings, both of which are necessary for autonomy. Yet, unlike communitarian schools, the communal nature of the P4C classroom doesn't entail homogenisation and the loss of individuality because it embraces the notion that it is the interaction of individual differences that gives rise to inquiry and the intersubjective meanings that will enable students to autonomously interact with their socio-cultural environment. Thus, P4C emulates Dewey's belief that "the intermingling in the school of youth of different races, different religions, and unlike customs creates for all a new and broader environment", which facilitates growth and autonomy (1916, 21).

For this reason, the classroom Community of Inquiry aims to be inclusive of cultural and individual differences. Community of Inquiry participants do not merely adapt to the ideas and methods of the dominant group, as is often the case with dominant notions of school community. As explained in Chapter 3, the Community of Inquiry procedures, including the logical principles that guide inquiry, are not absolute and a priori. They are those practices that the classroom community, or other communities, have found effective in past inquiries and which have consequently been formalised so that they can be used to guide future inquiry. They are socio-culturally constructed and fallible. This means that the Community of Inquiry procedures should reflect the diverse perspectives of the communities from which they evolve, and the Community of Inquiry participants are required to critically reflect on these procedures and reconstruct them if they are found to be exclusive or ineffective for creating intersubjective meanings. This disputes Ellsworth's description of classroom dialogue as resembling the continuity editing of classical Hollywood cinema. Continuity editing's function is to hide the artificial, constructed nature of the film by making the transition from what one shot to another appear seamless and natural. Ellsworth claims that in the same way, classroom dialogue often conceals its own culturally constructed processes in order to make the transition from one perspective to another appear natural and unproblematic (1997, 89). The aim of the Community of Inquiry is not to transmit ideas seamlessly from one individual to another but to have diverse ideas interact and be transformed into new, more common, intersubjective ideas. Dialogue and thinking that is critically aware of the socio-cultural origins of its own processes is more refined and inclusive and consequently will be more conducive of intersubjective meanings. Thus, the Community of Inquiry actually values a diversity of thinking styles because of the fact that they make the contextual nature of the processes of dialogue conspicuous and open to philosophical investigation. Diversity fosters the procedural thinking that is at the heart of P4C's Community of Inquiry (see Chapter 3).

Since Community of Inquiry participants recognise the importance of interdependency and individual differences, P4C also cultivates the development of care, empathy, open-mindedness, reasonableness, respect for others, as well as a host of other affective and social skills that are necessary for autonomy and citizenship (see Chapter 5). Importantly, the Community of Inquiry not only facilitates caring attitudes but also facilitates the student's ability to elicit care, assistance, support and empathy from others. This is because the P4C classroom normalises and values interdependency, enabling students to feel comfortable displaying confusion, asking questions and asking others for assistance. This in turn provokes others to develop caring and empathetic skills and dispositions in response to those who signal a need for assistance and care.

Unlike individualistic and communitarian schools, which can present care and interdependency as incompatible with rights and rules, P4C rejects the problematic justice/care dualism. The caring, interdependent nature of the Community of Inquiry doesn't eliminate the need for classroom rules and procedures, which provide guidelines and standards for how individuals should behave and treat each other, as well as for what counts as good thinking. In the Community of Inquiry, the relationship between rights, rules and care is actually one of operational co-dependency. For example, recognition of another's need and right to participate in the inquiry is a reason to actively engage them in dialogue. The recognition of such a right is a prompt to treat them with care and respect so as to sustain open lines of communication. In turn, our capacity for care and empathy enables us to recognise that others have certain needs, interests and rights, including the right to inquire with others. The student's capacity for empathy and care enables them to formulate, understand and effectively perform communal inquiry procedures, such as offering others assistance when they are having trouble understanding or expressing themselves. In turn, having such standard procedures initiates and promotes such caring action, especially in situations where feelings of empathy and care may initially be lacking.

As we have seen, it is often argued that appeals to rights and general rules can be adversarial and culturally imperialistic, and, consequently, impede the development of care and altruism. When appeals to rights or rules involve making aggressive demands of others or interfere with one's ability to be altruistic, it is because they are seen as natural, absolute, infallible and, thus, exempt from critical reflection and revision. However, the rights and rules that guide the Community of Inquiry are not natural and absolute but contextual, fallible and always open to inquiry. It is accepted that in some situations they may be inappropriate or fail to promote an inclusive, communal inquiry and, as such, may need to be restricted, revised or relinquished. For example, Bandman explains that the child's right to inquire and ask questions, which implies that adults have a responsibility to respond to them, is not absolute and unlimited because certain inquiries may be inappropriate—for example, when children ask questions that aim to elicit personal information from another, or where the questions may touch on a subject which is painful or sensitive to another, or in situations where the information that children are trying to elicit from another could be dangerous to themselves (e.g., a child inquires about how to make a bomb) (1993, 34). While there are other rules and rights that it is difficult to imagine will ever be inappropriate or undesirable, what is important is that the Community of Inquiry remains open to the fact that if they ever did become problematic, they need not simply be retained under the assumption that they are natural and unalterable. This doesn't mean that such rules, procedures and rights have no authority, justification and stability. Their justification is their past and present success at fulfilling their purpose (e.g., promoting communal inquiry) and their general acceptance, practice and importance to the classroom community and other communities beyond the school provides them with their force. Having such generally accepted rights and rules means that P4C students can draw on them to protect their interests, as well as those of others. Since these rights are not absolute, it is also possible for P4C participants to surrender their rights so as to act purely for the sake of another or for some greater cause. Thus, in the Community of Inquiry, rights and rules don't impede the development of caring and altruistic dispositions but neither does the caring, interdependent nature of the inquiry delimit the need for general rights and rules.

Since the rules and rights that guide the Community of Inquiry are contextual and fallible, they are less likely to appear oppressive to students, as the rules in individualistic schools often do. The rules and procedures that guide the Community of Inquiry gain acceptance from the participants because they use them and experience their positive consequences. If the participants find them problematic or inferior, they are able to critique and reconstruct them. Thus, as with Summerhill, the students can shape the procedures that govern their own learning experience. Consequently, they are more likely to understand, value and promote these procedures (Dewey 2004a, 23). However, in contrast to individualistic schools like

Summerhill, the Community of Inquiry procedures are not constructed as means to constraining and controlling students' natural inclinations to be antisocial and individualistic. Rather, in P4C, the classroom procedures and rules are outgrowths and formalisations of the social, interdependent and caring nature of individuals engaged in communal inquiry. Since they reflect and promote communal inquiry, they are clearly seen to facilitate student autonomy rather than constrain it. This is why P4C theorists and teachers often claim that students care for the procedures of inquiry (Splitter and Sharp 1995, 19). These procedures have current use and immense value to students, who recognise that their own growth, and that of others, is dependent on them.

The Role of the Facilitator in the Community of Inquiry

The claim that students in the Community of Inquiry construct their own meaning and care about the procedures of inquiry and each other is sometimes taken to imply that P4C teachers are merely neutral spectators or equal participants. For example, Berrian states, "With me as listener, the students are free to interact with each other. That's exactly what I want them to do. I want them to forget that I'm there. The important thing is for them to express their opinion and give a reason for their point of view" (1985, 44). However, without some degree of teacher intervention, the Community of Inquiry would probably lose direction, fail to make progress and fail to be an educational experience for the students (Sprod 2001, 69; Murris 2000, 40, 44). Thus, unlike Summerhill teachers, the P4C teacher is not thought to occupy a position equal to that of students. The teacher has some degree of authority because of her more developed capacity for philosophical inquiry and her responsibility to provide and maintain a learning environment that provokes and scaffolds rigorous, purposeful and increasingly more sophisticated communal inquiry (Sprod 2001, 69–74; Murris 2000, 41).

The P4C teacher fulfils this responsibility in several ways, all of which require her to be an active participant in the inquiry. First, the P4C teacher is responsible for selecting the texts, materials and content, which will stimulate puzzlement, reflection and inquiry. The teacher should also promote and model the logical and caring procedures that enable communal inquiry, such as taking turns, giving reasons, listening to the speaker and empathising. Since students are less experienced inquirers, the teacher will need to assist students to formulate questions and ideas, self-correct, construct criteria, clarify concepts, construct alternatives, find reasons, make connections and draw inferences, while being careful not to completely impose their own ideas on students. One way the teacher does this is through open-ended questioning, which provokes critical reflection, deeper thinking and a search for reasons and explanations (Splitter and Sharp 1995, 48–58). The teacher must also be able to identify and articulate the philosophical aspects of children's dialogue, as well as the logical moves that children make. This implies that P4C teachers must have some background in philosophy because they must be familiar with different philosophical problems and positions, as well as with the thinking methods and fallacies covered in logic (Murris 2000, 44).

Often the Community of Inquiry will prematurely or uncritically reach a settlement or adopt a view that is problematic. In these cases, the teacher has a responsibility to facilitate deeper thinking and the formulation of more reasonable judgments. However, since students are likely to see the teacher as an authority, teacher interventions run the risk of indoctrinating students. Thus, teachers need to be careful and not forceful in their interventions. They should not simply claim that a position is wrong, but identify procedural problems with the way it was attained, suggest or give defences for alternative positions, present possible problems with the position and suggest counter arguments. Simply allowing students to prematurely accept positions, or accept positions that are unjustified and problematic fails to facilitate inquiry, growth and autonomy. However, teachers must also provide students with plenty of opportunities and time to think of ideas, arguments, questions, problems and methods by themselves. Students must also feel that they can question or disagree with teachers, including over their choice of curriculum materials or in regards to classroom procedures. Like all Community of Inquiry participants, the teacher must accept their own fallibility and be willing to provide reasons and self-correct. Teachers must gain their students' trust and cooperation by providing reasons and making choices that demonstrate that they have their students' best interests in mind, not by presenting themselves as infallible authorities or disciplinarians. If the Community of Inquiry refuses to accept certain content or procedures (e.g., listening to each other), they should be able to experience, and critically reflect on, the consequences of that decision (Sprod 2001, 69–74, 167–172; Splitter and Sharp 1995, 135–140; Murris 2000).

The Global Community of Inquiry

Like Dewey, P4C advocates intend for the classroom Community of Inquiry to expand outwards, making connections with other communities that lead to mutual transformations and growth (Splitter and Sharp 1995; Burgh, Field and Freakley 2006). The desired result would be that the Community of Inquiry and its participants develop meanings and habits that are more sophisticated and inclusive of different cultures and people, while other communities are also transformed to be more reflective of the democratic practices and ideas promoted in the P4C classroom. However, such connections and mutual transformations are not an inevitable result of establishing classroom communities of inquiries. Even if students value and depend on the Community of Inquiry in the classroom, this is no guarantee that they will interact with other communities and apply collaborative inquiry practices beyond the school. The connections between P4C's democratic classroom, the whole school and the local and global community must be actively created within schools. Students must have the opportunities to experience the reconstructive potential of communal inquiry and philosophical practice with communities beyond the classroom as part of their everyday learning experience. In fact, since such interaction with other communities and different individuals is essential to one's growth and capacity for autonomy, students have a right to engage with other communities as part of their education (Bandman 1993, 37). This is implied by Dewey's claim that,

> It is the office of the school environment to balance the various elements in the social environment and to see to it that each individual gets an opportunity to escape from the limitations of the social group in which he was born, and to come into living contact with a broader environment. (2004a, 20)

As with communitarian schools, the Deweyian ideal of the self, society and citizenship necessities a type of service learning program where students can participate in the community beyond their classroom. However, unlike traditional service learning programs, a Deweyian type of service learning would require that students actively engage with those individuals affected by the social problem in a caring, communal inquiry so as to reconstruct the problem. As with the Hull House residents, the students would be benefited as much as those they assist because they would develop habits and meanings that would enable them to live a more autonomous, meaningful life. In the Chapter 8, I will provide a more detailed account of what a P4C approach to service learning might look like.

However, first we must look at another way in which P4C's anti-dualism has the potential to help foster democratic communities. In the next chapter, it will be shown that P4C rejects traditional gender stereotypes, especially gendered notions of knowledge and knowing, which are reflected in dominant pedagogies and ideals of curriculum. In doing so, P4C offers a classroom environment and pedagogy that is more inclusive and, thus, more democratic than many other approaches to schooling.

7   A Response to Male/ Female Dualism
Reconstructing Gender in Philosophy for Children

Philosophy for Children (P4C) reconstructs traditional gender stereotypes, which link caring, imaginative, concrete, social and connected thinking with femininity, and abstract, rationalistic and individualistic thinking with masculinity. Dominant educational ideals tend to privilege 'masculine' ideals of thinking, and this has disadvantaged females because schooling appears to be opposed to 'femininity'. However, the educational and epistemological exclusion or devaluing of the 'feminine' also disadvantages males by denying them access to abilities and attributes necessary for good thinking. In contrast, P4C challenges the traditional gendering of the curriculum, which maintains that supposedly concrete, emotive and imaginative subjects like arts, English and the humanities are feminine, while seemingly more rational subjects like mathematics and science are masculine. As such, P4C has the potential to respond to current concerns over the educational performance of males, especially in relation to literacy and behavioural problems, as well as perennial concerns about the comparatively low participation rates of females in mathematics and science. Before we can assess how P4C may help overcome these problems, we need to examine how dominant educational ideals reinforce dominant gender stereotypes and how this negatively affects the educational experiences of both males and females.

GENDER, DUALISM AND EDUCATION

In Chapter 1, it was explained that the dominant Western epistemological construct reflects 'masculine' experiences and desires and is defined in opposition to the 'feminine'. According to this dominant epistemology, the only legitimate means of attaining knowledge is through pure Reason, devoid of emotion, concrete experience, imagination and corporeality, which are considered obstacles to Reason. While Reason is associated with 'masculinity', all that is opposed to Reason is associated with the 'feminine'. Thus, knowledge and Reason are defined via an exclusion of the 'feminine'. While the faculties and attributes associated with femininity have been considered useful for the reproductive and caring activities of the private, domestic sphere, they are thought to be opposed to the public, political realm. It is only 'masculine' theoretical, rational knowledge that is thought of as suitable for public consumption and the paid workforce.

This has consequences for education because the fundamental goal of education has been to educate individuals so as they may participate as autonomous citizens in the productive, public realm. As such, traditional education tends to privilege the 'masculine' and devalue the 'feminine' (Martin 1982, 108). This is most noticeable in the traditional curriculum hierarchy described in Chapter 1. Mathematics and the physical sciences (i.e. physics and chemistry) are typically considered to be 'masculine' subjects in virtue of their greater emphasis on abstractness, theory and rationality. As Davies explains,

> Proper hard, non-subjective subjects like Maths, science and technology provide a haven of acceptable (male) knowledge which confirm that true knowledge lies outside oneself and independent of any subjectivities, independent of those emotions which need to be held in check. They are rational, cool, controllable, abstract, distant, and unquestionably hegemonic. (1996, 214)

These 'masculine' subjects are considered prestigious, demanding, and socially and vocationally valuable. As Teese et al. argue, they are prerequisites for some of the most high status university courses and professions, and their supposedly objective assessment methods (e.g., multiple-choice tests) are thought to enable a more reliable assessment and ranking of students than the seemingly more subjective assessments that characterise the arts and humanities (e.g., argumentative essays, creative writing). Performing well in these subjects is taken as a good indication of a student's abilities, more so than a good performance in other subjects (Teese et al. 1995, 10). These subjects maintain a higher status than subjects traditionally considered 'feminine' (e.g., arts, humanities, social sciences, etc.). As Gilbert and Gilbert explain, this gendered curriculum hierarchy perpetuates patriarchy:

> These divisions [public/private, mental/manual labour] have given rise to claims that feminine intuition, emotion and expressivity are naturally associated with the humanities, while maths and science attract boys because of the kind of rationality involved in these subjects. The prejudice that boys are naturally interested or talented in these subjects, and the recognition that they are high status subjects that will give boys access to desirable male careers, has been a factor in the position of power that men have traditionally held in the workforce. (1998, 122)

THE PARTICIPATION AND PERFORMANCE
OF GIRLS IN MATHS AND SCIENCE

Given the gendered nature of the curriculum, it is not surprising that females are less likely to participate in mathematics and science subjects. When females have participated, they have tended to be less successful at these subjects than their male counterparts. Given the high social and academic status that these subjects have, lower participation and performance in them has been particularly detrimental for females. Consequently, the participation and performance of females in maths and the sciences was a focus of early gender equity polices and strategies, which appear to have had some success. Since the late 1980s, when most of these policies and strategies were introduced in Australia, females have shown significant improvements in their participation and performance in mathematics and science (see Teese and Polesel 2003; Teese et al. 1995).

Nonetheless, serious concerns remain about the accessibility of these subjects to females. Female students still participate in mathematics and physical science subjects to a much lesser degree than males.[1] For example, in the 2011 New South Wales Higher School Certificate, only 2,135 females enrolled in physics compared to 7,247 males (NSWBOS 2011).[2] Males are also over-represented in the more advanced maths subjects in the final years of schooling. For example, in 2011, females accounted for only 34% of the students enrolled in the Year 12 subject Specialist Mathematics, which is the most demanding of the four maths subjects offered in the state of Victoria (VCAA 2011a, 2011b). Research by Teese et al. suggests that females tend to 'under-enrol' in maths by selecting courses below their capabilities. That is, females either underestimate their own abilities in mathematics or they don't value more demanding math subjects. In contrast, males tend to over-enrol in maths and, as such, they are over-represented in the lowest performing group of students in the more challenging maths courses (1995, 56). Females do now achieve higher average marks in many senior maths and science subjects in Australia. However, this is explained by the fact that it is predominantly a very select group of high-achieving, middle-class girls that enrol in these subjects in the first place, while the group of boys who enrol in them is larger and more diversified in terms of background and ability. Thus, not all girls have achieved greater access to these subjects. In all but the highest socio-economic backgrounds, boys still participate in these subjects in much greater numbers (Teese et al. 1995, 82–91). While females enrol in humanities and arts subjects in greater numbers than males, and generally perform significantly better in them, this doesn't act as a substitute for their poorer participation in maths and science because the arts and humanities don't have the vocational, academic and social status and benefits that maths and science do.

Problematically, many of the strategies and policies aimed at improving the participation and performance of females in maths and science have not challenged the gendering of these subjects or the privileging of them in the curriculum. Encouraging females into traditionally masculine subjects and occupations on the grounds that they are intellectually, economically and socially valuable could actually be seen to validate patriarchal ideals by reinforcing the superiority of the 'masculine' over the 'feminine'. As Kenway et al. explain,

> The almost exclusive hierarchy of mathematics and science and technology accepts the dominance of masculine values and knowledge and reinforces what many students already know, that those subject areas most associated with the masculine are to be valued over those most associated with the feminine. Far from breaking down gendered dualisms of hard/soft, male/female, powerful/powerless, it underlines and exaggerates them. (1997, 73)

Strategies that merely encourage girls to participate in traditionally male subjects also fail to critique the more implicit sexism in the way these subjects are taught. Girls may simply be expected to adapt to 'masculine' pedagogies and content. For example, maths and science subjects can seem 'masculine' because they place an "emphasis on technical knowledge, on solutions to problems which are justified in abstract rather than personal terms, on an individual, competitive approach to problems rather than a collaborative one" and on deductive reasoning over induction (Gilbert and Gilbert 1998, 121). The assessment methods relied upon in these subjects also appear to favour 'masculine' thinking styles. Research suggests that boys do better on multiple-choice and short-answer tests, as well as on high-risk public exams, which are the most commonly used assessment methods in maths and science. In contrast, females generally do better with open-ended essay questions, assessments requiring greater language ability and class-based projects. These are the dominant forms of assessment used in English, the arts and humanities but are still seldom used in maths (Teese and Polesel 2003). Thus, while females tend to have a competitive edge on the types of assessments used in English, the arts and humanities, again, these subjects are not as lucrative as the maths and sciences. This is why Teese et al. argue that "English does not work for girls in the way that maths and science so demonstrably serve to maximize some boys' chances of high achievement in their final exams" (1995, 105).

THE DISADVANTAGE OF GIRLS ACROSS THE CURRICULUM

It isn't just maths and science that can appear to devalue and exclude the 'feminine'. Since girls often participate and perform well in English, the arts and humanities, it is often believed that these are gender-neutral or feminised subjects. However, as explained in Chapter 1, these subjects can also privilege 'masculine' experiences and values. For example, the curriculum of such subjects, especially the traditional humanities like history and literature, often emphasises abstract theory; old and, thus, more established and 'certain' texts and knowledge; and argumentation as opposed to concrete experiences, contemporary issues, imagination and emotionality. The curriculum of such subjects may also focus on a study of male authors, theorists and historical figures. For example, much history curricula focuses on male activities and exploits. As one female student explains,

> We wouldn't normally do anything about women in Social Studies because mostly in Social Studies we learn about history. It would be pretty good if we did I guess but I don't really know if we could because I don't really know about any woman that was anything in history. (interviewed by Kenway et al. 1997, 77)

It's not just the content of these subjects that can reflect 'masculine' experiences and ideals, but also the pedagogical and assessment methods used. While the arts and humanities are more likely to emphasise classroom discussions, group work, school-based projects and essay writing, this may not necessarily advantage females. Essay writing and classroom discussions often emphasise abstract, depersonalised and aggressive forms of argumentation, which are associated with dominant 'masculine' ways of knowing. Many of the female college students interviewed by Belenky et al. expressed frustration that they were expected to put feelings and concrete experiences aside in order to produce essays that emphasised dispassionate objectivity, abstract ideas and logical rigour (1986, 200). The problem is that schooling, regardless of the subject area, has traditionally been focused on the cultivation of ideals of thinking and knowing that are incompatible with dominant notions of femininity. Consequently, many female students lack confidence in themselves as learners; underestimate their abilities; enrol in subjects less demanding than what they appear capable of; display greater dependency on teachers; are often more cautious and conservative in their responses on tests; are less likely, or less able, to contribute to classroom discussions; and appear reluctant to challenge, critique or disagree with teachers or other students (Teese and Polesel 2003; Teese et al. 1995, 97; Slade 1994, 30; Belenky et al. 1986, Ch. 2; Gilbert and Taylor 1991).

THE PARTICIPATION AND PERFORMANCE OF BOYS IN ART AND THE HUMANITIES

Just as females have been reluctant to participate in 'masculine' subjects, males participate less in the arts and humanities and tend to be less successful in these subjects when they do participate. For example, in 2011, male students only accounted for about 18% of the 3,975 students enrolled in the New South Wales Year 12 subject Society and Culture', and of the 9,717 students enrolled in the subject Visual Arts, only about 29% were male (NSWBOS 2011).[3] In recent times, there has also been considerable concern about boys' levels of literacy and engagement with the English curriculum. In international tests conducted by the Organisation for Economic and Cooperative Development in 2009, girls outperformed boys on the reading tests in all 70 participating nations by an average of one school year's progress. The size of the gender gap is much wider in some countries than in others (OECD 2010, 59). Australia's own national assessment program has shown that 3.1% more Year 9 girls met the reading benchmark in 2011 (ACARA 2011). While this gender difference may not seem very alarming, it has received considerable attention from the media and educational researchers.

At least part of the problem seems to be that subjects like English, art and the humanities can seem to conflict with dominant notions of masculinity. Reading is often perceived to be a passive and, therefore, feminine activity. This perception is supported by the fact that many teachers still treat reading as a means to taking in or memorising information rather than as a process of constructing meaning. Furthermore, school literature may focus on 'feminine' themes, such as personal relationships and emotions, while writing in English may emphasise imaginativeness, introspection, personal responses to texts, empathising with characters, describing feelings and so on. This conflicts with dominant notions of masculinity which stress the suppression of emotions, activeness and a focus on things "outside the self, rather than in the self" (Gilbert and Gilbert 1998, 214).

Males may also be reluctant to engage in such subjects because they are aware that these subjects have lower academic, social and vocational value. As Lingard and Douglas argue, the higher value attributed to 'masculine' subjects makes it very difficult to encourage boys to consider supposedly inferior 'feminine' subjects (1999, 166). Boys seem to have a more instrumental approach to schooling, with their subject choices revealing an emphasis on gaining paid work, particularly in the most high status jobs and positions, while girls, who tend to select from a boarder group of subjects, may have broader educational goals and be more likely to select subjects based on their current interests and abilities (Gilbert and Gilbert 1998, 121, 135–138; Glaser 1994, 15).

BOYS AND ANTI-SOCIAL BEHAVIOUR

Another area of concern is male students' greater tendency for anti-social and disruptive behaviour both in and out of the classroom. Research suggests that in Australia about 80 per cent of the students suspended or excluded from school are boys and boys far are more likely to be suspended for violence. Boys are also far more likely to drop out of school

(Commonwealth of Australia 2002). While there are many important factors that contribute to anti-social and disruptive classroom behaviour, including family background, boredom, learning problems, substance abuse and behavioural disorders, dominant ideals of femininity and masculinity are also contributors. A common explanation for boys' behavioural problems is that schooling expects and rewards behaviour that is 'feminine' and which conflicts with dominant notions of masculinity. For example, students are expected to be docile, obedient, quiet, still, orderly, neat and cooperative; display care for their work and for others; and passively receive information. This conflicts with the notion that boys should be robust, energetic, assertive, emotionally neutral and independent (McClean 1997). Thus, boys and young men may see disruptive and anti-social behaviour as a way to demonstrate risk-taking, independence, activeness, assertiveness, confidence, autonomy and dominance.

It is sometimes claimed that the reason schools promote 'feminine' behaviour is because teaching is a female-dominated profession and schools have become increasingly feminised. However, the 'feminine' notion of good behaviour promoted by schools has more to do with the fact that schools assume and promote a dominant notion of childhood that bears striking similarities to dominant notions of femininity. Like women, children are considered to lack rationality, autonomy and independence. Consequently, like women, children are expected to submit to the authority of more rational, autonomous individuals—adults and men. Thus, the problem is not so much that schools value the feminine and see masculinity as subversive. The problem is that there is an inherent conflict between dominant notions of masculinity and dominant notions of childhood, which forces boys to choose between being a good student and being 'masculine' (Gilbert and Gilbert 1998, 208).

THE RECUPERATIVE MASCULINIST RESPONSE

One response to these problems has been to argue that schools must reaffirm ideals of masculinity so that boys can freely and positively develop a masculine sense of self rather than having to define themselves in opposition to the supposedly feminised environment of the school. This often translates into calls for more male teachers, more masculine literature on the English curriculum (e.g., comics, action novels, etc), more active modes of learning and an emphasis on sports (Lingard and Douglas 1999, 133).

This recuperative masculinist position is highly problematic. First, the recuperative masculinist position uncritically accepts and affirms a particular notion of masculinity, as biologically determined, without considering the problematic nature of this notion of masculinity. The notion of masculinity that recuperative masculinists assert is hegemonic masculinity. However, as we have seen, this patriarchal notion of masculinity, along with its feminine counterpart, seem to be causal factors in many of these educational and social problems. Second, the uncritical acceptance and essentialising of hegemonic masculinity means that boys and men who don't conform to this ideal are seen as subversive and inferior. Boys who aren't physically strong and active, emotionally detached and assertive, and who don't appear to be ruggedly individualistic and independent are excluded from hegemonic masculinity. This can actually perpetuate self-esteem problems, social alienation and behavioural problems. This is most evident in relation to the issue of sexuality. Since hegemonic masculinity is characterised by hyper-heterosexuality, boys who are gay or bisexual, or even those who are perceived to be whether they actually are or not, are often subject to harassment, violence and other forms of marginalisation (Lingard and Douglas 1999, 144). Third, this position involves the uncritical acceptance of particular pedagogies and curricula simply because boys prefer them. For example, Buckingham recommends competitive learning environments for boys because "boy's are naturally competitive" and they get better results on standardised tests when learning in competitive environments (2004, 24). However, the fact that boy's prefer competition, or get higher marks in competitive learning environments, doesn't make competition a good pedagogical method. When students are primarily motivated by competition, their aim is not to understand or do something well but to beat other people. If students' only motivation for learning something is to outdo someone else, once the exam is finished and the prizes are given out, they are unlikely to continue to develop their knowledge or skills or even remember what has already been learnt. Furthermore, as explained in Chapter 6, competitiveness is associated with rugged individualism and can undermine cooperation. This may just perpetuate boys' behavioural problems. Another example is the call for more 'masculine' texts on the English curriculum. It is common to hear parents and teachers comment that as long as boys are reading it doesn't matter what they read. Surely it matters if students are uncritically reading texts that promote patriarchal gender stereotypes, violence, homophobia, racism or misogyny.

Thus, rather than simply accepting dominant notions of gender and affirming ideals of schooling that accommodate and facilitate them, we should critically reflect on existing pedagogical methods, curriculum content and dominant gender stereotypes in order to reconstruct them and create learning environments that facilitate skills and knowledge that will enable all students to live autonomous, meaningful lives. P4C offers a pedagogy and curriculum that can help us overcome many of these gender problems in education. Rather than simply reinforcing traditional gender stereotypes, P4C reconstructs them and promotes methods of thinking that emphasise the way traditionally masculine and feminine attributes are actually intertwined and interdependent in the process of inquiry and the acquisition of knowledge. P4C's anti-dualism results in a pedagogy that scaffolds all students to become reasonable, autonomous, critical, caring and collaborative thinkers, regardless of their sex.

PHILOSOPHY FOR CHILDREN'S RECONSTRUCTION OF GENDERED EPISTEMOLOGIES

There is some concern that P4C promotes traditional philosophical ideals and practices that reflect white, male, middle-class perspectives. In particular, there is a concern that P4C's emphasis on logic and philosophical inquiry may promote notions of Reason and argumentation that are adversarial and defined in opposition to the emotions, imagination, the corporeal and the subjective (Field 1997; Macoll 1997; Haynes 1994; Valentino 1998, 29; Birkhahn 1997, 39). As Macoll explains,

> I have to confess that I have often felt, as a feminist philosopher, some disquiet in advocating philosophy in schools, for the following reason: would you wish on young women or small girls a practice of philosophy, which you yourself have come to see as deeply imbued with disguised, gendered ideals and associations, which are, if not wrong, at the very least, not appropriate for everyone? (1997, 6)

However, as we have seen, P4C incorporates Dewey's epistemology to create a classroom "environment in which a number of traditional gender dualisms break down" and where undesirable philosophical ideals and methods are reconstructed (Glaser 1994, 16; see also Sharp 1993; Redshaw 1994a, 1994b; Haynes 1994; Splitter and Sharp 1995; Field 1997; Macoll 1997; Collins 2001). In Chapter 3, it was shown that P4C's pragmatist notions of truth and meaning reconstruct Reason/experience, object/subject, abstract/concrete and mind/body dualisms. In the P4C classroom, all thinking is a way of making sense of concrete experiences and, thus, is embodied, situated and subjective. However, it is understood that the reconstruction of experience simultaneously involves abstract and objective thinking, including identifying and adhering to general logical principles. Thus, P4C rejects the idea that the objective and abstract is severed from 'feminine' subjectivity, corporeality and the concrete and, thus, rejects the very notion that subjectivity, corporeality and the concrete are unique to women's ways of knowing. In Chapters 4 and 5, it was shown that P4C's notion of thinking rejects the dominant notion of Reason as opposed to the 'feminine' emotions and imagination. Rather, P4C assumes that reason, emotion and imagination are intertwined and functionally co-dependent. Attempts to completely isolate these faculties or attributes from one and other or to suppress any of them will always be unsuccessful and result in methods that are impoverished and ineffective for constructing meaning. As such, P4C rejects the assumption that imagination and emotion are more relevant to women's ways of knowing. In Chapter 6, it was demonstrated that P4C's classroom community of inquiry rejects individual/community dualism, instead emphasising the relational, communal nature of all thinking, the self and autonomy. P4C rejects the dominant ideal of autonomy as rugged individualism, opposed to 'feminine' dependency and connectedness and, in doing so, rejects the very notion that dependency and connectedness are 'feminine'.

Far from disadvantaging girls and women, P4C's focus on logic and philosophical inquiry may benefit female students in particular. Of particular value is the fact that the P4C's model of philosophy facilitates cooperative inquiry rather than the competitive style of school debating or adversarial method of philosophy described by Moultan (1983). As explained, many female students lack confidence in themselves as reasoners. The explicit and implicit exclusion of females from certain activities and disciplines, such as maths, science and logic, has undoubtedly contributed to this. P4C can particularly benefit those who have less-developed thinking skills and/or who simply lack confidence in themselves as reasoners because it is specifically designed to scaffold an ideal of thinking which doesn't reinforce traditional gendered notions of thinking. Haynes (1994) argues that facilitating the development of reasoning skills promotes feminist goals because the capacity to think for oneself frees both females and males from complete dependence on, and control by, others.

P4C's anti-dualistic epistemology also challenges the traditional gendered and hierarchical structure of the curriculum. Since P4C assumes that all subjects involve an ideal of thinking, which deconstructs traditional gender stereotypes, it rejects the gendering and ranking of subjects. If *all* students were required to engage in philosophical Communities of Inquiry in all classes, they would come to see traditional gender dualisms as fallacious and problematic. For example, students would see that the emotions and imagination are neither 'feminine' nor unique to English and art class but are actually key attributes of all good thinking in all subjects. Since P4C involves students inquiring into epistemology and the process of thinking itself, the problematic nature of traditional gendered ideals of knowing can also be made explicit and critically explored as a part of the inquiry itself. As such, the integration of P4C across the curriculum has the potential to help overcome the gender differences in participation rates and levels of achievement in different subjects. Of course, many dominant social values, institutions and practices beyond the school reinforce these gender stereotypes. This is why schooling must also enable students to openly inquire into gender issues more broadly, as well as gendered ideals of thinking and learning.

There is some concern that the reading material used in Lipman's P4C program may reinforce sexist stereotypes and thinking. Slade (1994) has argued that while most of the P4Ccharacters have gender-neutral names and don't display typical male and female ways of thinking, speaking and acting, the first P4C book, *Harry Stottlemeier's Discovery*, does reinforce traditional gender stereotypes. The story revolves around a male character named Harry who is trying to discover the principles of syllogistic logic. As Slade argues, Harry is stereotypically male in that he demonstrates thinking that is abstract, deductive and innovative. The text also suggests that Harry is competitive and lacking in interpersonal skills (1994, 30–31). The main female character is Lisa, who supports Harry's project but is also sceptical. At one point, Lisa quotes a line of poetry and emphasises the importance of the imagination as complementary to Harry's analytic technique. Thus, Lisa exemplifies a traditional feminine role. She is caring and supportive of male activities and values the imagination and emotion as much as deductive reasoning (1994, 31). Slade gives many more examples of how the characters in this narrative reflect traditional gender stereotypes.

While this is concerning, these texts are not essential for practicing P4C. Furthermore, as both Slade and Velasco argue, what is important is that P4C students are encouraged to question such representations of gender (Slade 1994, 31; Velasco 1997; see also Macoll 1997, 44). In the P4C classroom, the shared reading of the text is followed by a student-centred philosophical inquiry in which these gender stereotypes can and must be critically examined (Velasco 1997, 44). Thus, the important thing is that P4C fosters critical literacy and a critical examination of ideals of gender embedded in curriculum materials.

DISCUSSING GENDER IN THE PHILOSOPHICAL COMMUNITY OF INQUIRY

The P4C classroom is an ideal environment for discussing gender issues because it facilitates the necessary critical thinking skills, while also providing relevant philosophical subject matter (Collins 2001; Turgeon 1998). The many sub-disciplines of philosophy include problems and information relevant to gender issues. First, feminist philosophy provides various critiques of how epistemologies, social practices, public institutions, political systems and values can be patriarchal, as well as racist and classist. Feminist philosophy also suggests feminist alternatives, which may be assessed and implemented by students. Aesthetics and media ethics enable students to analyse how gender and sexuality is constructed and represented in different art forms and popular culture, and the ethical implications of this for those working in the media. The study of epistemology and logic enables students to critique how different ideals of knowledge and thinking may be gendered. Importantly, as mentioned, this may provoke and enable students to question the traditional gendering of the curriculum. Political philosophy can facilitate student inquiry into human rights, citizenship, autonomy, freedom, justice, equality, harassment and discrimination laws, democracy and multiculturalism—all of which are relevant to gender issues. The problems and theories of ethics can provide students with knowledge and skills for analysing the moral dimension of sexual harassment, sexual discrimination, bullying, violence and personal relationships. Ethical inquiry will also enable students to construct guidelines and standards for acceptable behaviour inside and outside the classroom. Metaphysics enables students to inquire into problems such as the nature of personhood, with an emphasis on how different notions of personhood may exclude certain people, such as women and children. Logic enables students to construct standards for good thinking, which can facilitate a meaningful and reasonable inquiry into these controversial and contentious issues.

GENDER, LITERACY AND COMMUNICATION SKILLS IN PHILOSOPHY FOR CHILDREN

P4C may also help improve boys' literacy skills and engagement with the English curriculum. Unlike traditional schooling, P4C makes it clear that reading is not a passive and 'feminine' activity of receiving information from a text. While traditional school textbooks are primarily designed to transmit information to students, texts used for P4C are open and problematic so as to provoke communal inquiry, where students are considered active participants in creating meaning (Othman and Hashim 2006; Jo 2001–2002). In the Community of Inquiry, it is assumed that students have a unique situatedness that will affect their interpretation of the text (Jo 2001–2002, 44–45). Attention is drawn to this multitude of interpretations because the whole class collaboratively reads the same text, and this shared reading is immediately followed by a communal inquiry, initiated by student questions. While the text will limit the number of possible of interpretations, if there was only one unambiguous response to the text, inquiry would be unnecessary. Inquiry is provoked as a means to critically comparing these competing interpretations (Othman and Hashim 2006, 27). Thus, P4C emphasises the fact that reading a text involves more than just correctly recognising words. It is an active and creative process of meaning making. As Lipman explains, reading involves a "collaboration between author and reader that results in a common product that goes beyond what the author has stated or implied" (2003, 175). This reading process may be particularly beneficial for boys because it is an active, autonomous activity that involves thinking that is both critical and creative. Furthermore, since P4C accepts that textual meaning is constructed and contextual, it facilitates critical literacy. Facilitating critical literacy is a fundamental goal of feminism because it requires students to look for sexism, class division, racism and other types of bias in texts.

Since reading is a process of constructing meaning and P4C focuses on facilitating the thinking skills needed for constructing meaning, it is not surprising that some research shows a correlation between P4C and improvement in reading ability (e.g., Othman and Hashim 2006; Tricky and Topping 2004). As Jo explains, constructing meaning from texts

involves making various connections, including connections between different words, between words and things, between premises and conclusions,
between things that are similar and things that are dissimilar, between the
general and the particular, between parts and wholes, between causes and
effects, and so on (2001–2002, 45). The study of formal and informal logic
in the P4C classroom, as well as P4C's emphasis on procedural thinking,
helps students understand why some inferences and connections are legitimate and meaningful and others are not. In the P4C classroom, students are
encouraged to break sentences down into their basic, logical form, examine
the different functions that each component of the sentence may have, and
uncover "hidden connections between the words" (Brown 1991, 11).

Lipman argues that standard reading comprehension tests look for three
abilities, all of which involve particular types of logical procedures. First,
they test to see "whether or not the reader understands what the passage
states" (2003, 176). This is demonstrated when the reader identifies another
passage that has an equivalent meaning to the first. This is a logical procedure of making a connection of synonymy between two separate things. Second, reading comprehension requires that the reader "infer what the passage
implies", which is also a logical procedure, requiring the ability to identify
what beliefs and meanings can legitimately be inferred from the text (2003,
176). Third, reading comprehension tests assess "whether or not the reader
grasps the *underlying assumptions* on which the passage is based" (2003,
176). This is also a logical procedure. It involves seeing the assertions made
in the text as the possible conclusions of valid or strong arguments and then
asking what the premises supporting those conclusions would be. Thus, the
reader tries to understand what reasons the author might have for making
such assertions. Lipman adds that analogical reasoning is of fundamental
importance. If readers can identify similarities between what is read and
other texts or ideas, then they also demonstrate comprehension of what has
been read, as well as the ability to go beyond the text and create new meanings (2003, 176). Thus, as Lipman explains, facilitating reasoning skills is
fundamental for facilitating reading comprehension:

> Reading comprehension can therefore be said to rest upon the formal
> skills of deductive inferential reasoning and upon such skills as ana-
> logical reasoning. It is likely that reading comprehension will be more
> effectively improved if these primary reasoning skills are strengthened
> than if attention is paid to syntactical lapses, vocabulary weaknesses,
> spelling deficiencies, and a lack of stylistic appreciation. This is because
> reasoning skills contribute directly to the reader's acquisition of mean-
> ing, and it is access to meaning that most effectively motivates the
> reader to continue pursuing the reading process. (2003, 176)

One would also expect that the emphasis placed on conceptual analysis
in P4C, as well as the study of philosophy of language, would facilitate

the development of language ability and literacy. Philosophy of language involves students investigating the nature and function of language, particularly when it is most ambiguous, problematic or obscure. For example, students can investigate the nature of metaphor, analogy and concepts that don't clearly correspond to concrete objects in the world (e.g., time, numbers, knowledge, freedom, beauty). Of course, these concepts are fundamental in P4C because they are the basis of philosophical puzzlement and inquiry. Conceptual analysis helps students understand the different contextual meanings that words can have and develop the ability to construct clear and precise definitions. The capacity for skilled conceptual analysis is imperative for reading comprehension, constructing and analysing arguments and for essay writing, which requires students to clarify how they are using or understanding concepts and to be consistent in their use of concepts. This helps students construct meaning from texts and avoid ambiguity in their writing and construction of arguments.

Participation in P4C's classroom Community of Inquiry should also help improve language, literacy and communication skills, simply because students are required to engage in a classroom dialogue and communicate their ideas to others, as well as listen to others speak (Jenkins and Lyle 2010). In order to participate in the inquiry, students learn that they need to choose and structure their words thoughtfully and carefully, give examples, provide reasons, listen to others and make connections between their own ideas and the ideas of others and the text. These skills don't just characterise good speaking and listening but also good writing and reading.

GENDER AND STUDENT BEHAVIOUR IN PHILOSOPHY FOR CHILDREN

By reconstructing dominant gender stereotypes, P4C may also help counter the disruptive classroom behaviour of boys. P4C challenges the notion that care, attentive listening, collaboration and learning are 'feminine' dispositions because such dispositions are explicitly identified as essential attributes that all good inquirers and autonomous individuals possess, regardless of their gender. Furthermore, P4C rejects the traditional view that well-behaved students are submissive, passive, silent and subordinate. It is understandable that students, both male and female, resist this ideal of the good student since it denies them any sense of autonomy and individuality. In contrast to traditional pedagogies, P4C is a more student-centred pedagogy, where students are active, autonomous participants in their own learning. As explained in Chapter 6, P4C rejects the child/adult dualism, which posits adults as fully autonomous and developed, while children are seen as dependent and deficit. In the P4C classroom, children have some degree of autonomy. The classroom inquiry is initiated by student questions and all students are encouraged to actively participate, give their own opinions, share their experiences and question others, including the teacher. Participation and effort is rewarded with meaningfulness and a greater capacity for independent thinking and this helps keep students motivated and engaged. In such an environment, students are less likely to be disruptive and resistant because they are less likely to feel oppressed, manipulated and bored.

Nonetheless, P4C could be improved in terms of its capacity to treat students as active, autonomous and valuable community members and in its ability to more fully engage all students so as to minimise student boredom and disruptive classroom behaviour. P4C could require students to take transformative action as a part of the inquiry process—that is, to engage in active citizenship by using their emerging philosophical knowledge and skills to respond to authentic social problems beyond the classroom and school. Such active learning experiences can help concretise and contextualise curriculum content and skills, rendering the learning process more meaningful and engaging. It also sends students the message that they are capable members of society, able to contribute to shaping and improving the world in which they live. Such learning experiences would also help P4C overcome one of the few problematic, gendered dualisms that it currently fails to address—the theory/practice dualism. As we have seen (Chapter 2), overcoming this dualism was a focus of Dewey's philosophy but seems to have been overlooked by Lipman and most other P4C theorists. P4C, with its focus on discussion and written texts, rather than action, may help perpetuate the problematic notion that thinking is primarily theoretical and disembodied. In the next chapter, we will examine this dualism in depth, including its problematic educational implications, before outlying a potential solution to P4C's problematic lack of practicality.

A Response to Theory/
Practice Dualism
Social Reconstruction Learning

We have seen that Dewey's theories of inquiry and education emphasise the interrelatedness of theory and practice, mind and body, thought and action, and abstract ideas and concrete experience (Chapters 2 and 3). Dewey's commitment to overcoming theory/practice dualism was most famously demonstrated at his Laboratory School at the University of Chicago where students learnt through undertaking practical, 'hands-on' activities like sewing, building, gardening and so on. While Lipman reiterates Dewey's rejection of theory/practice dualism, Philosophy for Children (P4C) does not involve students participating in the same type of active transformation of their environment as a part of the inquiry process. In this chapter, it will be argued that not only is P4C's lack of practicality inconsistent with Lipman's pragmatism, but it is educationally problematic. P4C's failure to overcome theory/practice dualism undermines its commitment to foster reflective thinking, active citizenship, democracy and a pragmatic attitude that is essential for living a meaningful life.

In order to develop a possible solution to P4C's problematic lack of practicality, an examination of service learning will be undertaken. Service learning is the most common type of practical learning implemented in schools and universities (Spring, Grim and Dietz 2009; Cipolle 2004). It involves students performing community service activities as a means to facilitating various learning outcomes (e.g., a sense of civic duty, compassion, problem-solving skills, etc.), while also making some positive contribution to the wider community. However, approaches to service learning vary and not all approaches are compatible with P4C's desirable educational goals. The literature identifies two broad approaches to service learning: one approach is politically conservative and prioritises the student's educational needs over the needs of the community, while the other is more concerned with bringing about genuine social change and reflects a more progressive political ideology. The first approach to service learning is often called 'traditional service learning', while the second approach is commonly referred to as a 'critical' or 'social justice approach'. It will be shown that the critical approach, which has its roots in Dewey's educational ideas, critical pedagogy and the curriculum ideology known as 'social reconstructionism', is both more consistent with the goals of P4C and more educational. However, critical service learning also has weaknesses. Not only will it be shown that P4C can be much improved through incorporating critical service learning, but I will argue that P4C can help critical service learning overcome some of its problems. This is because critical service learning needs to be able to facilitate the type of philosophical, collaborative inquiry that P4C is designed to foster. Thus, it will be argued that P4C and service learning are mutually dependent. They need each other in order to achieve their common Deweyian educational and social goals.

PHILOSOPHY FOR CHILDREN'S PROBLEMATIC LACK OF PRACTICALITY

As we have seen, Dewey describes inquiry as the process of intelligently interacting with our socio-cultural environment (see Chapter 2). Thus, inquiry is not a purely cognitive process; it necessarily involves transformative *action*. In fact, for Dewey, 'inquiry' is synonymous with 'reflective experience' and 'reflective action'. Dewey's rejection of theory/practice dualism is evident in his acceptance of the pragmatic maxim, which maintains that the meaning of an idea is determined by the consequences which result from it when it is applied to the problematic situation for which it was intended (see Chapter 3). Thus, experimentation and application are essential aspects of inquiry and the acquisition of meaning (Dewey 1938, 114, 146–147). Inquiry isn't limited to individual transformative action. As we have seen, Dewey thought communal inquiry was the superior mode of inquiry because our environment is essentially social and cultural (see Chapters 2 and 5). Thus, we have no choice but to consider the interests and actions of others if we are to interact with our environment in an intelligent manner. It is through conjoint reflective action that societies are able to transform themselves and their environment so as to create conditions that foster human flourishing. For Dewey, collaborative inquiry is social reconstruction—communities reconstructing common problems through collaborative, reflective and transformative action.

This notion of communal inquiry as social reconstruction is at the heart of Dewey's educational ideas. Recognising that the way people learn, grow and construct meaning was essentially through conjoint action and collaborative problem solving, Dewey wanted the school to be a continuation of the social activities that characterise community life outside of the school. He argued that each school must become

> an embryonic community life, active with the types of occupations that reflect the life of the larger society, and permeated throughout with the spirit of art, history and science. When the school introduces and trains each child of society into membership within such a little community,

saturating him with *the spirit of service*, and providing him with the instruments of effective self-direction, we shall have the deepest and best guarantee of a larger society which is worthy, lovely and harmonious. (1990, 29, italics added)

As discussed in Chapter 2, the Laboratory School's curriculum was organised around the interdisciplinary theme of social occupations (Tanner 1997, 60–62). Students at the school learnt through participating in practical, everyday, social activities, such as sewing, gardening, cooking, carpentry, running a shop, farming, photography and so on. This 'hands-on' curriculum enabled students to learn traditional disciplinary knowledge in a contextualised manner, while simultaneously developing communication, inquiry and manual skills. Students could see how the content of science, history, geography, English, maths and art was created to enable individuals to more intelligently interact with their environment because they learnt this disciplinary content through applying it to the types of concrete social problems that gave rise to it in the first place. However, I argued that this curriculum didn't go far enough because students were not required to take action that would actually contribute to the reconstruction of current social problems. As such, the students were not fully participating in collaborative inquiry as a form of social reconstruction. In particular, while Dewey's 'embryonic' community life may be sufficient for primary students, I think it is inadequate for older students who need an opportunity to reconstruct more complex and authentic social problems (see Chapter 2).

In theory, Lipman agrees with Dewey's rejection of theory/practice dualism. He too accepts the pragmatic maxim, stating that "to stop the idea from becoming a meaningless abstraction, consider how to demonstrate its practical bearings" and "the dialogue in a community of inquiry is aimed at practical results" (2008, 111; see also Gregory 2011, 200). Lipman doesn't just think that the outcomes of inquiry should be applied to concrete situations. Like Dewey, he suggests that inquiry itself is reflective action: "When, however, practice comes to be permeated with critical thinking, so that we reflect critically on what we do before, while, and after we do it, mere practice becomes self-correcting practice and self-correcting practice is inquiry" (Lipman 2008, 49).

However, unlike the Laboratory School, P4C does not incorporate this pragmatist notion of inquiry. Traditional P4C pedagogy and curriculum materials do not include the type of hands-on, practical problem solving activities that students were engaged in at the Laboratory School. P4C does not require students to actively transform their environment, either within the school or beyond the school. A typical P4C class involves the shared reading of a narrative, containing philosophically puzzling ideas, followed by a classroom communal inquiry initiated by student questions and responses to the text. Students are certainly expected to apply the ideas, methods and solutions developed in P4C classrooms, in that they are expected to alter their own behaviours as a result of these inquiries. For example, as a result of a communal inquiry into the nature of justice, students form a judgment about what 'justice' means and are expected to implement that notion of justice in their everyday experiences. However, they are not necessarily required to use their notion of justice to solve a specific, concrete problem as a part of the classroom Community of Inquiry process. For example, they are not required to identify real cases of injustice in the school (e.g., bullying) or wider community (e.g., Third World poverty) and take action to transform the unjust situation in some way. While some P4C teachers probably do use P4C as a launching pad for such transformative action, this is not a standard feature of P4C pedagogy and curriculum. As Cevallos-Estarellas and Sigurdardottir explain,

> In the description of the Community of Inquiry we have drawn there is nothing that requires the participants to act out, in the larger community, what they deliberate in the Community of Inquiry. The outcomes of the Community of Inquiry, it seem to us, tend to be purely intellectual, like the clarification of an idea, the discovery of a new perspective, or the development of a better understanding of a concept. Sometimes the inquiry results in a conclusion about the topic at hand . . . however, seldom is it asked what is to be done with the conclusion once it is reached. (2000, 56)

The problem is not merely the theoretical inconsistency displayed by Lipman. This lack of practicality is educationally and philosophically problematic. It means that P4C has not fully overcome the problematic theory/practice, mind/body, thought/action, abstract/concrete dualisms inherent in traditional education and epistemology. As we have seen, such dualisms lead to impoverished notions of thinking, knowledge, the self, autonomy and so on. As both Lipman and Dewey recognise, all good thinking is simultaneously concrete, abstract, practical, theoretical, experiential, reasonable, emotional and imaginative. The meaningful reconstruction of experience involves the interrelated use of all these capacities. Any curriculum or pedagogy which privileges the theoretical and the mental over the practical and the bodily cannot fully foster good thinking skills and meaningfulness. As Lipman himself states, "[S]tudents would think better if they could be provided with conditions that would encourage the application of their thinking to the world in which they lived" (2003, 208). The world in which they live is not limited to the classroom. Even the discussion of concrete experiences in the Community of Inquiry is insufficient because inquiry itself involves the active transformation of the socio-cultural environment—it involves the testing and application of ideas in concrete experience. Dialogue, as important as it is, does not constitute transformative action, application or changed behaviour.

By not requiring students to test and apply their newly developed philosophical ideas and methods beyond the classroom, P4C runs the risk that students will come to see these ideas and methods as only relevant in philosophy class or as meaningless altogether. Students may enjoy the philosophical discussions, ideas and arguments, but they may fail to appreciate the important role that philosophical inquiry can play in the meaningful reconstruction of everyday experiences and the improvement of the world in which they live. Students may come to see philosophy as a fun, novel subject that has limited vocational value and application to the 'real' world. Given that this is already a common misconception of philosophy, P4C ought to be actively challenging it, not reinforcing it.

Most P4C theorists and practitioners seem to assume that the attitudes, values, skills and knowledge learnt in the P4C class will naturally flow out of the classroom Community of Inquiry into the wider community beyond the school (e.g., Splitter and Sharp 1995). This assumption mirrors a mistake inherent in traditional pedagogy: students are taught a set body of abstract knowledge and are just expected to know how to apply that knowledge to everyday situations beyond the classroom. However, classrooms and schools are insulated and relatively controlled environments, unlike the multitude of complex and diverse environments outside the classroom. There is no guarantee that ideas and methods that work in the classroom will be applicable or useful in other situations or that students will know how to modify them for different situations. The concrete experiences and perspectives available to students in the classroom are limited, and classroom learning experiences are largely contrived in the sense that they are initiated and constructed by the teacher, the curriculum and the school. Burgh et al. state, "His [Lipman's] curriculum avoids substantive issues of immediate concern to students by creating a totally artificial environment, rather than one that uses real cases, as the basis for discussion" (2006, 101). This has its benefits, such as enabling students to inquire into manageable problems in a safer, controlled environment. However, there are many philosophical ideas and methods that students and teachers will never be able to properly examine, test or apply in the classroom Community of Inquiry because relevant authentic experiences are unlikely to arise. Requiring students to deliberately engage with communities beyond the classroom would widen their field of experience substantially and enable students to respond to more diverse and complex, real world problems.

Another concern is that by not requiring students to go out into the greater community and engage in transformative action, P4C perpetuates the dominant belief that students are merely future citizens, incapable of positively contributing to their community. As explained in Chapter 6, schooling based on futurity devalues young people and their current experiences. This is exactly the type of schooling that P4C opposes and is critical of. One of P4C's stated goals is to foster autonomy and active citizenship (Splitter and Sharp 1995; Sharp 1991). However, as Holdsworth

(2000) argues, teaching for active citizenship requires giving students roles of value that have a real effect on the decision-making processes of their society. Likewise, Cevallos-Estarellas and Sigurdottir argue that in order to promote active citizenship P4C must require students to take action:

> Through the Community of Inquiry we can certainly familiarize students with the deliberation process, but we have to add the activism factor to it. We have to show students how the process they take part in when working in a Community of Inquiry is relevant to their role as democratic citizens, and we have to encourage them to take action when they realize what is important to them. (2000, 56)

Not encouraging young people and children to undertake transformative action beyond the classroom also seems to undermine the often-made claim that the classroom Community of Inquiry is a model of democracy. The Deweyian notion of democracy that P4C embraces necessitates intercultural inquiry. The classroom Community of Inquiry must engage in inquiry with diverse communities beyond the classroom in order to be democratic in this sense. Furthermore, as Holdsworth (1996) argues, denying children and young people the opportunity to participate in the decision making procedures of their community and shape the world they live in is, in itself, undemocratic.

If P4C were able to incorporate the practical, active dimension of inquiry, it may also be able to overcome some common problems that plague the teaching of philosophy in schools. Philosophy is often assumed to be a very 'intellectual' subject, and, as such, many schools consider it to be a subject for academically minded and 'middle-class' students—those on the university track. In some cases, it has been adopted merely as a gifted education curriculum. In 2011, a P4C teacher in Perth told me that her school used Year 7 students' performances on maths tests to decide which students would be streamed into philosophy class, which was a curriculum only offered to 'high achievers'. In my own state (Victoria), private schools and schools in affluent suburbs seem much more likely to include philosophy on the curriculum. However, P4C was never intended to be a special curriculum for those on the university track. It was intended for *all* students because all people need the skills, knowledge and attitudes that P4C aims to develop in order to live ethical and meaningful lives. If P4C was more obviously practical, applied and involved 'hands-on' learning, it would probably appeal to a broader group of students and schools. Dewey recognised how curriculum that appeared overly theoretical, abstract and intellectual was exclusive and this was another reason he emphasised the practical dimension of inquiry and learning:

> The simple facts of the case are that in the great majority of human beings the distinctively intellectual interest is not dominant. They have

the so called practical impulse and disposition . . . If we were to conceive our educational end and aim in a less exclusive way, if we were
to introduce into educational processes the activities which appeal to
those whose dominant interest is to do and to make, we should find the
hold of the school upon its members to be more vital, more prolonged,
containing more culture. (1990, 27–28)

Another problem that plagues the practice of P4C is one already explored
in Chapter 3. The Community of Inquiry can appear aimless and as failing to make any real progress towards solving the problems inquired into.
This is largely because many P4C teachers assume that there are no right
answers to the philosophical problems explored and that every student's
opinion is equally valid. This is another reason why philosophy is sometimes perceived to be a trivial subject, good for practicing thinking skills
but having no other serious implications for 'real life'. Since P4C participants do not have to take action, there is nothing to really stop them from
going around in circles, endlessly criticising, rejecting arguments and opinions and settling for relativism. Questioning and being critical is good but
not if it merely leads to indecisiveness, a lack of practicality, a constant
search for perfect solutions or a failure to come up with positive theories
and ideas that enable transformative action. Freire's criticisms of reflection
and words severed from action, which he describes as mere "verbalism",
aptly describes the dialogues that take place in many philosophy classes:

Within the word we find two dimensions, reflection and action, in such
radical interaction that if one is sacrificed—even in part—the other
immediately suffers. There is no true word that is not at the same time a
praxis. Thus, to speak a true word is to transform the world. An unau-
thentic word, one which is unable to transform reality, results when
dichotomy is imposed upon its constitutive elements. *When a word is
deprived of its dimension of action, reflection automatically suffers as
well; and the word is changed into idle chatter, into verbalism, into an
alienated and alienating "blah."* It becomes an empty word, one which
cannot denounce the world, for denunciation is impossible without
a commitment to transform, and there is no transformation without
action. On the other hand, if action is emphasized exclusively to the
detriment of reflection, the word is converted into activism. (1993, 68,
italics added)

Mirroring Dewey's criticisms of theory practice/dualism, Freire argues for
praxis, a notion of inquiry and dialogue as reflective, transformative action.
If P4C participants were required to undertake such reflective action in order
to address some immediate, concrete problem, then the inquiry would have a
clear aim and complete relativism would be unacceptable. They would have to
reach some degree of consensus in order to take meaningful action to address

the problem. They could not endlessly search for perfect solutions because they would need to select from the best options currently available to them and do the best they could at the time to transform the problematic situation. This pragmatic attitude is something we want to foster—we want students to question, to be critical and careful thinkers, but we also want them to be able to make practical judgments and act on them so that they can effectively interact with their environment. We want their actions to be permeated with reflection and their thinking to be pragmatic and transformative. Without this active dimension, P4C cannot adequately foster the desirable Deweyian notion of inquiry as social reconstruction.

SERVICE LEARNING

Service learning offers a potential solution to P4C's problematic lack of practicality, as well as Dewey's failure to provide students with opportunities to respond to contemporary social problems in a transformative manner. 'Service learning' is a name given to an extraordinary number of diverse programs and curricula taught at all levels of schooling, including the tertiary level, and across all disciplinary areas. Broadly speaking, service learning involves students going out into the community to perform some type of community service activity. Common types of action that students perform include creating or maintaining recreational spaces like playgrounds, skate parks or community gardens; organising or assisting with community events like fetes, festivals, dances, music performances, art exhibitions, film festivals, markets, public forums, community meetings, conferences, sporting events and theatre productions; creating or delivering services like those offered by libraries, youth groups, tutoring services, childcare, soup kitchens and homeless shelters; and creating media productions, such as pamphlets, newspapers, films, radio programs, booklets, instructional material and websites. There are also more controversial activities that involve political activism or participation, including writing letters to members of government, constructing petitions, organising and attending protests, participating in local government meetings and so on.

Service learning differs from other types of community service in that the activities students perform are embedded in the academic curriculum and are intended to have educational benefits for the student participants (Cipolle 2004). For example, social studies students may help out in a homeless shelter when studying topics like poverty, community, social services, government policy, non-for-profit organisations, citizenship and so on. Science students might collect and test soil and water samples from local parklands and report the results to their local council as a means to learning about the impact of urbanisation on their natural environment, while simultaneously acquiring important scientific knowledge and skills. The extent to which different service learning programs are embedded in the curriculum varies greatly. As Tanner notes, all too often, programs called service learning "are merely add-ons to the curriculum rather than a true part of it" (1997, 4). Nonetheless, service learning is intended to have educational benefits for students, as well as benefits for the community being served. Some of the many claimed educational benefits of service learning are that it fosters an altruistic and caring attitude; tolerance for people from culturally and socially diverse backgrounds; leadership and communication skills; a sense of civic duty; critical thinking and problem solving skills; the ability to apply curriculum content to 'real-world' contexts; and better retention of curriculum content (Kielsmeier 2011; Luo et al. 2011; Gonsalves 2010; Bernacki and Jaeger 2008; Kahne and Sporte 2007; Billig, Root and Jesse 2005; Billig 2000, Eyler and Giles 1999). It has also been claimed that service learning can lead to improved grades and test scores (Gonsalves 2010; Furco and Root 2010; Billig 2000; Melchior 1999; Astin & Sax 1998).[1] Because it is embedded in the curriculum, the community service undertaken is not usually voluntary. It is generally a course requirement that students must satisfy in order to pass.

The nature and quality of service learning varies greatly. Many service learning theorists and practitioners have noted that there is little consensus about the aims, objectives and methods of service learning (Mitchell 2008, 50; Butin 2003, 1674; Bickford and Reynolds 2002, 230; Eyler and Giles 1994, 78; 1999, 3). Thus, the term 'service learning' is understood and applied in diverse and often conflicting ways. This lack of agreement stems, in part, from undeveloped theoretical foundations (Sheckley and Keeton 1997, 33; Eyler and Giles 1994, 77). Given Dewey's emphasis on reflective action, experiential learning, and connecting schools to the wider community, it is not surprising that Dewey is frequently cited as a key figure in the service learning literature (see Kielsmeier 2011; D'Arlach, Sánchez and Feuer 2009; Tilley-Lubbs 2009; Rocheleau 2004; Hoppe 2004; Cipolle 2004; Ward and Wolf-Wendel 2000; Deans 1999; Eyler and Giles 1994; 1999; Tanner 1997, 4–5; Kahne and Westheimer 1996; Giles 1991). This is even though Dewey himself did not explicitly recommend that students engage in community service as a regular part of their schooling. Critical pedagogy theorists, particularly Freire, are also frequently cited as providing a theoretical basis for service learning (see Tilley-Lubbs 2009; D'Arlach et al. 2009; Cipolle 2004; Ginwright and Cammarota 2002; Deans 1999). However, as Tanner points out, Dewey's educational ideas are clearly incompatible with some service learning programs (1997, 4). The same can be said of Freire, whose educational ideas are strikingly similar to Dewey's. Thus, before we look at service learning as a potential solution to P4C's lack of practicality, we need to distinguish between different approaches to service learning and identify a notion of service learning that is consistent with the educational ideals of Lipman and Dewey that are being advocated here.

A review of the service learning literature reveals two broad approaches. In her recent review of this literature, Mitchell (2008) identifies a *critical* and a *traditional approach* to service learning. The critical approach is primarily defined by its explicit social justice aim and social change orientation, while the traditional approach emphasises service without attention to systemic and structural inequalities and is more concerned with charity work than with bringing about social change. Mitchell's two notions of service learning align with the two notions of service learning identified by Kahne and Westheimer (1996): the *charity orientation* (traditional) and the *change orientation* (critical). While the 'charity' orientation focuses on giving, civic duty and additive experiences, service learning with a change orientation emphasises care, social reconstruction and transformative experiences. Similarly, Marullo and Edwards (2000) distinguish between a *social justice approach* to service learning, which is critical and change orientated, and a *charity approach*, which tends to reproduce the status quo. Many other service learning theorists make a similar distinction between a traditional, charity-based approach and a critical, change-orientated approach (e.g., Moely, Furco and Read 2008; Wang and Roberts 2006; Cipolle 2004; Bickford and Reynolds 2002; Ward and Wolf-Wendel 2000; Robinson 2000; Morton 1995). This conceptual framework will be used to outline a comprehensive and critical account of these two broad approaches to service learning in order to identify which approach is most suitable for P4C. I will adopt Mitchell's terminology, referring to 'traditional service learning' and 'critical service learning'. Although, I will outline each one separately, the traditional and critical approaches are not mutually exclusive or exhaustive. While there are types of service learning that epitomise each approach, there are also service learning programs that fall somewhere between the two or which integrate elements of both types of service learning. They should be considered two opposite ends of a spectrum.

TRADITIONAL SERVICE LEARNING

Traditional approaches to service learning are the most common type of service learning practised in schools and universities. This approach focuses more on the learning than the service element of service learning, in that it prioritises the educational benefits for the students over any potential benefits to the community (Mitchell 2008, 53). The service offered to the community is not actually intended to transform problematic or unjust social structures or conditions. It is focused on charity—on addressing immediate individual needs and problems by providing specific goods and services, such as serving food to the homeless, providing company to the elderly, collecting and distributing clothes and furniture to the poor, fundraising for environmental organisations, providing literacy and numeracy tutoring, and so on. Thus, traditional service learning aims more to alleviate the symptoms of social problems rather than transform their root causes. As such, there is little critical examination of systematic and structural problems or injustices that underpin and cause social problems like poverty, homelessness, social isolation, environmental degradation, adult illiteracy and so on. Students are not required to evaluate the effectiveness of current social, economic and political structures or consider alternative, more just and effective possibilities. They may not even be required to critically evaluate the effectiveness of the government or non-for-profit agencies, sectors and polices directly relevant to the service they perform. In fact, such critical examination may even be actively discouraged because it is seen to reduce the focus on altruism, charity and civic duty (Kahne and Westheimer 1996, 595). Traditional service learning usually involves students participating in pre-arranged and pre-existing community service programs and, as Robinson points out, it is usually "established, professional and mainstream organisations and agencies" that students are placed with (2000, 145). Thus, students do not participate in creating or designing the services and activities they perform. For these reasons, traditional service learning is associated with a conservative political agenda and the promotion of volunteerism, civic duty and obedience rather than political and social activism. As Marullo and Edwards explain,

> Most of the community service that takes place is perceived to be an act of charity by the actor, intended to achieve a noble (albeit small) outcome that improves the life of individual service recipients at the expense of the volunteer who can afford to make such a private contribution. Such acts are perceived to be moral rather than political acts. Volunteers in a charitable operation do not seek to alter stratification systems that produce inequality, only to temporarily reallocate surplus assets that they control. (2000, 900)

Kahne and Westheimer (1996) provide a typical example of this type of service learning from their yearlong study of two dozen K–12 teachers who participated in a university-based program to promote service learning in schools. As a part of their study of democracy and citizenship, students in Mr. Johnson's 12th grade U.S. government course were required to undertake some community service of their own choosing. This involved students finding existing community service programs or organisations where they could work as volunteers. Examples of the service performed included a student who worked at a centre that cared for babies whose mothers had used crack cocaine during their pregnancy; another prepared and distributed survival kits to the homeless; while another student volunteered at a hospital by performing low-skilled tasks that assisted doctors and patients. As Kahne and Westheimer explain, the focus was on charity and on the students developing a sense of altruism and civic duty. There was "only minimal attention to any systematic analysis of the ills his students were helping alleviate" because "his students were not asked to articulate an understanding of the conditions and contexts that might have contributed to the loss of a family's home or to a pregnant mother's decision to turn to crack cocaine" (1996, 593).

PROBLEMS WITH TRADITIONAL SERVICE LEARNING

The most obvious problem with such service learning is that the types of action students engage in do not appear to have significant or long-lasting benefits for the recipients of the service because students only treat the symptoms of social problems while leaving their underlying causes intact. Marullo and Edwards describe such service as "placing band aids on haemorrhaging wounds and ignoring the source of the haemorrhage". They add that while "such Band-Aids are needed to prevent the victims from bleeding to death . . . the danger lies in equating this type of service with solving the problem" (2000, 902). Many critics argue that this type of service learning can sometimes do more harm than good because it normalises and reinforces unjust social conditions by accepting them and covering up their effects, which are actually the things that render them noticeably problematic to everyone else. Thus, by continually alleviating the symptoms of social problems, traditional service learning may actually help conceal major structural problems and unjust systems, reducing the likelihood that more radical, and often expensive, action will ever be taken so as to eliminate the root cause of the problem. Robinson seems to be making this point by claiming that traditional service learning can "normalize and civilize the radical tendencies for defiance and unrest that rest within the communities we serve" (2000, 146). This is why charity work is often promoted by conservatives. Kahne and Westheimer state that when George Bush senior voiced his support for voluntary community service back in 1990, it was as "an alternative to government programs", and Bush "made no mention of changes that address the structural injustices that leave so many in need" (1996, 595). Cipolle argues that such service learning is often considered an alternative to government intervention, adding it "often replaces public sector workers" (2004, 19).

When it is not obvious that the service performed provides any long-lasting benefits to the service recipients, there is also a concern that disadvantaged communities are actually being exploited for the benefits of students and teachers. Such service learning can seem like an anthropological expedition or "cultural safari" where the community acts as a "social laboratory with human guinea pigs whom students can go out and look at, prod, and snicker at as they 'learn' about social problems in the classroom" (Marullo and Edwards 2000, 908; see also Bickford and Reynolds 2002, 232; Forbes 1999).

This raises another common criticism of traditional approaches to service learning: they are characterised by a hierarchical relationship between the providers of the service and the recipients. Since traditional service learning involves students providing some type of service to marginalised or disadvantaged individuals, it supports a "position of privilege for those doing the serving" (Butin 2003, 1682). As Rosenberger (2000) points out, the term 'service' is problematic for the very reason that it suggests inequality rather than reciprocity because the server does something *for* the server rather than *with* them. In this giver/receiver relationship, the receiver is positioned as a passive object of charity. They have little to no involvement in creating or implementing solutions to the social problems or in articulating the problems in the first place. They are not empowered to help themselves or their own community, or even consulted to ensure that the services they are provided with are genuinely helpful. Consequently, the community service performed is often based on "unexamined, preconceived assessments of the community and the characteristics and needs of its residents" (J. Ward 1997, 140). The hierarchical nature of such service may actually reinforce negative preconceptions that students have about the recipients of the service—for example, that they are deficit, incapable, dependent, uneducated, unintelligent, lazy or just generally useless, not to mention stereotypes students may already harbour about particular minorities. This is why Cipolle believes that "when students from the dominant culture participate in service-learning with charity as the goal, they can see themselves as better and cling to their racist, sexist, or classist assumptions" (2004, 19). This is particularly problematic when students lack a critical understanding of the structural and systematic problems and injustices that underpin social problems. Students may believe they live in a meritocracy, and, as such, problems like poverty, illiteracy and homelessness must be personal problems caused by the individual's own lack of ability or effort. Thus, there is a genuine risk that traditional service learning may encourage students to blame the victim (Marullo and Edwards 2000, 903).

The hierarchical relationships of traditional service learning makes it difficult for this pedagogy to achieve its goal of fostering altruism and care. As Ward explains, "[T]his 'I give/they receive' orientation to the helping relationship often betrays a 'better than/less than' dynamic that impedes the development of real caring relationships in which mutual expectations, responsibilities and benefits are shared by both those who help and those being helped" (1997, 144). Sometimes, caring, reciprocal relationships do develop in traditional service learning. However, they are conceived as merely personal relationships. Relationships and attitudes of care and empathy are not utilised as a means to understanding the social problem or as necessary for the collaborative construction of solutions. In traditional service learning, care and empathy are severed from critical thinking and reflective action, depriving these attributes of their full cognitive force and social value. The notion of care fostered by traditional service learning is not the same as the notion of caring thinking promoted by Addams, Dewey and P4C (see Chapters 5 and 6). As Lipman explains, caring thinking occurs when "our emotions shape and direct our thoughts, provide them with a framework, with a sense of proportion, with a perspective, or better still with a number of different perspectives" (2003, 261–262). This type of caring is not deliberately fostered by traditional service learning because students' emotional responses need not inform their critical examination of social problems or the construction of solutions.

While traditional service learning prioritises the needs of the student over the needs of the community, it seems unlikely that such service experiences would foster higher-order thinking skills like critical and creative thinking. As explained, students are not required to undertake a critical inquiry into the social problems and issues or to engage in problem solving. Since the service activities are usually prearranged, students are simply handed ready-made solutions and are not even required to critically reflect on the effectiveness of their action. In traditional service, any reflection that does take place is often tokenistic and uncritical. It usually focuses on how the students have benefitted from their experience (Kahne and Westheimer 1996). No wonder Tanner claims that many service learning programs "are not based on Dewey's idea that service is part of student's intellectual as well as social development. In fact, some programs convey the exact opposite—that doing has nothing whatsoever to do with thinking" (1997, 4).

For the same reasons, traditional service learning is also unlikely to foster active and critical citizenship. Students are not engaged in political action or in utilising or criticising existing political procedures and systems. If anything, traditional service may actually discourage active citizenship by suggesting that social problems like poverty are really just personal problems that can ultimately only be fixed by the individuals changing their attitudes and behaviours. Furthermore, since students are only required to uncritically perform prearranged service activities, traditional service learning may actually foster passivity, docility and obedience. As Robinson explains,

> If service-learning merely inputs students into service-jobs that deal with the fall out of the system, then it is poor training for critical citizenship, political reasoning or social transformation . . . A service-learning language of individualistic therapy and 'helping,' rather than a language of political resistance, conflict and social transformation, silences students as agents of political and social change. (2000, 145)

Traditional service learning may also discourage active citizenship because students often resent such service learning experiences. Due to the problems already outlined, combined with the fact that it is usually compulsory, traditional service learning can be a rather negative experience for both students and service recipients. Resentment can stem from the fact that students lack any sense of ownership over the service they perform, and even if students feel that the service is problematic, they are not encouraged to express these concerns or to explore alternatives. The apparent impotency of the action taken may foster apathy among students. These feelings can be exacerbated if the recipients fail to demonstrate their appreciation for the service. In some cases, service recipients even exhibit hostility or resentment towards the students who can seem like privileged outsiders (Bickford and Reynolds 2002, 232; Marullo and Edwards 2000, 901). Such negative experiences are made worse when the service is not fully integrated into the curriculum. If both the social and educational benefits of the service seem dubious, students will likely feel that they are being forced to perform free labour. Hence, Tanner's claim that service learning can seem more like a "penalty" to students (1997, 4). Some American students have even challenged the legality of compulsory service learning on the grounds that it is "government-sponsored forced labour and therefore violates the 13th Amendment of the Constitution, which bars involuntary servitude" (Hernadez 1994).

THE CRITICAL APPROACH TO SERVICE LEARNING

While the traditional approach to service learning is dominant in practice; the critical approach is favoured amongst service learning theorists. The most distinctive feature of this approach is its commitment to social change. It has a more progressive political agenda. It places as much emphasis on the social problems and the benefits to the community as it does on student outcomes. Since critical service learning is genuinely committed to transformative action, there is a focus on the root causes of social problems. The aim is not merely to alleviate the individual symptoms of social problems but to challenge, destabilise and ultimately "deconstruct systems of power so the need for service and the inequalities that create and sustain them are dismantled" (Mitchell 2008, 50). Hence, the reason this approach is also referred to as the 'social justice approach'. Marullo and Edwards use a well-known proverb to effectively articulate this fundamental difference between the critical and traditional approach:

> One of the oft quoted adages about service is taken from the biblical wisdom about feeding the hungry: give people a fish and you feed them for a day, but teach them to fish and you feed them for a lifetime. Charity work tends to stop at feeding the hungry a meal or after presenting a fishing workshop. Justice work, by contrast, sees education as part of an empowerment process, which, to extend this analogy, would include securing access to productive fishing grounds, an equitable food distribution system, and the political resources needed to advocate for their continuation. Justice work is empowering in that the poor or those in need are treated as equal partners in the determination of what services

and resources are needed and how they can be attained. The goal of the justice advocate should always be that those in need will no longer face such needs—colloquially referred to as 'working oneself out of a job'. (2000, 901)

While traditional service learning tends to accept the status quo, the critical approach assumes that the status quo is problematic, and, as such, students are required to approach the world with a critical and creative outlook. Students are encouraged to critically examine the effectiveness of existing social and political conditions, social values and ideologies, policies and existing community and charitable organisations. Students must also critically analyse their own work in the community in order to assess its effectiveness at reconstructing social problems. This includes students developing a critical awareness of the hierarchical nature of traditional server/served relationships. As we have seen in Chapter 4, a critical outlook goes hand in hand with an imaginative outlook. If students are constantly seeking out problems, then they must also be able to imagine alternative, less problematic possibilities and means for realising these possibilities. This seems to be what Wade (2001) means when she describes this type of service learning as 'service for an ideal' as opposed to 'service for an individual'. Students must imagine a more ideal version of reality and take action to bring about this ideal.

Critical service learning is also more conducive to fostering genuine collaboration and reciprocity. Solutions that fail to incorporate the interests and perspectives of all those affected by the issue will not to be fully supported by the community and, as such, are unlikely to be effective at solving the problem. Furthermore, as Marullo and Edwards explained, lasting social change entails that "community members should be empowered to do as much of the work themselves" so that their need to be provided with services and goods by others is removed or reduced (2000, 907). This collaborative approach counteracts the hierarchical relationships that characterise traditional service learning. In fact, the term 'service learning' is really an inappropriate name for the critical approach because the members of the community are not recipients of services provided by students. Rather, they are active political agents working collaboratively with students to improve their own situation and the lives of others. The community members are not seen as deficit and dependent but as possessing valuable resources, such as essential skills, knowledge and insights into the social problem that must be utilised for effective social reconstruction to occur (Ward and Wolf-Wendel 2000, 771). Mitchell states that "incorporating community knowledge . . . can provide "insider" information about community needs and concerns and make linkages to root causes that may be more difficult for faculty and students who enjoy a more privileged status" (2008, 56). The aim isn't to just use community knowledge and skills but to develop and enrich community knowledge and skills because students and teachers also introduce new skills, knowledge and perspectives to the community. This is a reciprocal relationship where all students, teachers and community members are expected to learn, grow and be transformed. Thus, as Flower (2002) argues, the critical approach necessitates students, teachers and community members engaging in intercultural, collaborative inquiry. As such, a focus on dialogue is another distinguishing feature of the critical approach. As we have seen, dialogue differs from mere conversation in that it is essentially aimed at problem solving, is guided by reason and aims at the creation of intersubjective meaning. The critical approach's collaborative working through of social problems is dependent on effective dialogue.

It should be evident that the critical approach is better positioned to foster active citizenship, critical and creative thinking, problem-solving skills, caring thinking, cultural awareness and an improved understanding of social problems and political processes. Students are not handed fixed and ready-made 'solutions' that they must uncritically accept and apply to pre-selected social problems. This is a much more student-centred pedagogy, in the sense that teachers and community service workers act as facilitators and participants, rather than merely as experts, disseminating knowledge and handing out action plans. This is not to deny the fact that teachers and members of the community will often have more sophisticated problem-solving skills and relevant knowledge that they should teach to students. The difference is that with the critical approach, students play a central role in identifying problems, suggesting possible action, critically examining and comparing the suggested actions, and formulating a judgment about which action to take, all the while critically reflecting on the process and the effectiveness of the action they decide to take. Unlike the traditional approach, such service learning necessitates critical and creative thinking. Thus, it is not surprising that research by Wang and Rodgers (2006) found that critical approaches to service learning resulted in the development of more complex thinking skills than did traditional service learning. This type of service learning also requires students to acquire a more thorough understanding of the complex, root causes of social problems in order to construct and apply effective solutions. This in-depth understanding of the issues, along with the need for collaborative relationships, means that the critical approach is much more likely to foster greater cultural awareness and caring relationships. Since students are actually required to engage in communal inquiry with members of the community, any misconceptions and stereotypes students possess are more likely to be challenged and transformed. Students are more likely to become critically aware of their own situatedness and biases. Not only are such relationships good for service learning, but it is this problematising of one's experiences that leads to inquiry and growth in the first place. As we have seen (Chapter 5), this is one of the reasons Dewey argued that communities must be inclusive of differences because exposure to difference provokes critical self-reflection.

While it is uncommon to see this type of service learning practiced in mainstream schools, some theorists have provided recent examples of service learning that reflect a more critical orientation. One such example is provided by Bland (2012). Bland describes a project involving Year 10 students (15–16 year olds) from low socio-economic backgrounds who worked collaboratively with teachers and university staff to research barriers to tertiary education within their own school community in Queensland, Australia. The problem was directly related to students' own interests because student participants were from "schools with historically low progression to tertiary education" (2012, 80). With the support of teachers and academics, students devised plans for how to research and respond to this social problem. One research group collected and analysed data about the understandings and attitudes that their peers had in regards to tertiary education. Discovering that their peers had many misconceptions about tertiary education, the group created a DVD, which could be used by schools, universities and other relevant organisations to better inform young people. The DVD won two awards, and students have presented their research at several conferences. According to Bland, "[T]he DVD has had a profound impact on the school, encouraging other students to investigate tertiary options, and, as the reputation of the DVD grew, new respect has been generated for its creators among school staff, with relationships between the teachers and the students improving greatly" (2012, 84). Thus, the students undertook research to identify potential root causes of the problem and took transformative action that targeted the causes. The students were not mere participants in pre-arranged community service work. They helped articulate the problem and created and implemented a solution. They worked collaboratively with university staff, who taught them valuable research skills and knowledge about tertiary education and the university staff gained invaluable insights into the attitudes and understandings that students from low socio-economic backgrounds, and young people in general, have in regards to tertiary study. The solution aimed to better inform and, thus, empower those affected by the social problem, including the student participants themselves. The students were also empowered because they developed invaluable new research and communication skills, knowledge and self-confidence. A truly critical approach would have required students to investigate unjust conditions and structures that may contribute to this problem, and it is suggested by Bland that students, teachers and academics did critically examine such issues as a part of the project. This example illustrates that the critical approach doesn't require immensely time-consuming, complex or expensive action because students are not required to completely solve every aspect of the social problem investigated. They only need to take some action that aims to reconstruct some aspect of the problem.

It is commonly assumed that this approach to service learning is only suitable for social studies curricula. However, it can be incorporated into any subject are. For example, Gustein and Peterson (2006) have identified middle school maths teachers that have adopted a critical service learning approach. In these examples, students use various maths skills and content, "such as calculation with integers, decimals, and percents; graphing and algebra; probability and statistics; measurement and data analysis; and mathematical reasoning and reporting", as a means to responding to social issues in their local neighbourhood. The problems investigated were identified by students themselves or by the teacher based on the teacher's knowledge of the student's experiences and interests. For example, one project involved students comparing the density of liquor stores in their inner-city neighbourhood compared to the destiny of liquor stores in the suburbs. This project was a result of the students frequently encountering drunks on their way to and from school. In some, but not all, of the examples in the book, students were required to undertake transformative social action, which often included disseminating their new knowledge and values through creating and distributed flyers, sending reports to newspapers, giving presentations at their school advisory council, sending letters and reports to local council and peer teaching younger students.

Because of the obvious political nature of this pedagogy, the best examples of critical service learning actually come from non-traditional educational institutions. For example, Robinson rightly identifies Jane Addams' Hull House settlement as an example of this educational ideal (2000, 148 –149). As we have already seen in Chapter 6, Hull House aimed to reconstruct problems impacting the local community (e.g., poverty, inequality, sanitation, access to healthcare, workers' rights, women's rights, immigration policy, war, etc.), while simultaneously developing new knowledge and methods which could be used to improve society at large and foster democracy. The residents and visitors of Hull House included members of the local community, community service workers, activists, as well as researchers and scholars, such as Dewey and Addams. All were simultaneously teachers and students, engaged in collaborative inquiries aimed at reconstructing real social problems. These collaborative inquiries contributed to a wealth of new knowledge and even the development of whole academic fields (see Chapter 6).

Another famous example is the Highlander Folk School in Tennessee, which was founded by Myles Horton in 1932. Like Hull House, Highlander is not a conventional educational institution in that it doesn't teach state mandated curricula, and it originally only catered for adult students. The school now offers programs for children and youth but not as an alternative to regular schooling. Highlander was originally created in order to educate local farmers, factory workers and miners so that they could unite and take action to overcome their own oppression and exploitation at the hands of industrialists and landowners (Schiro 2008, 135). The school later played a key role in the civil rights movement of the 1950s and '60s. Rosa Parks, along with other key figures in the civil rights movement, was a student at the school. The school's involvement in the civil rights movement was so significant that it was investigated by the FBI and temporarily shut down in 1961.[2] Today, the school continues to tackle contemporary social justice issues, such as environmental sustainability and immigration.[3] Influenced by the ideas of Paulo Freire, Highlander aims to make students critically conscious of their own oppression and of how their own behaviours and beliefs may contribute to injustices and social problems. The students, with the assistance of teachers, undertake systematic analyses of social justice issues and identify effective means for reconstructing these problems so that they can return to their schools, communities and workplaces and educate and recruit others to take collaborative action to address the problems. Such action has included striking, picket lines, petitions and protests, as well as the development and provisions of services (e.g., during the civil rights movement, they provided free literacy classes to African Americans, partially to overcome the problem of many African American's being excluded from voting on the grounds that they were illiterate). The focus is on empowering participants to design and implement their own solutions to social problems in a collaborative manner. The pedagogy used in classes, which are called workshops, is student-centred, collaborative, and dialogue and inquiry based. There is also a strong emphasis on art and music.

Because critical service learning is the preferred approach amongst service learning researchers and theorists, the philosophical and pedagogical ideas that underpin it are more conspicuous and developed than are those of traditional service learning. Many of those who advocate for this approach to service learning draw on critical pedagogy for inspiration, particularly the ideas of Paulo Freire but also Henry Giroux, Ira Shor, bell hooks, Peter McLaren, Michael Apple and many others. Critical pedagogy is characterised by its acceptance of a social constructivist epistemology; a socio-cultural notion of the self; a curriculum focused on criticising the status quo and on social justice issues; learning through dialogue and collaborative inquiry; the political and cultural dimensions of schooling; and the potential of the school to transform society. The similarity between the critical approach to service learning and critical pedagogy is demonstrated by Giroux' description of critical pedagogy:

> Central to any viable notion of critical pedagogy is enabling students to recognise "how knowledge is related to the power of self-definition" and to use the knowledge they gain to both critique the world in which they live and, when necessary, to intervene in socially responsible ways in order to change it. Critical pedagogy is about more than a struggle over assigned meanings, official knowledge, and established modes of authority: it is also about encouraging students to take risks, act on their sense of social responsibility, and engage the world as an object of both critical analysis and hopeful transformation. (2011, 14)

The similarities between the two educational ideas are most prominent when one compares the writing and social action of Myles Horton, founder of the Highlander School, to that of Paulo Freire. Just before Horton died, the two collaborated, publishing a dialogue emphasising their similar views and experiences.[4] Paulo Freire's own work with illiterate adults in Brazil and other parts of the world is another example of critical service learning. His students were engaged in the type of transformative social action prescribed by proponents of critical service learning. The students developed literacy skills through a critical exploration of social problems that affected their own communities, such as alcoholism, violence, poverty and so on. Through collaborative inquiries, teachers and students would identify and articulate social problems and develop plans for reconstructing such problems. The aim was not just to promote literacy but also to provoke oppressed communities to become critically conscious of their own oppression and of the systems, structures, behaviours and values that caused this oppression, and to ultimately take action to emancipate themselves and their communities.

The only obvious difference between critical service learning and critical pedagogy is that not all proponents of critical pedagogy explicitly argue that students themselves should undertake transformative social action outside of the school as a part of their normal learning. However, the basic tenets of critical pedagogy seem to entail that students should engage in such transformative action during their schooling. In general, critical pedagogy tends to be more theoretical, while proponents of critical service learning provide clearer, practical guidelines for exactly how students can engage with their world in a critical and transformative manner. Hence Hoops' claim that "service learning provides an opportunity to actualize the goals posed by critical pedagogy" (2011, 3).

Another important educational tradition associated with critical service learning is the curriculum theory referred to as social reconstructionism, which emerged in the 1920s.[5] Major proponents of social reconstructionism include George Counts, Harold Rugg and Theodore Brameld. Like proponents of critical pedagogy and critical service learning, social reconstructionists assume society is problematic and in need of reconstruction. Examples of social problems that social reconstructionists often target are "racism, war, sexism, poverty, pollution, worker exploitation, global warming, crime, political corruption, population explosion, energy shortages, illiteracy, inadequate health care, and unemployment" (Schiro 2008, 133). Like critical pedagogy theorists, social reconstructionists argue that these problems are maintained and reproduced by dominant ideologies and values that are deeply ingrained in our social and political structures and institutions. Social reconstructionists critique many of the same ideologies targeted by proponents of critical pedagogy, such as patriarchy, Eurocentrism, capitalism and liberal individualism. Also like critical pedagogy, social reconstructionists consider schools to be one of the social institutions that reproduce such ideologies and social problems. However, both theories also consider schools to be potential means for reconstructing society so that it is more just. Like proponents of critical service learning, social reconstructionists emphasise students undertaking transformative social action as a part of their regular schooling.

Thus, the key tenets of social reconstructionism are virtually indistinguishable from those of critical pedagogy and critical service learning. This isn't surprising given that all three educational ideals have their roots in Dewey. What is surprising is how infrequently these different groups of educational theorists are connected in the literature and how little acknowledgement proponents of critical pedagogy and critical service learning have given to social reconstructionism, which is the oldest of the three theories. There are some exceptions to this. For example, in his textbook on curriculum theory, Schiro (2008) categorises critical pedagogy theorists as social reconstructionists, failing to distinguish between the two traditions. McLaren notes that critical pedagogy has its roots in social reconstructionism, as well as critical theory, although he fails to elaborate on the considerable similarities between the two educational theories (2007, 185). Kahne and Westheimer (1996) and Robinson (2000) acknowledge the influence of the social reconstructionists on critical approaches to service learning.[6] The lack of attention given to social reconstructionism by proponents of critical pedagogy and critical service learning may simply reflect an unawareness of social reconstructionism. The fact that many critical pedagogy theorists don't fully acknowledge their debt to Dewey has probably contributed to this by obscuring the theoretical foundation that critical pedagogy shares with social reconstructionism. Critical pedagogy theorists frequently acknowledge the influence of Dewey's ideas but rarely explain, in any detail, the nature or extent of this influence.

Thus, not surprisingly, the critical approach to service learning suggests a means for realising Dewey's own educational and philosophical ideals. Kahne and Westheimer are correct to claim that Dewey's ideas support such an approach to service learning:

> For past reformers, such as John Dewey, William Kilpatrick, George Counts, and Paul Hanna, the transformative potential of this approach was of prime importance. These curriculum theorists and education reformers wanted students to engage in service learning projects so that they would recognise that their academic abilities and collective commitments could help them respond in meaningful ways to a variety of social concerns. For Dewey, this idea was the essence of democratic education. He argued for the creation of "miniature communities" in which students would work together to identify and respond to problems they confronted. The value of this approach extended far beyond the service students might provide for the elderly or the ways they might clean up the environment. It lay in the analytic and academic skills, the moral acuity, and the social sensitivity they would develop as they learned to assess critically and respond collectively to authentic problems. (1996, 592)

Critical service learning seems to be what was missing from the curriculum at Dewey's Laboratory School. It could have provided the opportunity for students to undertake collaborative inquiries as a means to reconstructing more complex and authentic social problems beyond the limited environment of the school. As argued in Chapter 2, these are the types of problems and inquiries that would have benefitted older students in particular. It could have opened up more relationships between the school and the wider community, providing more opportunities for intercultural inquiry, which is a cornerstone of Dewey's notion of democracy. Intercultural inquiry is also a cornerstone of Dewey's notion of growth because, as we have seen, it leads to critical self-reflection and the problematising of experience. If the aim of education is growth, then it seems that critical service learning should play an essential role in every school.

Given its Deweyian roots, it is not surprising that the critical approach to service learning is most compatible with the educational goals and ideals of P4C. The focus on problem solving through communal inquiry, critical self-reflection, autonomy, democracy, caring thinking and constructing meaning are common features of both educational ideas. In contrast, the traditional approach to service learning seems more likely to undermine many of these educational ideals and, thus, it is not an appropriate solution to P4C's lack of practicality. However, while the critical approach to service learning overcomes many of the problems with traditional service learning, it is not without its problems. Before we can look at how P4C and critical service learning can be integrated it is necessary to outline some of the criticisms of, and potential weaknesses with, the critical approach.

PROBLEMS WITH CRITICAL SERVICE LEARNING

One concern with the critical approach to service learning is that students may take action that is not very effective or that may even be detrimental to the community. This reflects not only a concern for the community but also a concern about the potential negative impact this may have on students. Their increased input into the analysis of the problem and decision about what action to take means that students can bear considerable responsibility for failures. Bickford and Reynolds express this concern, stating that "students might choose to write letters of protest for a liberating-action project to businesses, legislative bodies, and other institutions. But what if no one receives a response? Students might be discouraged, apathetic, or outraged" (2002, 246). Since traditional service only requires students to participate in prearranged activities, it can appear less risky, complex and demanding of students and teachers. However, I'm not convinced that critical service learning's increased difficulty is such a problem. This may just foster attitudes of persistence and hard work, a more realistic understanding of the complexity of social problems and a realisation that social reconstruction is never finished—it is a permanent attitude or way of being in the world that fosters human flourishing. Furthermore, as we have seen, the activities performed in traditional service learning programs may also have a detrimental effect on the community. Thus, the concern over the critical approach probably has more to do with the fact that students may participate in activities not already sanctioned by some mainstream agency or organisation and, as such, their actions may be deemed controversial and may attract unwanted public scrutiny. Nonetheless, with any service learning, measures must be put in place to minimise potential mistakes or harm and advocates of the critical approach are yet to fully develop such measures.

Another problem with the critical approach to service learning is that there is little attention given to the explicit teaching or scaffolding of inquiry skills. Most proponents of this type of service learning seem to assume that if students are provided with the opportunity to solve authentic social problems, they will naturally develop the requisite inquiry skills. Clearly, sophisticated inquiry skills don't just result from exposure to problems. If this were the case, there wouldn't be so many adults with inadequate problem solving skills and poor judgement. If students are to engage in effective social reconstruction, they must be supported by curricula and pedagogy specifically designed to foster the development of good thinking. If thinking skills are not deliberately taught, students will be exposed to problems that they are ill-equipped to deal with, causing them to feel overwhelmed and increasing the likelihood that their action will be unsuccessful.

The critical approach to service learning also lacks clear procedures for fostering the types of caring collaborative communities needed for effective social reconstruction. This concern is expressed by Rosenberger, who states that "much of the service learning literature shares a commitment to building mutual relationships . . . What is missing, however, is an approach for creating such relationships" (2000, 37). As explained in Chapter 6, communities have the potential to be exclusive, oppressive and homogenising. This is a particular concern when people from very different and unequal positions are bought together and expected to collaborate. The more diverse the community, the more potential there is for disagreement and hostility. Given that critical service learning necessitates intercultural inquiry, it is essential that clear procedures are developed to foster inclusive, caring communities.

Another common criticism of this type of service learning is that it may lead to political indoctrination. There is a concern that this pedagogy enables teachers to use students to act out their own political agendas. However, I am not convinced that this is anymore of a problem for critical service learning that it is for any other pedagogy. Critical service learning requires students to analyse the problems themselves and construct and enact solutions. They are not simply told what the causes of the problem are, nor are they told what action to take. Thus, in some cases, teachers may even have to accept that their students' understandings of social problems are different to their own. As Bickford and Reynolds explain,

Students must be free to choose the arenas in which they engage in social work. Although we may hope that our students are or will become progressive thinkers, we must accept the possibility that a student will support an issue or cause we find abhorrent. We only educate; we cannot insist that a student's ideological affiliations match our own. Of course, we may ask the student to justify his or her choice based on course readings. By exploring students' rationales for activism projects, we might also help students recognise and claim their own assumptions and ideologies. (2002, 246)

In order to avoid the accusation of indoctrination, Bickford and Reynolds actually underestimate the level of teacher intervention needed for effective social reconstruction. I believe teachers are *obligated* to ask students to justify their choices, opinions and actions. We certainly wouldn't allow students to take whatever action they pleased. Teachers, community members and other students should criticise and block action that is unjustified or too problematic. However, they should do this by providing good reasons for why such action is inappropriate not by simply disallowing or dismissing it without justification. They should also allow for all opinions and suggestions to be critically examined rather than simply forbidding particular topics. Furthermore, teachers influence students through the selection of topics and curriculum materials and through the design of learning activities. Most teachers already have, and should continue to have, this level of influence over students. However, all teachers should try to expose students to a variety of opinions and perspectives, not just the ones they themselves agree with, and they must teach students to distinguish between good and bad arguments so students can form their own reasonable opinions and values. Of course, most school teachers are also required to teach to some state or national mandated curriculum, which aims to promote certain values and beliefs anyway (e.g., the values associated with democracy). Even the most seemingly neutral curricula will promote some values and ideas over others. As a maths teacher who had adopted a critical service learning pedagogy claimed, "[T]eaching maths in a neutral manner is not possible. No math teaching—no teaching of any kind, for that matter—is actually 'neutral'" (Schiro 2008, 142). Critical pedagogy theorists and social reconstructionists rightly reject the notion of value neutral curriculum. Thus, it is not obvious that critical service learning is more inclined to commit political indoctrination than any other type of schooling. In fact, it may even be less inclined to do so than traditional pedagogies. For one, it requires that teachers' values and agendas are out in the open where they can be subjected to public scrutiny, not hidden behind the closed doors of the classroom. This is less dangerous than teachers claiming objectivity and neutrality while communicating values, disguised as absolute truths, to students so that these values are never subject to critique from students, parents or members of the public. Furthermore, as explained, traditional service learning requires students to uncritically support dominant types of community service work and existing policies. Surely this is more a form of political indoctrination than is the critical approach where students are expected to critically compare alternative ideas and actions.

A related concern about critical service learning has to do with its suitability for children and young people. Much of the literature promoting this approach to service learning is focused on university students. At what age should students be exposed to such complex social issues? A common perception is that children should be allowed to be children—they should not be burdened with such depressing and difficult problems. This belief rests on an assumption that young children would not concern themselves with such problems if they were not deliberately exposed to them by adults. This assumption is untrue. Children, even very young children, worry about all sorts of social problems and injustices, including war, terrorism, bullying, environmental sustainability, poverty, discrimination, substance abuse, violence and so on. They are exposed to such things more now than in the past due to the fact that they now have easier access to news and information. Assuming that children and young people don't have such concerns amounts to dismissing their concerns and failing to provide them with tools for adequately understanding and responding to such issues. While the critical service learning pedagogy sees the world as problematic and in need of reconstruction, it is also a positive and hopeful pedagogy because it sees these problems as solvable. Far from burdening children with depressing insurmountable problems, this educational ideal encourages children to see themselves as active, autonomous individuals, capable of collaborating with others to shape their social-cultural environment in a positive manner. The opposing viewpoint teaches children that they are too young, too powerless or that the problems are too big and too complex—that they should simply wait for more capable community leaders, like politicians, to fix these problems, if they can be fixed at all. This message is far more depressing than the one critical service learning sends. That being said, clearly the social problems explored and the action taken needs to suit the age and capabilities of the student, just as any curriculum must.

Another problem with the critical approach to service learning is one already mentioned—the fact that the name 'service learning' is actually inappropriate. This name better describes traditional service learning, where students literally provide some service to the community. It doesn't capture the critical, collaborative, reciprocal, inquiry-based and transformative action that characterises the critical approach. Since social reconstructionism predates both critical service learning and critical pedagogy and its name appropriately captures the aims and method of this pedagogy, I propose that this pedagogy be referred to as 'social reconstruction learning'. 'Social reconstruction learning' also appropriately recognises the considerable influence that Dewey's ideas have had on this educational ideal.

PHILOSOPHY FOR CHILDREN AS SOCIAL RECONSTRUCTION LEARNING

While some of the criticisms of the critical approach are unfounded, others highlight weaknesses with the pedagogy that need to be addressed. In particular, the ambiguity regarding how to teach the thinking skills necessary for effective social reconstruction; how to foster the caring, collaborative relationships necessary for effective social reconstruction; and how to deal with the problem of students taking ineffective or even detrimental action are all legitimate concerns that need to be attended to. In this section, it will be shown that P4C can help the critical approach overcome these problems because its pedagogy and curriculum have been deliberately designed to foster the collaborative inquiry needed for effective social reconstruction.

Since P4C is specifically focused on the facilitation of thinking skills, it can provide social reconstruction learning with the pedagogical tools and curriculum that it needs to scaffold thinking. As we have seen (Chapter 3), one of the values of the discipline of philosophy (particularly logic) is that it provides students and teachers with an invaluable metacognitive language and set of tools for critically evaluating and discussing the procedures of inquiry. It is not possible to teach thinking unless we have a language and body of knowledge that describes, explains and evaluates the process of thinking itself. How else could teachers and students properly identify and evaluate different thinking moves or procedures? In P4C, students learn methods, ideas and concepts necessary for developing good thinking skills through engaging with learning materials that have logical and epistemological themes and problems embedded in them. A large number of learning resources and activities have been designed by those working in the field of P4C specifically for the purpose of scaffolding reflective thinking.[7] Second, it has also been argued that the public nature of the Community of Inquiry renders the processes of thinking conspicuous, encouraging students to observe, reflect on and discuss each other's thinking moves and strategies. Furthermore, the individual's own thoughts are exposed to the different views and criticisms of others, provoking them to critically reflect on their own thinking. The aim is for students to internalise such social procedures so that they become conscious of the efficacy of their own thinking processes without the need for such external prompts (see Chapter 2). The effective analysis and reconstruction of social problems requires exactly this type of metacognitive thinking.

P4C also provides well-developed procedures and methods for fostering the type of caring, collaborative and reciprocal relationships that effective social reconstruction necessitates). As explained in Chapter 5, empathy, open-mindedness and care for others and the procedures of inquiry are actively facilitated. P4C participants come to realise that such dispositions and capabilities are needed to build trust, without which, the Community of Inquiry could not operate as people would be unwilling to risk sharing their thoughts. Since the aim in the Community of Inquiry is to construct common solutions to common problems, participants learn that they need others to participate in order to construct ideas that are more intersubjective and effective. One of the roles of the facilitator is to explicitly emphasise why such relationships and caring attitudes are essential and to actively reinforce them through identifying and discouraging behaviour that negates them (e.g., not taking turns to speak, ignoring points made by others, fidgeting while others are speaking, ridiculing or dismissing serious contributions, refusing to provide reasons for one's opinions, refusing to self-correct when given good reasons to do so, etc.) and by identifying and promoting behaviour that fosters them (e.g., building on each other's ideas, changing one's opinion in light of ideas or criticisms provided by others, asking each other questions, assisting others to explain or develop their ideas, making connections between different contributions; encouraging others to participate, etc). In the Community of Inquiry, students themselves are expected to identify and actively encourage these positive behaviours and discourage negative ones, gradually reducing the need for teacher intervention. Thus, the Community of Inquiry provides a framework for the type of intercultural inquiry that social reconstruction learning necessitates.

For social reconstruction learning, the classroom Community of Inquiry would need to be extended to include relevant members of the community who would be considered equal participants in the classroom inquiry. Community members should come into the classroom to engage in communal inquiry and students and teachers should leave the classroom to engage in communal inquiry with members of the community in their own environment. Thus, the Community of Inquiry can help foster the development of trusting, reciprocal relationships between teachers, students and community members, which is needed for the analysis of social problems and the construction of intersubjective solutions that actually incorporate the needs and perspectives of both students and community members. Participation in the Community of Inquiry would be a form of social reconstruction in itself because it should result in all participants developing essential knowledge, skills and attitudes necessary for living meaningful and autonomous lives.

P4C can also help reduce the potential for students taking action that is detrimental or damaging. The deliberate teaching of thinking skills and the focus on intersubjective solutions and continuous critical self-reflection can support the development of more thoughtful, reasonable solutions and actions. The communal nature of the inquiry means that suggested solutions are going to be subject to criticism and analysis from multiple perspectives. This will reduce the likelihood of oversights or mistakes that may result from student's having narrow or bigoted perspectives. In general, the community can act as a kind of quality control measure because it forces participants to justify their ideas and get support from the rest of the community before they take action. This will make it harder to reach an agreement about what action to take but it will reduce the chances of the action being ineffective or harmful.

This doesn't mean that participants must reach consensus about what action to take (see Chapter 3). The Community of Inquiry may agree to break up into smaller groups with each group taking different action to tackle a social problem. In the true spirit of the Community of Inquiry, we should not allow different groups to take action that undermines or counters the actions of another group. However, the Community of Inquiry could accept that there are multiple valuable, non-conflicting ways of responding to the problem. If a suitable agreement about what action(s) to take cannot be reached, then this should prompt a reconsideration of how the social problem has been articulated, and perhaps the Community of Inquiry will need to focus on another aspect of the problem. I have argued that one of the benefits of concrete problem solving is that it renders an inability to reach enough agreement to take action unacceptable. Concrete problems require transformative action so endless discussions and indecision is not an acceptable option. P4C's acceptance of fallibilism supports this pragmatic attitude because the aim of the Community of Inquiry is not to find absolute truths or perfect solutions but to construct workable solutions that have the potential to effectively reconstruct the problem at hand. The Community of Inquiry doesn't need to believe that their action will completely solve the problem for eternity. Given the limited time and resources available to most students and teachers, the Community of Inquiry will probably only be able to tackle a small part of the social problem. They are unlikely to develop a permanent or even far-reaching solution. They will likely have to accept that their action has limitations. They may not even be sure that their proposed action will make any significant difference at all but this doesn't justify a failure to take any action. The Community of Inquiry participants will need to do the best they can with the options and resources available to them and they will have to critically evaluate the effectiveness of their action as a part of the inquiry process. Even action which is not very successful is beneficial because at least the Community of Inquiry will understand why this action didn't work, and can then eliminate one option and consider better alternatives. They will be one step closer to having a better understanding of the problem and of taking effective action.

While integrating P4C and social reconstruction learning may be beneficial to both pedagogies, is it really possible to integrate the two without diminishing the traditional aims, knowledge and methods of philosophy? Besides a focus on good thinking, does the discipline of philosophy really have anything to offer concrete social problems? Philosophy is typically considered a highly abstract and theoretical discipline. While many areas of philosophy seem to have clear and direct implications for concrete social problems, notably applied ethics and political philosophy, other areas seem remote. Many years ago, during a conference presentation, another philosopher stated that it would be extremely difficult to connect philosophy of mind to concrete social problems. If this is true, what would this mean about the place of philosophy of mind on the school curriculum? Should it be excluded from the curriculum or only taught as a rather novel but less significant area of philosophy, consisting of puzzling content that is really only good for fostering the development of higher order thinking skills?

Philosophical problems or theories that have no bearing on concrete experience and social problems shouldn't be part of the school curriculum. Such content would appear meaningless to students in the same way that a lot of traditional school curriculum content does due to its apparent irrelevance to lived experience. That being said, I believe that little if any disciplinarily content is totally irrelevant to lived experience. Rather, the problem is that disciplinary content is often presented to students as abstract and fragmented parcels of information ready to be stored away in their memories in case they should ever come across a situation in which it may be of some use. This was Dewey's criticism of traditional curricula. We have seen that a common misconception about Dewey is that he believed traditional subjects had no place on the school curriculum. Yet the curriculum at the Laboratory School consisted of traditional school subjects, including history, geography, science and art. While Dewey was critical of the way these subjects were traditionally taught, he believed that they encapsulated our culture, which consists of the common knowledge, values, methods, tools and ideas that have been generated by past and future communities so as to enable humans to more intelligently interact with their environment. Dewey believed disciplinary content should be taught as knowledge, skills, methods and values that were constructed in response to everyday problems—namely, the problem of how to more effectively interact with our social environment. Hence, the reason that in Dewey's school children would learn geometry in order to build a functioning garden shed; biology in order to effectively grow a kitchen garden; chemistry in order to dye fabrics for a garment; and so on.

Dewey's critique of the discipline of philosophy mirrors his critique of traditional school curriculum content. He didn't believe the discipline of philosophy had no bearing on lived experience. He believed that the problems of philosophy could be found in "widespread social conditions and aims" (2004a, 318). He believed philosophical problems contained emotional, imaginative and practical dimensions because they grew out of human aims, hopes and activities. This is true of even the most seemingly remote and abstract areas of philosophy. Take, for example, Dewey's own explanation of the origins of the mind/body problem, the problem of other minds and epistemological scepticism. Dewey states that in ancient Greek, medieval and barbarian societies, individuals desired to be free of the authoritarianism which had become the way of life. Rather than uncritically accepting information and instructions from authorities, individuals desired to experience things for themselves. This provoked libertarian societies that emphasised the rights of individuals to achieve knowledge for themselves, free from the coercion and interference of society and nature. As a consequence, the individual mind was conceived of as opposed to a potentially coercive external world, including its own body and other people. This created an apparent gap between mind and body—a pseudo-epistemological gap that philosophers became preoccupied with bridging. The apparent failure to bridge this gap gave rise to the doctrines of solipsism and scepticism (2004a, 279–289). While Dewey's explanation of the mind/body problem is contestable, it exemplifies his notion of philosophy as grounded in "widespread social conditions and aims". The problem, Dewey says, is that a preoccupation with attaining certainty in the form of absolute truths, has led philosophers to articulate, examine and theorise such problems in an overly abstract and technical manner. That is, the quest for certainty has "reduced philosophy to a show of elaborate terminology, a hair-splitting logic, and a fictitious devotion to the mere external forms of comprehensive and minute demonstration" (2004b, 12). Philosophical problems were stripped of their practical, emotional and imaginative origins because the practical, imaginative and emotional all suggest contingency and uncertainty:

> Philosophy has arrogated itself to the office of demonstrating the existence of a transcendent, absolute or inner reality and of revealing to man the nature and features of this ultimate and higher reality. It has therefore claimed that it was in possession of a higher organ of knowledge than is employed by positive science and ordinary practical experience, and that is marked by a superior dignity and importance—a claim which is undeniable if philosophy leads man to proof and intuition of a reality beyond that open to day-by-day life and the special sciences. (2004b, 14)

Hence, Dewey proposed a reconstruction of philosophy, which would resituate philosophical problems within the social conditions and aims from which they originated. If philosophical problems are social problems, then philosophical inquiry is a form of social reconstruction. Dewey describes what a reconstructed history of philosophy would look like, a history of philosophy "not as an isolated thing but as a chapter in the development of civilisation and culture":

> Instead of the disputes of rivals about the nature of reality, we have the significant record of the efforts of men to formulate the things of experience to which they are most deeply and passionately attached. Instead of impersonal and purely speculative endeavours to contemplate as remote beholders of the nature of absolute things-in-themselves, we have a living picture of the choice of thoughtful men about what they would have life to be, and to what ends they would have men shape their intelligent activities. (2004b, 15)

Given the social importance of this reconstructed notion of philosophy, one wonders why philosophy was not on the curriculum at the Laboratory School. It is surprising that Dewey did not consider reconstructing philosophy for the school curriculum, especially given that the other disciplines included on the Laboratory School curriculum had to be similarly reconstructed so as to draw out their concrete, social, practical, imaginative and emotional aspects. Lipman has done some of the work needed to rectify this oversight by developing P4C. However, as explained, Lipman didn't go far enough. His approach to teaching philosophy lacks the valuable practical dimension central to Dewey's curriculum.

So what might a social reconstructionist philosophy curriculum look like? Lisman and Harvey's (2006) edited collection presents many good examples and ideas about how to integrate philosophy and service learning, although the examples are focused on tertiary education and are not necessarily examples of a social reconstructionist approach. A social reconstructionist philosophy curriculum would ideally be a semester or year-long course based on a broad social issue. Starting with a broad issue, such as inequality, has both educational and practical benefits. It allows the teacher to develop a unit outline and identify and prepare relevant sub-topics, themes, texts and learning experiences beforehand. However, because it is a broad topic rather than a specific social problem (e.g., poverty, homelessness, unemployment, racism), it still provides students with the opportunity to identify concrete examples or specific case studies of inequality that they would like to investigate, thus enabling the teacher to develop a course that takes into account the student's interests and understandings. Starting with a broad topic also maximises the options available for taking transformative action. Students need to know from the outset that they are expected to undertake transformative action as a part of the course. This means they can be considering and evaluating possible problems they could tackle throughout the course, allowing them plenty of time to approach relevant community members or organisations that they must engage in communal inquiry with.

After establishing the procedures of the classroom Community of Inquiry, a good starting place would be a collaborative analysis of the key concept (e.g. inequality) so as to develop a working definition of the term, which would allow the Community of Inquiry to identify and examine some concrete examples and case studies of inequality. As a class, two or three case studies or more specific examples should be selected as focus points throughout the rest of the course (e.g., Third World poverty, homelessness in the local community, particular incidents of racism or sexism or social/political exclusion, etc.). The Community of Inquiry should undertake some initial research and reading into these specific case studies and issues, which would ideally include having relevant people from outside the school visit and participate in the classroom Community of Inquiry, as well as taking relevant field trips to develop some understandings about these issues. Throughout the course, these case studies can act as concrete, specific problems that will ground the more abstract ideas, theories and texts discussed in class. This doesn't mean other cases and examples cannot also be explored later on. Starting with a broad social issue, and with some cases rather than some philosophical theories or texts, means that philosophical content will only make it onto the syllabus if it has the potential to contribute to a better understanding of the issue and the construction of a solution.

As an example of how philosophical content may be relevant to social issues, I will use the broad issue of inequality as a starting point for suggesting a philosophy-based reconstructionist curriculum. The following are possible philosophical units of work that might be included in such a course (keeping in mind that all good teachers adapt curriculum as they are implementing it so as to respond to emerging student interests and needs and, in this case, the needs and interest of relevant community members):

1. *What needs and interests do people have?* This question seems like a good starting point because in order to determine what it means for people to be treated equally, we need some understanding of human interests and needs. This unit would include an exploration of questions like, Are there universal human needs and interests? Which needs and interests are most fundamental? What different needs and interests do different people and groups have (e.g., children, women, refugees, etc.)? What are some of the ways in which such interests and needs are blocked or denied? Such questions would be relevant to any of the more specific social problems the Community of Inquiry may focus on, such as Third World poverty or homelessness. There are various areas of philosophy that would help the Community of Inquiry examine and answer such questions. Some consideration of the nature of the self and personhood, reality, experience, the mind and body, gender, race and culture would be necessary to answering such questions well. Philosophical literature on the good life, happiness and the meaning of life would also be relevant. It wouldn't be possible to examine every relevant philosophical issue or text. The teacher needs to select just a few that will assist students to critically examine these issues and answer the question. Some texts and activities may be selected in advance while others may be included in response to ideas and problems that arise in the classroom community of inquiry or as a result of student suggestions.

2. *What capacities and resources enable individuals to satisfy their needs and interests?* This question could provoke an inquiry into many areas of philosophy, especially the topics of freewill and autonomy. Epistemology, philosophy of mind and logic are also relevant because knowledge and the capacity for inquiry or rationality may also be things that enable individuals to satisfy their needs and interests. This

could provoke a Community of Inquiry into what knowledge is and what effective inquiry looks like, as well as into the role of experience, the imagination and emotions in inquiry and knowing. This can be linked back to the focus case studies by examining how these particular individuals may not have equal opportunity to develop or exercise such capacities or to access and construct knowledge.

3. *Are we obligated to assist others to satisfy their needs and interests?* If so, what is the nature of this obligation? Is it limited to not interfering with other peoples' opportunities to satisfy their own needs and interests? Are we required to actively support or promote others' abilities to satisfy their own needs and interests? What happens when different needs and interests conflict? An examination of such ethical issues is essential for exploring any cases of inequality.

4. *What type of society is most likely to support the satisfaction of human needs and interests?* This question prompts an exploration of topics in political philosophy. What types of government, laws and economic systems are most likely to provide people with equal opportunities to satisfy their needs and interests? Key topics would be a consideration of the nature of justice, rights, citizenship, democracy, community, capitalism and so on. Again, students would then need to take the political theories and concepts explored in the readings and dialogue and use them to analyse and pose solutions to specific case studies of inequality.

5. *What type of education would foster such a society?* This question is at the heart of philosophy of education. Philosophers of education like Rousseau, Locke, Dewey and Plato took an interest in education because they were concerned with identifying the type of education that would foster their ideals of society and the good life. Students are likely to have an interest in this issue too given that education is so central to their current experiences. This question should also provoke a consideration of the nature of mind and epistemology because in order to work out what education should be, we must understand how individuals learn, and this, in turn, requires an understanding of how the mind works and interacts with the world, as well as an understanding of what knowledge is and how it is acquired. Logic is also relevant because if an aim of education is to foster the capacity for inquiry or reasonableness, then one would need some conception of what good thinking is in order to outline ideal pedagogies and curricula.

The Community of Inquiry must constantly move between philosophical texts and theories and analyses of concrete social problems or case studies, with the overriding aim of articulating the causes and nature problem and identifying some possible transformative action that may be taken. While students should be considering possible action they can take throughout the course, the teacher should set a deadline for the Community of Inquiry to decide on a specific problem they want to respond to. This deadline would need to be far enough into the course to allow time for students to developed their philosophical skills and understandings enough to make a more informed decision about what problem they want to address. However, it needs to be early enough in the course to allow for the considerable amount of time that planning and undertaking transformative action would take, especially because they need to undertake action in collaboration with relevant community members. There are a multitude of possible actions students could take as a part of the type of course described above, and it will depend on the age and abilities of the students, as well as the local community and resources available. For younger students, they may tackle concrete cases by taking action within the school community (but beyond their own class). Many of the types of service learning activities already mentioned could be suitable action, depending on the specific problem students investigated. It may even be the case that students come to the conclusion that volunteering with a mainstream community organisation or helping implement an existing service is the most effective action they can take (e.g., working in a homeless shelter, assisting with an established adult tutoring program). However, they would have to form this judgment as a result of undertaking a careful philosophical inquiry into the social issue, supported by philosophical literature and methods. Furthermore, they would continue to engage in collaborative philosophical inquiry during and after the action. The action doesn't come at the conclusion of the inquiry—it is part of it. This will support their critical evaluation of the effectiveness of the action, enabling them to make recommendations for future action. This is what traditional service learning doesn't allow for and what social justice approaches to service learning aim at but often fail to realise because of a lack of clear pedagogical procedures and curriculum content that can actively foster the communal inquiry necessary for effective social reconstruction.

As a result of inquiring into topics similar to those described above, senior secondary school students in one of my philosophy classes came to the conclusion that in a just society, all schools must teach philosophy. The students had undertaken a project where they had to design a type of schooling that would foster their idea of a just society. They had studied political philosophy for several weeks and had a series of questions to guide their design. There was a general consensus that the teaching of philosophy was essential for fostering the thinking skills, dispositions and social skills needed for their ideal society. As a result of discussions about P4C with a primary teacher in our school, I approached my philosophy students to see if they would be interested in designing some philosophical curriculum materials for the primary students. They would then work with the primary teachers and use the materials to facilitate philosophical inquiry with the primary students. Thus, my students would have an opportunity to test out and evaluate their idea. The primary teachers and students would also have presumably benefitted from the experience. My students were enthusiastic about the suggestion. The fact that the action was suggested by the teacher is irrelevant. As long as students are able to critically assess it and reject it if they think it is unsuitable, it doesn't matter who suggests the action. However, our plan was never enacted due to the fact that it was already late in the year when the idea emerged, and there were time constraints as a result of the state mandated, content-heavy curriculum. It was a struggle just to cover all the content on the curriculum in our allocated class time before the end of year exam. Hence, there was simply no time left for active citizenship and social reconstruction. I left school teaching soon after this to take up an academic position. This incident demonstrates the way dominant school structures and educational ideas can impede such teaching, which explains why the educational ideas of people like Dewey and Freire have had little to no impact on mainstream schooling. These ideas don't comfortably fit into existing structures and ideologies. This doesn't mean teachers should give up. Teachers need to be prepared to have to adapt such educational ideas, implement them gradually and partially, and constantly justify and explain the value of these ideas and practices because colleagues may perceive them to be unorthodox and even dubious.

Conclusion

It has been argued that many problems in educational theory and practice, as well as in philosophy, are connected to problematic dualisms. Drawing on the ideas of John Dewey, Philosophy for Children (P4C) and feminist philosophy, I have examined how these dualisms have detrimental consequences for education. Dualisms such as subject/object, Reason/experience, Reason/imagination, Reason/emotion, mind/body, subject/object, abstract/concrete, theory/practice, absolute/relative and individual/community underpin debates about the nature of truth, meaning, the self and knowledge in relation to education. In particular, they give rise to the competing doctrines of relativism and absolutism in education, which are both problematic and incompatible with the desirable educational goals of Dewey and P4C. Traditional schooling also incorporates Reason/emotion and Reason/imagination dualisms, which make it impossible for schools to facilitate reflective thinking, moral reasoning, autonomy and democratic citizenship, all of which require an integration of reason, emotion and imagination. Community/individual dualism gives rise to individualistic or communitarian school practices. While individualism fails to promote the social skills, caring disposition and interdependency required for autonomy and democratic citizenship, communitarian schools can suppress or exclude differences, which also undermines a notion of democracy that prioritises intercultural inquiry and inclusivity. Theory/practice dualism leads to schooling that fails to facilitate reflective and intelligent action because it excludes the essential practical aspect of all thinking. All of these dualisms reinforce problematic gender stereotypes in schools and the gendered nature of the traditional curriculum. This underpins problems such as the reduced participation of females in maths and the physical sciences and the disengagement of male students with the English curriculum. By examining the way these dualisms are assumed in various educational ideas and methods, a new understanding of many educational problems has been developed. Many responses to these educational problems fail because they don't reconstruct the dualisms which underpin the problems. Any effective solution to these fundamental problems cannot leave these underlying dualisms intact.

These dualisms may also underpin other serious educational problems that I have not had the space to explore here. For example, these dualisms likely support other educational inequalities, such as the serious disadvantages that Australian indigenous students face in mainstream schools, as well as the problems faced by students from low socio-economic backgrounds and students from many other marginalised groups. As mentioned in Chapter 1, the subordinate dualistic categories on the right side of the table of dualisms (body, emotion, practice, concrete, imagination, particular, etc.) are not just associated with 'femininity' but also with other marginalised groups, including non-whites, the working class and people with low socio-economic status. For example, the mind/body and theory/practice dualism is clearly associated with race and class inequality because particular classes and races are associated with manual, physical labour. This contrasts the 'superior' work associated with the professions and the middle class, which is often considered to be more theoretical, abstract and cognitive. This is perpetuated through the traditional curriculum hierarchy, which maintains that seemingly more abstract and theoretical subjects are more valuable and educational than subjects perceived to be largely practical and concrete. The relationship between these dualisms and other types of social and educational inequalities needs to be explored in more detail.

It has been argued that the anti-dualistic ideas of Dewey, feminist philosophy and P4C provide the basis for a response to these educational problems. P4C transforms the classroom into the type of Community of Inquiry that Dewey described as the basis of all thinking, meaning, knowledge, autonomy and democracy. In order to examine the influence of Dewey on P4C and the educational benefits of this, a detailed account of the philosophical ideals embedded in P4C has been provided. Such a detailed analysis of the theoretical foundations of P4C had not yet been provided. Lipman acknowledged Dewey's influence on P4C but never fully articulated the nature and extent of this influence. A thorough understanding of P4C's theoretical foundations has enabled a clarification of some of the more contentious aspects of P4C. For example, a major problem with P4C stems from confusion about whether it assumes relativism and absolutism. Some P4C practitioners assume that the Community of Inquiry is an opportunity for students to freely express their thoughts and opinions, all of which are considered equally valuable. While others assume that the Community of Inquiry involves students inquiring into problems that have fixed and final outcomes which students must eventually accept. It has been shown that neither of these assumptions is compatible with P4C's Deweyian goals and ideals, and that both are unacceptable as educational ideals. Rather, P4C assumes a pragmatist middle-ground notion of truth. This notion of truth incorporates the desirable aspects of both relativism and absolutism and is consequently best able to facilitate reflective thinking, autonomy, community and democracy. We have also seen that while P4C is ideal for facilitating emotional intelligence, it could be improved through the development of philosophical curriculum materials specifically designed to foster inquiry into the emotions and the skills needed for emotional intelligence. Similarly, it has also been shown that P4C is well positioned to respond to gender inequalities in education. However, again, there needs to be a specific emphasis placed on these issues in the classroom. Students need to explore gender issues, and other interrelated social issues, including the gendered nature of different epistemological ideals and the school curriculum.

This theoretical analysis of P4C has also drawn attention to P4C's problematic acceptance of theory/practice dualism. This is one dualism that P4C doesn't appear to challenge, and this is a serious problem with the pedagogy because it undermines all of P4C's educational goals. In particular, the exclusion of practicality means that P4C can't fully facilitate the development of reflective thinking and action, meaningful learning and active democratic citizenship. P4C's focus on dialogue and texts as opposed to transformative action also perpetuates the notion that philosophy is an elitist, overly intellectual and, thus, exclusive subject, as well as the common assumption that philosophy lacks vocational and practical value. I have attempted to overcome this problem by integrating P4C with a critical, social justice approach to service learning that I have called 'social reconstruction learning'. This more practical P4C pedagogy would involve students engaging in philosophical communal inquiries with members of the wider community in order to reconstruct real social problems. The type of communal inquiry and philosophical skills and knowledge promoted by P4C are essential for such social reconstruction. Thus social reconstruction learning and P4C are interdependent ideals. This integrated pedagogy not only improves P4C's ability to meet its educational goals, but it also offers a solution to many of the problems that plague service learning. As a form of social reconstruction learning, P4C will be better able to foster the Deweyian notion of collaborative, imaginative, emotional, reasonable, active inquiry that it was originally designed to foster. As such, it will be more likely to foster the type of democratic communities that are necessary for growth and meaningfulness.

Notes

NOTES TO THE INTRODUCTION

1. For other discussion of Dewey's influence on P4C, see Cam (2008).

NOTES TO CHAPTER 1

1. I will a use a capitalised 'Reason' in order to refer to this problematic ideal of reason and to distinguish it from unproblematic notions of reason, such as the ideal of reasonableness in the P4C literature.
2. This list has been compiled from lists in F. Mathews (1998, 519) and Plumwood (2002, 20). This list doesn't exhaust the possible dualistic pairs, but just lists some of the most fundamental ones in Western thought.
3. Chodorow's object-relations psychoanalysis suggests that the traditional nuclear family gives rise to gendered, dualistic thinking. It is important to emphasise that Keller's critique is of the dominant ideal of the scientific method rather than scientific practices themselves, which, as Keller acknowledges, differ greatly among scientists (1983, 125).
4. For example, see Polesel's (2008) discussion of vocational education in schools in Australia and Quin's (2003) discussion of media studies in schools.
5. The Core Knowledge Foundation website provides examples of this type of curriculum and pedagogy, as well as research and information about schools that implement it: http://www.coreknowledge.org/

NOTES TO CHAPTER 2

1. For a good example of the selective nature of vision, see this well-known television advertisement about drivers being aware of cyclists. As the add states, "It's easy to miss something you are not looking for" (http://www.youtube.com/watch?v=pTv4yD6BKlA).
2. By 'language', Dewey means that which communicates. Thus, not only written and verbal speech but also "gestures . . . rights, ceremonies, monuments and the products of industrial and the fine arts" (1938, 46).

NOTES TO CHAPTER 3

1. Matthews doesn't mean that Plato has a banking theory of education. Rather, Plato has what is sometimes referred to as a 'midwife' model of learning, where the teacher aims to draw knowledge and understanding

out of the student, such as Socrates does through various questioning techniques in Plato's dialogues. However, the knowledge drawn out is supposed to be absolute. Once it's recalled by the student, it is not subject to revision and should be accepted by all. This is also the reason that in the Platonic dialogues, Socrates frequently uses leading questions and an aggressive inquiry style that actually directs his 'co-inquirers' to the 'one right answer'. Hence, most of these dialogues are not good examples of the type of open, collaborative inquiry promoted by P4C. This is even though many P4C theorists emphasise the influence of Socratic dialogue on P4C.

2. This is why Dewey's theory is often mistakenly used to support both absolutism and relativism (Schleifer 1996–1997).

3. Borg (1992) uses an example of a murder that is not witnessed by anyone as a counterexample to Dewey's pragmatic theory of truth. Borg claims that on Dewey's view the murder hypothesis could never be shown to be true because there are no witnesses to verify the claim that a murder had happened. This is a misunderstanding of the pragmatic theory of truth. So long as the murder hypothesis solved the mystery better than any alternative ideas, which means it satisfies the known facts of the case and the inquirer's expectations, it is true. However, there is always the possibility that new information may falsify the hypothesis at a later time.

4. Dewey's notion of experience is difficult to articulate and is frequently misunderstood and misrepresented. This is because as Gatens-Robinson points out, "In rejecting the dualisms of object and subject, mind and world, Dewey struggled to express himself through a language in which those distinctions are built in" (2002, 195). As Dewey himself realised, the common misunderstanding of his notion of experience is the source of many of the misunderstandings of his theory of truth.

NOTES TO CHAPTER 5

1. While the reconstruction of a problematic situation should bring about some feelings of satisfaction, the knowledge acquired through reconstructing the situation may not be personally agreeable or pleasing (See Chapter 3). Scheffler describes "the joy of verification" but states that not all verification may be accompanied by elation since "soberly predicted events may be so dreadful as to occasion not joy but sorrow or despair" (1991, 10–11).

2. The research was conducted over a year long period in three Montreal schools with 30 children making up the experimental P4C groups and 42 children making up the control groups. The P4C students attended a one hour-long P4C session per week. The session included the reading of a story followed by a collaborative inquiry. They used emotional intelligence tests designed by E. B. Freeman.

3. The school where P4C appeared to have no affect was a high socio-economic school where emotional recognition abilities were already elevated.

NOTES TO CHAPTER 6

1. Etzioni actually recommends that service be undertaken for a year after schooling is completed, which means that it would not be an opportunity for students to reflectively practice and develop the types of problem solving skills, attitudes, values and disciplinary content that we would expect them to learn at school from an early age.

2. This notion of a global community reflects that described by Mason, which doesn't require the breakdown of other important, more localised or national communities (2000, 175).
3. For example, Addams co-founded the Women's International League of Peace and Freedom (Whips 2004, 127).
4. For an account of how the philosophies of Dewey and Addams are similar to contemporary ethics of care theories, see Leffers (1993).
5. Kiss (1997), Held (1995) and Gilligan (1982) argue for the value of both rights and care. Kymlicka (2002) also argues that both are compatible and interconnected.

NOTES TO CHAPTER 7

1. As explained in Chapter 1, biology is an exception as it has long been considered a more feminine science subject than physics and chemistry. This is because it clearly deals with the concrete, material world and reproduction.
2. The HSC is a certificate awarded to students who complete the final year of schooling (Year 12) in New South Wales, Australia.
3. Exceptions are subjects like geography and economics, which, unlike other humanities subjects, could be seen as more 'masculine' because they emphasise quantification and measurement and appear to be more vocationally orientated (see Teese et al. 1995, 31).

NOTES TO CHAPTER 8

1. However, as Eyler and Giles (1999) point out, when the service learning is optional, the higher grade point averages of university students who participate in service learning could reflect the fact students who participate in service are more motivated and engaged students to begin with.
2. The documentary *You Got to Move: Stories of Change in the South*, directed by Lucy Massie Phenix (1985), provides a good overview of Highlander during this period, including an account of the FBI investigation. Files from the FBI investigation can also be viewed online at the FBI website: http://vault.fbi.gov/Highlander%20Folk%20School.
3. More information about Highlander's current programs can be found at the website: http://www.highlandercenter.org/programs.asp.
4. The book *We Make the Road by Walking: Conversations on Education and Social Change* (1990) is a dialogue between Horton and Freire.
5. The social reconstructionist approach to curriculum is also sometimes referred to as social meliorism (e.g., Kliebard 2004).
6. Another possible explanation for the general lack of acknowledgement given to social reconstructionism is that some proponents of the theory, such as Counts (1986) and Brameld (1977), promoted extreme leftist political views, which some modern proponents of service learning may wish to distance themselves from. Not only did the social reconstructionists conceive of schools as means to social reconstruction, but many of them recommended that schools reconstruct society along socialist lines. Even other progressive educators considered social reconstructionists like Counts and Brameld too radical (Kohl in Brameld 2009, xiii). Although, as McLaren (2007) points out, Marxism and socialism have also influenced critical pedagogy.
7. Some examples are Cam (1995, 2006), Golding (2002, 2006), Lipman (1992) and Wilks (1996, 2005).

References

Abowitz, Kathleen Knight. 1999. "Reclaiming Community." *Educational Theory* 49 (2): 143–160.

Addams, Jane. 1910. *Twenty Years at Hull House*. New York: The Macmillan Company.

———. 1964. *Democracy and Social Ethics*. Cambridge, MA: Harvard University Press.

Alcoff, Linda. 1988. "Cultural Feminism Versus Post-structuralism: The Identity Crisis in Feminist Theory." *Signs* 13:405–436.

———. 1995. "Is the Feminist Critique of Reason Rational?" *Philosophical Topics* 23 (2): 1–26.

Alcoff, Linda, and Elizabeth Potter, eds. 1993. Feminist Epistemologies. New York: Routledge.

Aleman, Ana M. 2002. "Identity, Feminist Teaching, and John Dewey." In *Feminist Interpretations of John Dewey*, edited by Charlene Siegfried Haddock, 113–129. University Park: Pennsylvania State University Press.

Angier, Roswell P. 1927. "The Conflict Theory of Emotion." *The American Journal of Psychology* 39 (1): 390–401.

Apple, Michael. 2009. "Controlling the Work of Teachers." In *The Curriculum Studies Reader*, edited by D. J. Flinders and S. Thornton 183–197. London: Routledge.

Aristotle. 1911. *The Nichomachean Ethics of Aristotle*. Translated by D. P. Chase. London: Dent.

Astin, A. W., and L. Sax. 1998. "How Undergraduates Are Affected by Service Participation." *Journal of College Student Development* 39 (3): 251–263.

Australian Broadcasting Commission (ABC) Radio National. 2004. "Is Small Really Lost?" (Radio transcript). *Encounter*. www.abc.net.au/rn/relig/enc/stories/s1237204.htm.

Australian Council for Education Research (ACER). 2002. *Boys in School and Society*, by John Creswell, Ken Rowe, and Graeme Withers. Melbourne: ACER www.acer.edu.au/research/teaching/documents/boysInSchoolSoc.pdf.

Australian Curriculum, Assessment & Reporting Authority (ACARA). 2011. *National Assessment Program: Literacy and Numeracy Report*. Sydney: ACARA. http://www.nap.edu.au/_Documents/National%20Report/NAPLAN_2011_National_Report.pdf.

Bandman, Bertram. 1993. "Children's Educational Rights." In *Thinking Children and Education*, edited by Matthew Lipman. Dubuque, 27–44. IA: Kendall/ Hunt Publishing.

Barrow, Robin. 1988. "Some Observations on the Concept of Imagination." In *Imagination and Education*, edited by Kieran Egan and Dan Nadaner, 82–85. New York: Teachers College Press.

Belenky, Mary Field, Blythe McVicker Clinchy, Nancy Rule Goldberger, and Jill Mattuck Tarule. 1986. *Women's Ways of Knowing: The Development of Self, Voice, and Mind*. New York: Basic Books.

Bell, Macalester. 2005. "A Women's Scorn: Toward a Feminist Defence of Contempt as a Moral Emotion." *Hypatia* 20 (4): 80–93.

Benjamin, Martin. 1978. "Moral Knowledge and Moral Education." In *Growing Up With Philosophy*, edited by Matthew Lipman and Ann Margaret Sharp, 311–325. Philadelphia: Temple University Press.

Benjamin, Martin, and Eugenio Echeverria. 1992. "Knowledge and the Classroom." In *Studies in Philosophy for Children: Harry Stottlemeier's Discovery*, edited by Anne Margaret Sharp and Ronald F. Reed, 64–78. Philadelphia: Temple University Press.

Berliner, David. C. 2009. "MCLB (Much Curriculum Left Behind): A U.S. Calamity in the Making." *The Educational Forum* 73 (4): 284–296.

Berliner, David C., and Sharon Lyn Nichols. 2007. *Collateral Damage: How High Stakes Testing Corrupts America's Schools*. Cambridge, MA: Harvard Education Press.

Bernacki, Matthew L., and Elizabeth Jaeger. 2008. "Exploring the Impact of Service-Learning on Moral Development and Moral Orientation." *Michigan Journal of Community Service Learning* 4 (2): 5–15.

Berrian, Annette. 1985. "Socrates in a New Package Helps Kids Learn to Think." *Thinking: The Journal of Philosophy for Children* 5 (3): 43–45.

Bickford, Donna M., and Nedra Reynolds. 2002. "Activism and Service-Learning: Reframing Volunteerism as Acts of Dissent." *Pedagogy: Critical Approaches to Teaching Literature, Language, Composition, and Culture* 2 (2): 229–252.

Bidulph, Steve. 1995. *Manhood: An Action Plan for Changing Men's Lives*. Sydney: Finch Publishing.

Billig, Shelley H. 2000. "Research on K–12 School-Based Service-Learning—the Evidence Builds." *Phi Delta Kappan* 81 (9): 658–671.

Billig, Shelley H., Sue Root and Dan Jesse. 2005. *The Impact of Participation in Service-Learning on High School Students' Civic Engagement*. College Park: Center for Information and Research on Civic Learning and Engagement (CIRCLE), University of Maryland.

Birkhahn, Tayla. 1997. "A Purple Sky: The Challenged Chance for Change." *Thinking: The Journal of Philosophy for Children* 13 (1): 37–41.

Bitting, Paul F., and Cheryl Southworth. 1992. "Reverence and the Passions of Inquiry." *Thinking: The Journal of Philosophy for Children* 10 (2): 13–18.

Bland, Derek. 2012. "Imagination for Reengagement from the Margins of Education." *Australian Educational Researcher* 39 (1): 75–89.

Bleazby, Jennifer. 2004. "Practicality and Philosophy for Children." *Critical and Creative Thinking: The Australasian Journal of Philosophy of Education* 12 (2): 33–42.

———. 2006. "Autonomy, Democratic Community and Citizenship in Philosophy for Children: Dewey and Philosophy for Children's Rejection of Community/Individual Dualism." *Analytic Teaching* 26 (1): 30–52.

———. 2008. "Philosophy for Children as a Response to Gender Problems in Australian Schools." *Thinking: The Journal of Philosophy for Children* 19 (2–3): 70–78.

———. 2011. "Overcoming Relativism and Absolutism: Dewey's Ideals of Truth and Meaning in Philosophy for Children. *Educational Philosophy and Theory* 43 (5): 453–466.

Boler, Megan. 1999. *Feeling Power: Emotions and Education*. New York: Routledge.

Bordo, Susan. 1987. *The Flight to Objectivity, Essays on Cartesianism and Culture*. Albany: State University of New York Press.

Borg, Karl. 1992. "Russell Vs. Dewey: Inquiry or Truth? Where Is the Little Word?" In *Children: Thinking and Philosophy: Proceedings of the 5th International Conference of Philosophy for Children*, edited by Daniela G. Camhy, 72–82. Sankt Augustin, Germany: Academia Verlag.

Brameld, Theodore. 1977. "Reconstructionism as Radical Philosophy of Education: A Reappraisal." *The Educational Forum* 42 (1): 67–76.

———. 2009. *The Use of Explosive Ideas in Education: Class, Culture and Evolution*. New York: The New Press.

Brown, R., and R. Fletcher, eds. 1995. *Boys in Schools: Addressing the Issues*. Lane Cove, Sydney: Finch Publishing.

Brown, Rexford G. 1991. "Cultivating a Literacy of Thoughtfulness." *Thinking: The Journal of Philosophy for Children* 9(4): 5–12.

Buchanan J. 1993. "Young Women's Complex Lives and the Idea of Youth Transitions." In *Youth Subcultures: Theory, History and the Australian Experience*, edited by R. White, 61–66. Tasmania: National Clearing House for Youth Studies.

Buckingham, Jennifer. 2000. *Boy Troubles: Understanding Rising Suicide, Rising Crime and Educational Failure*, St Leonards, NSW: The Centre for Independent Studies.

———. 2004. *Boy's Education: Research and Rhetoric*. Melbourne: The Centre for Independent Studies.

Buenaseda-Saludo, Mara. 2003. "Cultivating Social Imagination in the Community of Inquiry." *Thinking: The Journal of Philosophy for Children* 16 (3): 36–41.

Bundy, Murray. W. 1922. "Plato's View of the Imagination." *Studies in Philology* 19 (4): 362–403.

Buras, Kristen. L. 1999. "Questioning Core Assumptions: A Critical Reading of and Response to E.D. Hirsch's the 'Schools We Need and Why We Don't Have Them.'" *Harvard Educational Review* 69 (1): 67–93.

Burgh, Gilbert. 2003. "Democratic Education: Aligning Curriculum, Pedagogy, Assessment and School Governance." *Philosophy, Democracy and Education*, edited by Philip Cam, 101–120. Seoul: Korean National Commission for UNESCO.

Burgh, Gilbert, Terri Field, and Mark Freakley. 2006. *Ethics and the Community of Inquiry: Education for Deliberative Democracy*. Melbourne: Thompson Social Science Press.

Butin, Dan W. 2003. "Of What Use Is It? Multiple Conceptualisations of Service Learning Within Education." *Teachers College Record* 105 (9): 1674–1692.

Cam, Philip. 1995. Thinking Together: Philosophical Inquiry for the Classroom. Sydney: Hale & Iremonger.

———. 1997. "Philosophy in the Primary School." In *Philosophy and Democracy in Asia*, edited by Philip Cam, In-suk Cha and Mark Tamthai. Seoul: Korean National Commission for UNESCO.

———. 2006. *Twenty Thinking Tools*. Melbourne: ACER.

———. 2008. "Dewey, Lipman and the Tradition of Reflective Education." In *Pragmatism, Education and Children*, edited by M. Taylor, H. Schreier and P. Ghiraldelli, Jr., 163–181. New York: Rodopi.

Cevallos-Estarellas, Pablo, and Brynhildur Sigurdardottir. 2000. "The Community of Inquiry as a Means for Cultivating Democracy." *Inquiry Critical Thinking Across the Disciplines* 19 (2): 45–57.

Chodorow, Nancy. 1978. *The Reproduction of Mothering: Psychoanalysis and the Sociology of Gender*. Berkley: University of California Press.

Cipolle, Susan. 2004. "Service-Learning as a Counter Hegemonic Practice: Evidence Pro and Con." *Multicultural Education* 11 (3): 12–23.

Code, Lorraine. 1991. *What Can She Know? Feminist Theory and the Construction of Knowledge*. Ithaca, NY: Cornell University Press.
———. 1992. "Feminist Epistemology." In *A Companion to Epistemology*, edited by Jonathon Dancy and Ernst Sosa, 375–379. Oxford: Blackwell.
———. 1995. *Rhetorical Spaces: Essays on Gendered Locations*. New York: Routledge.
Collins, Louise. 2001. "Philosophy for Children and Feminist Philosophy." *Thinking: The Journal of Philosophy for Children* 15 (4): 20–30.
Counts, George S. 1986. "The Intangible Supports of Liberty." *The Educational Forum* 50 (3): 273–282.
Cunningham, Suzanne. 1995. "Dewey on Emotions: Recent Empirical Evidence." *Transactions of the Charles S. Peirce Society* 31 (4): 865–874.
———. 1997. "Two Faces of Intentionality." *Philosophy of Science* 64 (3): 445–460.
Damasio, Antonio R. 1994. *Descartes' Error: Emotion, Reason, and the Human Brain*. New York: Putnam.
———. 1996. "The Somatic Marker Hypothesis and the Possible Functions of the Prefrontal Cortex." *Philosophical Transactions of the Royal Society of London*, Series B (Biological Sciences) 351: 1413–1420.
———. 1999. *The Feeling of What Happens: Body and Emotion in the Making of Consciousness*. New York: Harcourt Brace & Company.
D'Arlach, Lucia, Bernadette Sánchez and Rachel Feuer. 2009. "Voices From the Community: A Case for Reciprocity in Service Learning." *Michigan Journal of Community Service Learning* 16 (1): 5–16.
Darwin, Charles. 1979. *The Expression of Emotions in Man and Animals*. London: Julian Friedmann Publishers.
Davey, Sarah. 2004. "Consensus, Caring and Community: An Inquiry into Dialogue." *Analytic Teaching* 25 (1): 18–51.
Davies, Bronwyn. 1996. *Power/Knowledge/Desire: Changing School Organisation and Management Practices*. Canberra: Department of Employment, Education and Youth Affairs.
Deans, Thomas. 1999. "Service Learning in Two Keys: Paulo Freire's Critical Pedagogy in Relation to John Dewey's Pragmatism." *Michigan Journal of Community Service Learning* 6 (1): 15–29.
Deganhardt, Michael, and Elaine McKay. 1988. "Imagination and Education for Intercultural Understanding." In *Imagination and Education*, edited by Kieran Egan, and Dan Nadaner, 237–255. New York: Teachers College Press.
Department of Education and Training (DET). 2003. *Educating Boys: Issues and Information*. Canberra: DET.
Descartes, Rene. 2006. *A Discourse on Method*. Translated by Ian Maclean. Oxford: Oxford University Press.
Dewey, John. 1916. *Essays in Experimental Logic*. New York: Dover Publications.
———. 1927. *The Public and Its Problems*. Chicago: The Swallow Press.
———. 1930b. *Human Nature and Conduct: An Introduction to Social Psychology*. New York: The Modern Library Publishers.
———. 1930a. *The Quest for Certainty: A Study of the Relation of Knowledge and Action*. London: George Allen & Unwin.
———. 1938. *Logic, The Theory of Inquiry*. New York: Henry Holt and Company.
———. 1939. *Freedom and Culture*. New York: G. P. Putnams & Sons.
———. 1956. *The Child and the Curriculum: The School and Society*. Chicago: Phoenix Books.
———. 1958a. *Art as Experience*. New York: Capricorn Books.
———. 1958b. *Experience and Nature*. New York: Dover Publications.

———. 1963. *Experience and Education*. New York: Collier Books.

———. 1967. *The Collected Works of John Dewey: The Early Works 1882–1898*, Volume 2, edited by Jo Ann Boydston. Carbondale: Southern Illinois University Press.

———. 1971. *The Collected Works of John Dewey: The Early Works 1882–1898*, Volume 4, edited by Jo Ann Boydston. Carbondale: Southern Illinois University Press.

———. 1972. *The Collected Works of John Dewey: The Early Works 1882–1998*, Volume 5, edited by Jo Ann Boydston. Carbondale: Southern Illinois University Press.

———. 1976. *The Collected Works of John Dewey: The Middle Works 1899–1924*, Volume 1, edited by Jo Ann Boydston. Carbondale: Southern Illinois University Press.

———. 1977. *The Collected Works of John Dewey: The Middle Works 1899–1924*, Volume 4, edited by Jo Ann Boydston. Carbondale: Southern Illinois University Press.

———. 1978. *The Collected Works of John Dewey: The Middle Works 1899–1924*, Volume 6, edited by Jo Ann Boydston. Carbondale: Southern Illinois University Press.

———. 1984a. *The Collected Works of John Dewey: The Later Works 1925–1953*, Volume 2, edited by Jo Ann Boydston. Carbondale: Southern Illinois University Press.

———. 1984b. *The Collected Works of John Dewey: The Later Works 1925–1953*, Volume 5, edited by Jo Ann Boydston. Carbondale: Southern Illinois University Press.

———. 1985. *The Collected Works of John Dewey: The Later Works 1925–1953*, Volume 6, edited by Jo Ann Boydston. Carbondale: Southern Illinois University Press.

———. 1986. *The Collected Works of John Dewey: The Later Works 1925–1953*, Volume 9, edited by Jo Ann Boydston. Carbondale: Southern Illinois University Press.

———. 1987. *The Collected Works of John Dewey: The Later Work 1925–1953*, Volume 11, edited by Jo Ann Boydston. Carbondale: Southern Illinois University Press.

———. 1988. *The Collected Works of John Dewey: Later Works 1925–1953*, Volume 13, edited by Jo Ann Boydston. Carbondale: Southern Illinois University Press.

———. 1989. *The Collected Works of John Dewey: The Later Works 1925–1953*, Volume 15, edited by Jo Ann Boydston. Carbondale: Southern Illinois University Press.

———. 1990. *The School and Society. The Child and the Curriculum*. Chicago: University of Chicago Press.

———. 1991. *The Collected Works of John Dewey: The Later Works 1925–1953*, Volume 17, edited by Jo Ann Boydston. Carbondale: Southern Illinois University Press.

———. 1997. *How We Think*. Mineola, New York: Dover Publications.

———. 2004a. *Democracy and Education*. Mineola, New York: Dover Publications.

———. 2004b. *Reconstruction in Philosophy*, Mineola, New York: The Beacon Press.

Dewey, John, and Arthur F. Bentley. 1949. *Knowing and The Known*. Connecticut: Greenwood Press Publishers.

Dewhurst, David. 1997. "Education and Passion." *Educational Theory* 47 (4): 477–487.

Egan, Keiran. 2007. "Imagination, Past and Present." In *Teaching and Learning Outside the Box*, edited by Keiran Egan, Maureen Stout and Keiichi Takaya, 3–20. New York: Teachers College Press.

Egan, Keiran, and Gillian Judson. 2009. "Values and Imagination in Teaching: With a Special Focus on Social Studies." *Educational Philosophy and Theory* 41 (2): 126–140.

Ellsworth, Elizabeth. 1997. *Teaching Positions: Difference, Pedagogy and the Power of Address*. New York: Teacher's College Press.

Elshtain, Jean Bethke. 1995. "Feminism, Family and Community." In *Feminism and Community*, edited by Penny A. Weis and Marilyn Friedman, 259–272. Philadelphia: Temple University Press.

Etzioni, Amatai. 1993. *The Spirit of Community: Rights, Responsibilities, and the Communitarian Agenda*. New York: Crown Publishers Inc.

Eyler, Janet, and Dwight E. Giles, Jr. 1994. "The Theoretical Roots of Service-Learning in John Dewey: Toward a Theory of Service-Learning." *Michigan Journal of Community Service Learning* 1 (1): 77–85.

———. 1999. *Where's the Learning in Service Learning?* San Francisco: Jossey-Bass Publishers.

Farson, Richard Evans. 1974. *Birthrights*. New York: Macmillan.

Fesmire, Steven. 2003. *John Dewey and Moral Imagination: Pragmatism in Ethics*. Bloomington: Indiana University Press.

Field, Terri. 1995. "Philosophy for Children and the Feminist Critique of Reason." *Critical and Creative Thinking: The Australasian Journal of Philosophy for Children* 3 (1): 9–12.

———. 1997. "Feminist Epistemology and Philosophy for Children." *Thinking: The Journal of Philosophy for Children* 13 (1): 17–22.

Fielding, Michael. 1976. "Against Competition: In Praise of a Malleable Analysis and the Subversiveness of Philosophy." *Journal of Philosophy of Education* 10 (1): 124–146.

Flower, Linda. 2002. "Intercultural Inquiry and Transformation of Service." *College English* 65 (2): 181–121.

Forbes, Kathryn, Linda Garber, Loretta Kensinger and Janet Trapp Slagter. 1999. "Punishing Pedagogy: The Failings of Forced Volunteerism." *Women's Studies Quarterly* 27 (3–4): 158–168.

Fraser, Nancy, and Linda J. Nicholson. 1990. "Social Criticism Without Philosophy: An Encounter Between Feminism and Postmodernism." In *Feminism/Postmodernism*, edited by Linda J. Nicholson, 19–38. New York: Routledge.

Fraser, Nancy, and Linda Gordon. 1997. "Decoding 'Dependency': Inscriptions of Power in a Keyword of the US Welfare State." In *Reconstructing Political Theory: Feminist Perspectives*, edited by Una Narayan and Mary L. Shanley, 25–47. Cambridge: Polity Press.

Frazer, Elizabeth, and Nicola Lacey 1993. *The Politics of Community: A Feminist Critique of the Liberal Communitarian Debate*. Buffalo: University of Toronto Press.

Freire, Paulo. 1993. *Pedagogy of the Oppressed*. New York: Continuum.

Furco, Andrew, and Susan Root. 2010. "Research Demonstrates the Value of Service Learning: Significant Studies Point to the Value of Service Learning, but the Field Needs More Experiential Research to Firmly Establish the Value of this Approach." *Phi Delta Kappan* 91 (5): 16–21.

Gardner, Susan T. 1995. "Inquiry is No Mere Conversation (or Discussion or Dialogue): Facilitation of Inquiry is Hard Work!" *Critical and Creative Thinking: The Australasian Journal of Philosophy for Children* 3 (2): 38–49.

———. 1998. "Truth in Ethics and Elsewhere." *Analytic Teaching* 19 (1): 78–88.

Garrison, Jim. 1996. "A Deweyian Theory of Democratic Listening." *Educational Theory* 46 (4): 429–451.

Gatens, Moira. 1991. *Feminism and Philosophy: Perspectives on Difference and Equality*, Bloomington: Indiana University Press.

Gatens-Robinson, Eugenie. 2002. "The Pragmatic Ecology of the Object: John Dewey and Donna Haraway on Objectivity." In *Feminist Interpretations of John Dewey*, edited by Charlene Seigfried Haddock, 189–209. University Park: Pennsylvania State University Press.

Gilbert, Pam, and Sandra Taylor. 1991. *Fashioning the Feminine: Girls, Popular Culture and Schooling*. Sydney: Allen and Unwin.

Gilbert, Rob, and Pam Gilbert. 1998. *Masculinity Goes to School*. Sydney: Allen & Unwin.

Giles, Dwight E., Jr. 1991. "Dewey's Theory of Experience: Implications for Service-Learning." *Journal of Cooperative Education* 27 (2): 87–90.

Gilligan, Carol. 1982. *In a Different Voice: Psychological Theory and Women's Development*. Cambridge, MA: Harvard University Press.

Ginwright, Shawn, and Julio Cammarota. 2002. "New Terrain in Youth Development: The Promise of a Social Justice Approach." *Social Justice* 29 (4): 82–95.

Giroux, Henry A. 2011. *On Critical Pedagogy*. New York: Continuum.

Glaser, Jen. 1994. "Reasoning as Dialogical Inquiry: A Model for the Liberation of Women." *Thinking: The Journal of Philosophy for Children* 11 (3–4): 16–17.

———. 2007. "Educating for Citizenship and Social Justice." In *Philosophical Foundations of Innovative Learning*, edited by D. Camhy. Sankt Augustin, 16–23. Germany: Academia Verlag.

Glover, Jonathon. 1999. *Humanity: A Moral History of the Twentieth Century*. London: Jonathan Cape.

Golding, Clinton. 2002. Connecting Concepts: Thinking Activities for Students. Melbourne: ACER Press.

———. 2005a. *Creating a Thinking School*. Melbourne: ACER.

———. 2005b. "Truth or Making Sense—What Is More Important in Education?" *Proceedings of the 34th Annual Conference of the Philosophy of Education Society of Australia*. Hong Kong: PESA. http://www.pesa.org.au/site/page/conference.html

———. 2006. *Thinking with Rich Concepts: Philosophical Questioning in the Classroom*. Melbourne: Hawker Brownlow.

Goleman, Daniel. 1996. *Emotional Intelligence: Why It Can Matter More Than I.* London: Bloomsbury.

Gonsalves, Susan. 2010. "Connecting Curriculum with Community: Service Learning Projects Apply Academic Skills and Knowledge to Address Real-Life Issues." *District Administrator* 46 (9): 64–71.

Gosselin, Collette. 2003. "In a Different Voice and the Transformative Experience: A Deweyian Perspective." *Educational Theory* 53 (1): 231–244.

Greene, Maxine. 1995. *Releasing the Imagination: Essays on Education, the Arts and Social Change*. San Francisco: Jossey-Bass Publishers.

Gregory, Maughn. 2002 "Constructivism, Standards, and the Classroom Community of Inquiry." *Educational Theory* 52 (4): 397–409.

———. 2007. "A Framework for Facilitating Classroom Dialogue." *Teaching Philosophy* 30(1): 59–84

———. 2011. "Philosophy for Children and Its Critics: A Mendham dialogue." *Journal of Philosophy of Education* 45 (2): 199–219.

Grimshaw, Jean. 1986. *Feminist Philosophy: Women's Perspectives on Philosophical Traditions*. Brighton: Wheatsheaf Books.

Gustein, Eric, and Bob Peterson. 2006. *Rethinking Mathematics: Teaching Social Justice by the Numbers*. Milwaukee, MI: Rethinking Schools.

Gutmann, Amy. 1982. "What's the Use of Going to School? The Problem of Educa-
tion in Utilitarian and Rights Theories." In *Utilitarianism and Beyond*, edited
by Amartya Sen and Bernard Williams. Cambridge: Cambridge University
Press.
———. 1987. *Democratic Education*. Princeton, NJ: Princeton University Press.
Hamrick, William S. 1989. "Philosophy for Children and Aesthetic Education."
Journal of Aesthetic Education 23 (2): 55–67.
Haralambous, Bronwen, Robert Fitzgerald, and Thomas Nielsen. 2007. "You Are
Now Leaving Flatland: Why We Need Imagination in Education." *Professional
Educator* 6 (4): 38–41.
Harding, Sandra. 1986. The Science Question in Feminism. Ithaca, NY: Cornell
University Press.
———. 1991. *Whose Science? Whose Knowledge?* Ithaca, NY: Cornell University
Press.
———. 1993. "Rethinking Standpoint Epistemology: What Is Strong Objectiv-
ity?" In *Feminist Epistemologies*, edited by Linda Alcoff and Elizabeth Potter,
49–82. New York: Routledge.
Harris, Stephen. 1997. "It Takes Imagination." In *Indigenous Education: Historical, Moral and Practical Tales*, edited by Stephen Harris and Merridy Malin,
5–16. Darwin, Australia: Northern Territory University Press.
Hart, Carol Guen. 1993. "Power in the Service of Love: John Dewey's Logic and
the Dream of a Common Language." *Hypatia* 8 (2): 190–113.
Hass, Marjorie, and Rachel Joffe Falmagne. 2002. "Representing Reason: Femi-
nist Theory and Formal Logic." In *Representing Reason: Feminist Theory and
Formal Logic*, edited by Rachel Joffe Falmagne and Marjorie Hass, 1–10. Lan-
ham, MD: Rowman & Littlefield.
Haynes, Felicity. 1994. "Male Dominance and the Mastery of Reason." *Thinking:
The Journal of Philosophy for Children* 11 (3–4): 18–23.
Heckman, Susan J. 1990. *Gender and Knowledge: Elements of a Postmodern
Feminism*, Cambridge: Polity Press.
Held, Virginia 1995. "Non-Contractual Society: A Feminist View." In *Feminism
and Community*, editors Penny A. Weiss and Marilyn Friedman, 209–231. Phil-
adelphia: Temple University Press.
Heldke, Lisa. 1989. "John Dewey and Evelyn Fox Keller: A Shared Epistemological
Tradition." In *Feminism and Science*, edited by Nancy Tuana, 104–116. Bloom-
ington: Indiana University Press.
Hernandez, Raymond.1994. "Group Sues School Districts Over Civic Service Pro-
grams." *New York Times*, April 20. http://www.nytimes.com/1994/04/20/us/
group-sues-school-districts-over-civic-service-programs.html.
Hirsch, E. D. 1989. *Cultural Literacy: What Every American Needs to Know*.
Melbourne: Schwartz Publishing.
———. 1996. *The Schools We Need and Why We Don't Have Them*. New York:
Doubleday.
Hook, Sidney. 1971. *John Dewey, an Intellectual Portrait*. Westport, CT: Green-
wood Press.
hooks, bell. 1981. *Ain't I a Women: Black Women and Feminism*. Boston: South
End Press.
Hoops, Joshua F. 2011. "Developing an Ethic of Tension: Negotiating Service
Learning and Critical Pedagogy Ethical Tensions." *Journal of Civic Commit-
ment* 16 (January): 1–16.
Holdsworth, Roger. 1996. "What Do We Mean by Student Participation?" *Youth
Studies Australia* 15 (1): 26–28.
———. 2000. "Schools that Create Real Roles of Value for Young People." *Pros-
pects* 30 (3): 349–362.

Holland, Nancy J. 1995. "Convergence on Whose Truth? Feminist Philosophy and the 'Masculine Intellect' of Pragmatism." *Journal of Social Philosophy* 26 (2): 170–183.

Holma, Katariina. 2004. "Plurealism and Education: Israel Scheffler's Synthesis and Its Presumable Educational Consequences." *Educational Theory* 54 (4): 419–431.

Holt, John. 1975. Escape From Childhood: The Needs and Rights of Children. Harmondsworth, UK: Penguin Books.

Hoppe, Sherry L. 2004. "A Synthesis of the Theoretical Stances." In *Service-Learning: History, Theory and Issues*, edited by Bruce W. Speck and Sherry L. Hoppe, 137–149. Westport, CT: Praeger.

Horton, Myles, and Paulo Freire. 1990. *We Make the Road by Walking: Conversations on Education and Social Change*. Philadelphia: Temple University Press.

Jaggar, Allison M. 1989. "Love and Knowledge: Emotion in Feminist Epistemology." In Gender, Body, Knowledge: Feminist Reconstructions of Being and Knowing, edited by Susan R. Bordo and Allison M. Jaggar, 145–171. New Brunswick, NJ: Rutgers University Press.

James, William. 1884. "What is an emotion?" *Mind* 9 (34): 188–205.

———. 1978. *Pragmatism/The Meaning of Truth*. Cambridge, MA: Harvard University Press.

———. 1983. *Principals of Psychology*. London: Macmillan & Co.

James, William, and Carl Georg Lange. 1922. *The Emotions*. Baltimore: Williams and Wilkins Company.

Jenkins, Philip, and Sue Lyle. 2010. "Enacting Dialogue: The Impact of Promoting Philosophy for Children on the Literate Thinking of Identified Poor Readers, Aged 10." *Language & Education* 24 (6): 459–472.

Jo, Seon-Hee. 2001–2002. "Literacy: Constructing Meaning Through Philosophical Inquiry." *Analytic Teaching* 21 (1): 44–52.

———. 2002. "Imagination in Community of Inquiry." *Thinking: The Journal of Philosophy for Children* 16 (2): 39–43.

Johnson, Ann. 1993. "Feeling-Talk in Preschool: Teacher Views of Emotional Expression and its Significance." *Analytic Teaching* 13 (2): 3–10.

Johnson, David W., and Roger T. Johnson. 1991. *Learning Together and Alone: Cooperative, Competitive, and Individualistic Learning*. Boston: Allyn and Bacon.

Johnson, Mark. 1993. *Moral Imagination: Implications of Cognitive Science for Ethics*. Chicago: University of Chicago Press.

Jonas, Hans. 1954. "The Nobility of Sight: A Study in the Phenomenology of the Senses." *Philosophy and Phenomenological Research* 14 (4): 507–519.

Kant, Emmanuel. 1964. *The Doctrine of Virtue*. Translated by Mary J. Gregor. New York: Harper & Row.

Kahne, Joseph, and Joel Westheimer. 1996. "In the Service of What? The Politics of Service Learning." *Phi Delta Kappan* 77 (9): 592–598.

Kahne, Joseph, and Susan E. Sporte. 2007. *Developing Citizens: The Impact of Civic Learning Opportunities on Students' Commitment To Civic Participation*. Chicago: Consortium of Chicago School Research.

Keller, Evelyn Fox. 1983. *A Feeling for the Organism: The Life and Work of Barbara McClintock*. San Francisco: W. H. Freeman.

———. 1985. *Reflections on Gender and Science*. New Haven, CT: Yale University Press.

Keller, Evelyn Fox, and Christine R. Grontowski. 1983. "The Mind's Eye." In *Discovering Reality: Feminist Perspectives on Epistemology, Metaphysics, Methodology, and Philosophy of Science*, edited by Sandra Harding and Merrill B. Hintikka, 207–223. Dordrecht: D. Reidel Publishing Company.

Kelly, A. V. 2009. *The Curriculum: Theory and Practice*. London: Sage.

Kennedy, David. 1995. "Philosophy for Children and School Reform: Dewey, Lipman, and the Community of Inquiry." In *Children Philosophy and Democracy*, edited by John P. Portelli and Ronald F. Reed, 159–177. Calgary, Canada: Detselig Enterprises.———. 1999. "Philosophy for Children and the Reconstruction of Philosophy." *Metaphilosophy* 30 (4).

Kennedy, David Knowles. 2006. "John Dewey on Children, Childhood and Education." *Childhood & Philosophy* 2 (4): 211–229. www.filoeduc.org/childphilo/n4/dewey.html

Kenway, Jane, Sue Willis, Jill Blackmore, and Leonie Rennie. 1997. *Answering Back: Girls, Boys, and Feminism in Schools*. Sydney: Allen and Unwin.

Kielsmeier, James. 2011. "Service Learning: The Time Is Now." *The Prevention Researcher* 18 (1): 3–7.

Kirkman, Robert. 2008. "Teaching for Moral Imagination.". *Teaching Philosophy* 31(4): 333–350.

Kiss, Elizabeth. 1997. "Alchemy or Fool's Gold? Assessing Feminist Doubts About Rights." In *Reconstructing Political Theory: Feminist Perspectives*, edited by Una Narayan and Mary L. Shanley, 1–24. Cambridge: Polity Press.

Kliebard, Herbart M. 2004. *The Struggle for the American Curriculum: 1893–1958*. New York: Taylor & Francis.

Kristjansson, Kristjan. 1981. "The Didactics of Emotion Education." *Analytic Teaching* 21 (1): 5–15.

Kunin, Madeleine M. 1997. "Service Learning and Improved Academic Achievement: The National Scene." In *Service Learning*, edited by Joan Schine, 149–160. Chicago: The National Society for the Study of Education.

Kymlicka, Will. 2002. *Contemporary Political Philosophy: An Introduction*. Oxford: Oxford University Press.

Lagemann, Ellen. 2000. *An Elusive Science: The Troubling History of Educational Research*. Chicago: University of Chicago Press.

Laird, Susan. 1988. "Women and Gender in John Dewey's Philosophy of Education." Educational Theory 38 (1): 111–129.

Laws, Stephen. 2006. *The War for Children's Minds*. London: Routledge.

———. 2009. "Religion and Philosophy in Schools." In *Philosophy in Schools*, edited by Michael Hand and Carrie Winstanley, 41–60. London: Continuum.

Leffers, M. Regina. 1993. "Pragmatists Jane Addams and John Dewey Inform the Ethic of Care." *Hypatia* 8(2): 64–77.

Levinson, Meira. 1999. *The Demands of Liberal Education*. Oxford: Oxford University Press.

Lingard, Bob. 2009. "Testing Times: The Need for New Intelligent Accountabilities for Schooling." *Queensland Teachers Union Professional Magazine* 24 (November): 13–19.

Lingard, Bob, and Peter Douglas. 1999. *Men Engaging Feminisms*. Buckingham, UK: Open University Press.

Lipman, Matthew. 1988. *Philosophy Goes to School*. Philadelphia: Temple University Press.

———. 1992. Harry Stottlemeier's Discovery. Adapted by Laurence J. Splitter. Melbourne: ACER Press.

———. 1995. "Using Philosophy to Educate Emotions." *Analytic Teaching* 15 (2): 3–10.

———. 2003. *Thinking in Education*. 2nd ed. Cambridge: Cambridge University Press.

———. 2008. "Philosophy for Children's Debt to Dewey." In *Pragmatism, Education and Children*, edited by Michael Taylor, Helmut Schreier and Paulo Ghiraldelli, Jr., 143–151. New York: Rodopi.

Lipman, Matthew, and Ann M. Sharp. 1978. "Can Moral Education be Divorced From Philosophical Education?" In *Growing Up With Philosophy*, edited by Matthew Lipman and Ann Margaret Sharp, 338–367. Philadelphia: Temple University Press.

Lipman, Matthew, Ann M. Sharp and Fredrick S. Oscanyan 1980. *Philosophy in the Classroom*. Philadelphia: Temple University Press.

Lisman, David C., and Irene E. Harvey, eds. 2006. *Beyond the Tower: Concepts and Models for Service Learning in Philosophy*. Sterling, VA: Stylus.

Lister, Ruth. 1990. "Women, Economic Dependency and Citizenship." *The Journal of Social Policy* 19 (4): 445–467.

Lorde, Audre. 1984. *Sister Outsider: Essays and Speeches*. Freedom, CA: Crossing Press.

Luo, Renfu, Yaojiang Shi, Linxiu Zhang, Chengfang Liu, Hongbin Li, Scott Rozelle and Brian Sharbono. 2011. "Community Service, Educational Performance and Social Responsibility in Northwest China." *Journal of Moral Education* 40 (2): 181–202.

Lloyd, Genevieve. 1984. *The Man of Reason: 'Male' and 'Female' in Western Philosophy*. Minneapolis: University of Minnesota Press.

Macoll, San. 1997. "Opening Philosophy." *Thinking: The Journal of Philosophy for Children* 11 (3–4): 5–9.

Martin, Jane Roland. 1982. "Excluding Women from the Educational Realm." In *The Education Feminism Reader*, edited by Linda Stone, 105–121. New York: Routledge.

Marshall, Thomas Humphrey. 1950. *Citizenship and Social Class, and Other Essays*. Cambridge: Cambridge University Press.

Marullo, Sam, and Bob Edwards. 2000. "From Charity to Justice: The Potential of University-Community Collaboration for Social Change." *American Behavioural Scientist* 43 (5): 895–912.

Mason, Andrew. 2000. *Community, Solidarity and Belonging*. Cambridge: Cambridge University Press.

Mathews, Freya. 1998. "From Epistemology to Spirituality: Feminist Perspectives." *The Journal of Dharma* 23 (4): 517–539.

Matthews, Michael R. 1980. *The Marxist Theory of Schooling: A Study of Epistemology and Education*. Sussex, UK: Harvester.

Matthews, Gareth B. 1979. "The Philosopher as Teacher: Philosophy and the Young Child." *Metaphilosophy* 10 (3–4): 354–368.

———. 1980. *Philosophy and the Young Child*. Cambridge, MA: Harvard University Press.

———. 1991. "The Philosophical Imagination in Children's Play." In *Imagination and Education*, edited by Kieran Egan and Dan Nadaner, 186–197. New York: Teachers College Press.

Mayhew, Katherine Camp, and Anna Camp Edwards. 1936. *The Dewey School: The Laboratory School of the University of Chicago 1896–1903*. New York: D. Appleton-Century Co.

McClean, Chris. 1997. "Engaging With Boy's Experiences of Masculinity: Implications for Gender Reform in Schools." In *Will Boys Be Boys? Boy's Education in the Context of Gender Reform*, edited by Jane Kenway. Deakin West: Australian Curriculum Studies Association.

McFall, Lynne. 1991. "What Is Wrong With Bitterness?" In *Feminist Ethics*, edited by Claudia Card. Lawrence: University of Kansas Press.

McKenna, Erin. 2002. "The Need for a Pragmatist Feminist Self." In *Feminist Interpretations of John Dewey*, edited by Charlene Haddock Seigfried, 133–158. University Park: Pennsylvania State University Press.

McLaren, Peter. 2007. *Life in Schools: An Introduction to Critical Pedagogy in the Foundations of Education*. Boston: Pearson Education.

McNeil, John D. 2009. *Contemporary Curriculum: In Thought and Action*. Hoboken, NJ: John Wiley & Sons.

Mead, George Herbert. 1967. *Mind, Self and Society: From the Standpoint of a Behavioural Scientist*. Chicago: University of Chicago Press.

Melchior, Alan. 1999. *Summary Report: National Evaluation of Learn and Serve America*. Waltham, MA: Centre for Human Resources. http://www.learnandserve.gov/pdf/lsa_evaluation.pdf.

Meyers, Dianna T. 1989. *Self, Society, and Personal Choice*. New York: Columbia University Press.

Miller, Marjorie C. 2002. "Feminism and Pragmatism: On the Arrival of a 'Ministry of Disturbance, a Regulated Force of Annoyance; a Destroyer of Routine, an Underminer of Complacency.'" In *Feminist Interpretations of John Dewey*, edited by Charlene Haddock Siegfried, 78–94. University Park: Pennsylvania State University Press.

Minnich, Elizabeth Kamarck. 2002. "Philosophy, Education and the American Tradition of Aspirational Democracy." In *Feminist Interpretations of John Dewey*, edited by Charlene Haddock Seigfried, 95–112. University Park: Pennsylvania State University Press.

Mitchell, Tania D. 2008. "Traditional vs. Critical Service Learning: Engaging the Literature to Differentiate Two Models." *Michigan Journal of Community Service Learning* 14 (2): 50–66.

Mitias, Lara M. 2004. "Philosophy-Process, Perspective, and Pluralism—for Children." *Thinking: The Journal of Philosophy for Children* 17 (1): 17–23.

Moely, Barbara E., Andrew Furco and Julia Read. 2008. "Charity and Social Change: The Impact of Individual Preferences on Service Learning Outcomes." *Michigan Journal of Community Service* 15 (1): 37–48.

Morton, Keith. 1995. "The Irony of Service: Charity, Project and Social Change in Service-Learning." *Michigan Journal of Community Service-Learning* 2 (1): 19–32.

Moultan, Janice. 1983. "The Paradigm of Philosophy: The Adversary Method." *Discovering Reality: Feminist Perspectives on Epistemology, Metaphysics, Methodology and Philosophy of Science*, edited by Sandra Harding and Merril B. Hintikka, 149–164. Boston: Kluwer.

Murris, Karin. 2000. "The Role of the Facilitator in Philosophical Inquiry." *Thinking: The Journal of Philosophy for Children* 15 (2): 40–46.

Narrayan, Una. 1988. "Working Together Across Difference: Some Considerations on Emotions and Political practice." *Hypatia* 3 (2): 31–47.

Neil, A. S. 1962. *Summerhill*. Harmondsworth, UK: Penguin Books.

New South Wales Board of Studies (NSWBOS). 2011. *Student HSC Entries by Sex*. Sydney: NSWBOS. http://www.boardofstudies.nsw.edu.au/ebos/static/EN_SX_2011_12.html.

Nussbaum, Martha C. 2001. *Upheavals of Thought: The Intelligence of Emotions*. New York, Cambridge University Press.

———. 2010. *Not for Profit: Why Democracy Needs the Humanities*. Princeton, NJ: Princeton University Press

Nye, Andrea. 1990. Words of Power: A Feminist Reading of the History of Logic. New York: Routledge.

O'Loughhlin, Marjorie. 1998. "Paying Attention to Bodies in Education: Theoretical Resources and Practical Suggestions." *Educational Philosophy and Theory* 30 (3): 275–297.

Oliver, Pam. 2002. "What Do Girls Know Anyway? Rationality, Gender, and Social Control." In Representing Reason: Feminist Theory and Formal Logic, edited by Rachel Joffe Falmagne and Marjorie Hass, 209–240. Lanham, MD: Rowman & Littlefield.

Olsen, Mark. 2001. "Citizenship and Education: From Alfred Marshal to Iris Marion Young." *Educational Philosophy and Theory* 33 (1): 77–94.

Organisation for Economic & Cooperative Development (OECD). 2010. *PISA 2009 Results: What Students Know and Can Do: Student Performance in Reading, Mathematics and Science, Volume 1.* http://www.pisa.oecd.org/dataoecd/10/61/48852548.pdf.

Oscanyan, Fredrick S. 1978. "The Role of Logic in Education." *Growing Up With Philosophy,* edited by Matthew Lipman and Ann Margaret Sharp, 259–273. Philadelphia: Temple University Press.

Othman, Moomala, and Rosnani Hashim. 2006. "Critical Thinking and Reading Skills: A Comparative Study of the Reader Response and the Philosophy for Children Approaches." *Thinking: The Journal of Philosophy for Children* 18 (2): 26–34.

Pacifici, Linda, and Jim Garrison. 2004. "Imagination, Emotion and Inquiry: The Teachable Moment." *Contemporary Pragmatism* 1 (1): 119–132.

Palermo, James, and Catherine D'Erasmo. 2001. "Teaching Empathy and the Teacher's Responsibility." *Thinking: The Journal of Philosophy for Children* 15 (4): 31–33.

Parfit, Derek. 1984. *Reasons and Persons.* Oxford: Clarendon Press.

Pearl, Arthur. 1978. "Towards a General Theory of Valuing Youth." In *The Value of Youth* , edited by Arthur Pearl, Douglas Grant and Ernst Wenk, 1–15. Thousand Oaks, CA: Responsible Action.

Phenix, Lucy Massie, and Veronica Selver (directors). 2011. *You Got to Move: Stories of Change in the South.* (DVD). Harrington Park: Milliarium Zero.

Plato. 1998. *The Republic.* Translated by R. Waterfield. Oxford: Oxford University Press.

Plumwood, Val. 1993. *Feminism and the Mastery of Nature.* London: Routledge.

———. 2002. "The Politics of Reason: Toward a Feminist Logic." In Representing Reason: Feminist Theory and Formal Logic, edited by Rachel Joffe Falmagne and Marjorie Hass, 11–70. Lanham, MD: Rowman & Littlefield.

Polesel, John. 2008. "Democratising the Curriculum or Training the Children of the Poor: School-Based Vocational Education in Australia." *Journal of Educational Policy* 23 (6): 615–632.

Quin, Robyn. 2003. "Questions of Knowledge in Australian Media Education." *Television & New Media* 4 (4): 439–460.

Quirk, Bill. 2005. *The Anti-Content Mindset: The Root Cause of the "Math Wars."* http://www.wgquirk.com/content.html.

Ravitch, Diane. 2010. *The Death and Life of the Great American School System: How Testing and Choice Are Undermining Education.* New York: Basic Books.

Redshaw, Sarah. 1994a. "Body Knowledge." *Thinking: The Journal of Philosophy for Children* 11 (3–4): 9–15.

———. 1994b. "Philosophical Applications: Cultivating Alternative Approaches to Dispute Resolution." *Thinking: The Journal of Philosophy for Children* 11 (2): 10–13.

Reid, Alan. 2005. *Rethinking National Curriculum Collaboration: Towards an Australian Curriculum.* Canberra: Australian Government, Department of Education, Science and Training. http://www.dest.gov.au/NR/rdonlyres/662870A8-BA7B-4F23-BD08-DE99A7BFF41A/2650/report1.pdf.

———. 2011. "The National Curriculum: A Case Study in Policy Catch-Up." *Professional Voice* 8 (3): 33–36

Richardson, Brenda. 1997. "Teaching for Presence in the Democratic Classroom." *Thinking: The Journal of Philosophy for Children* 13 (1): 26–32.

Robinson, Tony. 2000. "Dare the School Build a New Social Order?" *Michigan Journal of Community Service Learning* 7 (1): 142–157.

Rocheleau, Jordy. 2004. "Theoretical Roots of Service-Learning: Progressive Education and the Development of Citizenship." In *Service-Learning: History, Theory & Issues*, edited by Bruce W. Speck and Sherry L. Hoppe, 3–17. Westport, CT: Praeger.

Rosenberger, Cynthia. 2000. "Beyond Empathy: Developing Critical Consciousness Through Service Learning." In *Integrating Service Learning and Multicultural Education in College and Universities*, edited by Carolyn R. O'Grady, 23–. Mahwah, NJ: Lawrence Erlbaum Associates.

Rowan, Leonie, Michelle Knobel, Chris Bigum and Colin Lankshear. 2002. *Boy's Literacies and Schooling: The Dangerous Territories of Gender-Based Literacy Reform*. Buckingham, UK: Open University Press.

Russell, Dee. 1998. "Cultivating the Imagination in Music Education: John Dewey's Theory of Imagination and It's Relation to the Chicago Laboratory School." *Educational Theory* 48 (2): 193–210.

Sandel, M. J. 1982. *Liberalism and the Limits of Justice*. New York: Cambridge University Press.

Satish, Telgar. 1981. "The Relationship Between Knowledge and Emotions: Transcript of a Philosophy for Children Session in St Paul, Minnesota." *Thinking: The Journal of Philosophy for Children* 3 (3–4): 84–91.

Scheffler, Israel. 1974. *Four Pragmatists: A Critical Introduction to Peirce, Mead, James and Dewey*. London: Routledge & Kegan Paul.

———. 1991. *In Praise of the Cognitive Emotions*. New York: Routledge.

Schertz, Matthew. 2006. "Empathetic Pedagogy: Community of Inquiry and the Development of Empathy." *Analytic Teaching* 26 (1): 8–14.

Schiro, Michael. 2008. *Curriculum Theory: Conflicting Visions and Enduring Concerns*. Thousand Oaks, CA: Sage.

Schleifer, Michael. 1996–1997. "Philosophy and Community in Education: A Critique of Richard Rorty." Analytic Teaching 17 (2): 93–100.

Schleifer, Michael, and C. Martiny. 2005. *Talking About Values and Feelings with Young Children: How to Develop Good Judgment and Empathy*. Calgary, Canada: Temeron Press.

Schleifer, Michael, and Ginette Poirier. 1996. "The Effect of Philosophical Discussions in the Classroom on Respect for Others and Non-Stereotypic Attitudes." *Thinking: The Journal of Philosophy for Children* 12 (4): 32–34.

Schleifer, Michael, and Louis Courtemanche. 1996. "The Effect of Philosophy for Children on Language Ability." *Thinking: The Journal of Philosophy for Children* 12 (4): 30–31.

Schleifer, Michael, Marie France Daniel, Emmanuelle Peyronnet and Sara Lecomte. 2003. "The Impact of Philosophical Discussions on Moral Autonomy, Judgment, Empathy and the Recognition of Emotion in Five Year Olds." *Thinking: The Journal of Philosophy for Children* 16 (2): 4–12.

Schleifer, Michael, and Miriam McCormick. 2006. "Are We Responsible for Our Emotions and Moods?" *Thinking: The Journal of Philosophy for Children* 18 (1): 15–21.

Scolnicov, Samuel. 1978. "Truth, Neutrality and the Philosophy Teacher." In *Growing Up With Philosophy*, edited by Matthew Lipman and Ann M. Sharp, 392–405. Philadelphia: Temple University Press.

Scott, Marion. 1980. "Teach Her a Lesson: Sexist Curriculum in Patriarchal Education." In *Learning to Lose: Sexism and Education*, edited by Dale Spender and Elizabeth Sarah, 97–120. London: The Women's Press.

Sharp, Ann Margaret. 1987. "What Is a 'Community of Inquiry'?" *Journal of Moral Education* 16 (1): 37–45.

———. 1991. "The Community of Inquiry: Education for Democracy." *Thinking: The Journal of Philosophy for Children* 9 (2): 31–37.

———. 1993. "Peirce, Feminism and Philosophy for Children." *Analytic Teaching* 14 (1): 51–61.

———. 1994. "Feminism and Philosophy for Children: The Ethical Dimension." *Thinking: The Journal of Philosophy for Children* 11 (3–4): 24–28.

———. 2004. "The Other Dimension of Caring Thinking." *Critical and Creative Thinking: The Australasian Journal of Philosophy in Education* 12 (1): 9–15.

Sheckley, Barry G., and Morris T. Keeton. 1997. "Service Learning: A Theoretical Model." In *Service Learning*, edited by Joan Schine and Kenneth J. Rehage, 32–55. Chicago: University of Chicago Press.

Siegfried, Charlene Haddock. 1996. *Pragmatism and Feminism: Reweaving the Social Fabric*. Chicago: University of Chicago Press.

———, ed. 2002. *Feminist Interpretations of John Dewey*. University Park: Pennsylvania State University Press.

Sigurdardóttir, Brynhildur. 2002. "Imagination." *Thinking: The Journal of Philosophy for Children* 16 (2): 34–38.

Slade, Christina. 1994. "Harryspeak and the Conversation of Girls." *Thinking: The Journal of Philosophy for Children* 11 (3): 29–32.

———. 1997. "Conversing Across Differences: Relativism and Difference." *Analytic Teaching* 17 (2): 3–12.

Slavin, Robert E. 1985. "An Introduction to Cooperative Learning Research." In *Learning to Cooperate, Cooperating to Learn*, edited by Robert E. Slavin, Sharan Shlomo, Spencer Kagan, Rachel Hertz-Lazarowitz, Clark Webb and Richard Schmuck, 5–15. New York, Plenum Press.

Solomon, Robert C. 1998. "The Politics of Emotion." *Midwest Studies in Philosophy* 22: 1–19.

———. 2003, *Not Passions Slave: Emotions and Choice*. New York: Oxford University Press.

Spender, Dale. 1980. "Educational Institutions: Where Co-Operation Is Called Cheating." In *Learning to Loose: Sexism and Education*, edited by Dale Spender and Elizabeth Sarah, 39–48. London: The Women's Press.

———. 1982. *Invisible Women: The Schooling Scandal*. London: Writers and Reading Publishing.

Spelman, Elizabeth V. 1989. "Anger and Insubordination." In *Women, Knowledge and Reality: Explorations in Feminist Philosophy*, edited by Ann Gary and Marilyn Pearsall, 263–274. Boston: Unwin Hyman.

———. 1991. "The Virtue of Feeling and the Feeling of Virtue." *Feminist Ethics*, edited by Claudia Card, 213–232. Lawrence: University Press of Kansas.

Splitter, Laurence. 1997. "Philosophy and Civics Education." In *Philosophy and Democracy in Asia*, edited by Philip Cam, In-suk Cha and Mark Tamthai, 161–178. Seoul: Korean National Commission for UNESCO.

Splitter, Laurance, and Ann Margaret Sharp. 1995. *Teaching for Better Thinking*. Melbourne: ACER.

Spring, Kimberly., Robert Grimm, Jr. and Nathan Dietz. 2008. *Community Service and Service Learning in America's Schools*. Washington, DC: Corporation for National and Community Service, Office of Research and Policy Development. Retrieved on January 24, 2012 from: http://www.aces4kids.org/public/uploads/research-news/service_learning_corporation_for_national_and_community_service_.pdf.

Sprod, Tim 2001, *Philosophical Discussion in Moral Education: The Community of Ethical Inquiry*. London: Routledge.

Strike, Kenneth A. 1989. *Liberal Justice and the Marxist Critique of Education*. New York: Routledge.

———. 2000. "Liberalism, Communitarianism and the Space Between: In Praise of Kindness." *Journal of Moral Education* 29 (2): 133–148.

Sullivan, Susan. 2002. "The Need for Truth: Towards a Pragmatist Feminist Standpoint Theory." In *Feminist Interpretations of John Dewey*, edited by Charlene Haddock Seigfried, 133–159. University Park: Pennsylvania State University Press.

Tanner, Laurel N. 1997. *Dewey's Laboratory School: Lessons for Toda.* New York: Teachers College Press.

Tanesini, Alessandra. 1999. An Introduction to Feminist Epistemologies. Oxford: Blackwell Publishers.

Teese, Richard, and John Polesel. 2003. *Undemocratic Schooling: Equity and Quality in Mass Secondary Education in Australia.* Melbourne: Melbourne University Press.

Teese, Richard, Merryn Davies, Margaret Charlton and John Polesel. 1995. *Who Wins at School? Girls and Boys in Australian Secondary Education.* Melbourne: Australian Government Publishing Service.

Ternasky, P. Lance. 1993. "Coping With Relativism and Absolutism." In *Ethics for Professionals in Education: Perspectives for Preparation and Practice*, edited by Kenneth A. Strike and P. Lance Ternasky, 117–134. New York, Teacher's College Press.

Thayer, H. S. 1977. "Plato on the Morality of Imagination." *Review of Metaphysics* 30 (4): 594–618.

Thayer-Bacon, Barbara J. 1999. "Closing the Split Between Practical and Theoretical Reasoning: Knowers and the Known." *Educational Philosophy and Theory* 31 (3): 341–358.

———. 2003. "Pragmatism and Feminism as Qualified Relativism." *Studies in Philosophy and Education* 22: 417–438.

Thomas, John C. 1997. "Community of Inquiry and Differences of the Heart." *Thinking: The Journal of Philosophy for Children* 13 (1): 42–48.

Tilley-Lubbs, Gresilda. 2009. "Good Intentions Pave the Way to Hierarchy: A Retrospective Autoethnographic Approach." *Michigan Journal of Community Service Learning* 16 (Fall): 59–68.

Tricky, Steven., and Topping, Keith. J. 2004. "Philosophy for Children: A Systematic Review." *Research Papers in Education* 19 (3): 365–380.

Turgeon, Wendy C. 1998. "Metaphysical Horizons of Philosophy for Children: A Survey of Recent Discussions Within the Philosophy for Children Community." *Thinking: The Journal of Philosophy for Children* 14 (2): 18–22.

Twenge, Jena M., and W. Keith Campbell. 2009. *The Narcissism Epidemic.* New York: Free Press.

Valentino, Francesco. 1998. "The Thought of the Heart and Philosophy for Children." *Thinking: The Journal of Philosophy for Children* 14 (2): 29–34.

Velasco, Monica. 1997. "Language in Stories for Boys and Girls." *Thinking: The Journal of Philosophy for Children* 13 (2): 41–44.

Vesey, G. N. A. 1967. "Vision." The Encyclopaedia of Philosophy, Volume 8. Edited by Paul Edwards, 252–253. New York: Macmillan & the Free Press.

Victorian Curriculum & Assessment Authority (VCAA). 2011a. *VCE Unit Completion Outcomes—2011, Sociology.* Retrieved July 1, 2012 from, http://www.vcaa.vic.edu.au/vce/statistics/2011/section2/vce_sociology_11.pdf.

———. 2011b. *VCE Unit Completion Outcomes—2011, Specialist Mathematics.* Melbourne. Retrieved July 1, 2012 from http://www.vcaa.vic.edu.au/vce/statistics/2011/section2/vce_specialist_mathematics_11.pdf.

Vygotsky, Lev. 1978. *Mind and Society.* Cambridge, MA: Harvard University Press.

———. 1986. *Thought and Language.* Cambridge, MA: MIT Press.

Wade, Rahima 2001, "'And justice for all': Community Service-Learning for Social Justice." *Education Commission of the States.* Retrieved June 10, 2012 from http://www.ecs.org/clearinghouse/29/13/2913.htm.

Waghid, Yusef. 2005. "Action as an Educational Virtue: Toward a Different Understanding of Democratic Citizenship Education." *Educational Theory* 55 (3): 323–343.

Walby, Sylvia. 1994. "Is Citizenship Gendered?" *Sociology* 28 (2): 379–395.

Walkerdine, Valerie. 1988. The Mastery of Reason: Cognitive Development and the Production of Rationality. London; Routledge.

———. 1989. "Femininity as Performance." *Oxford Review of Education* 15 (3): 267–279.

Wallace, Alfred Russell. 1873. "Review of Darwin's 'The Expression of the Emotions in Man and Animals.'" Retrieved June 16, 2012, from http://people.wku.edu/charles.smith/wallace/S220.htm.

Wang, Yan, and Robert Roberts. 2006. "Impact of Service-Learning and Social Justice Education on College Students' Cognitive Development." *NASPA Journal* 43 (2): 316–337.

Ward, Janie Victoria. 1997. "Encouraging Cultural Competence in Service Learning Practice." In *Service Learning,* edited by Joan Schine, 136–148. Chicago: The National Society for the Study of Education.

Ward, Kelly, and Lisa Wolf-Wendel. 2000. "Community-Centred Service Learning: Moving From Doing For to Doing With." *American Behavioural Scientist* 43 (5): 767–780.

Ward, Lloyd Gordon. 1989. "The Dewey-Mead Analysis of Emotions." *The Social Science Journal* 26 (4): 465–479.

Warnock, Mary. 1976. *Imagination.* London: Faber & Faber.

Wertsch, James V. 1985. Vygotsky and the Social Formation of the Mind. Cambridge, MA: Harvard University Press.

West, Peter. 2002. *What Is the Matter With Boys? Showing Boys the Way Towards Manhood.* Marrickville, NSW: Choice Books.

Westbrook, Robert B. 1991. *John Dewey and American Democracy.* Ithaca, NY: Cornwell University Press.

Weiss, Penny A. 1995. "Feminism and Communitarianism: Comparing Critiques of Liberalism." In *Feminism and Community,* edited by Penny A. Weis and Marilyn Friedman, 161–186. Philadelphia: Temple University Press.

Whips, Judy D. 2004. "Jane Addam's Social Thought as a Model for a Pragmatist-Feminist Communitarianism." *Hypatia* 19 (2): 118–133.

White, Rob, and Johanna Wyn. 2004. Youth and Society: Exploring the Dynamics of Experience. South Melbourne: Oxford University Press.

Whitehouse, P. G. 1978. "The Meaning of Emotion in Dewey's Art as Experience." *The Journal of Aesthetics and Art Criticism* 37 (2): 149–146.

Wilks, Susan. 1996. Critical and Creative Thinking: Strategies for Classroom Inquiry. Melbourne: Eleanor Curtin Publishing.

———. 1997–1996. "Talking It Over Beats the Bullies: Confronting Social Issues in Australian Classrooms." *Analytic Teaching* 17 (1): 44–47.

———. 2005. *Designing a Thinking Curriculum*: Melbourne, ACER.

Williams, Bernard. 1973. "A Critique of Utilitarianism." In *Utilitarianism: For and Against,* edited by J. C. Smart and Bernard Williams, 75–87. Cambridge: Cambridge University Press.

Wilson, John. 1986. "Relativism and Teaching." *Journal of Philosophy of Education* 20 (1): 89–96.

Wright, Susan. 2000. "Challenging Literacies: The Significance of the Arts." *Proceedings of the Australian Association of Educational Research Conference.* Brisbane. Retrieved June 21, 2007, from www.aare.edu.au/00pap/wri00006.htm.

Wyn, Johanna. 1995. "'Youth' and 'Citizenship.'" *Melbourne Studies in Education* 36 (2): 45–65.

Yates, Lyn. 1993. *The Education of Girls: Policy, Research and the Question of Gender.* Melbourne: Australian Council for Educational Research.

———. 1997. "Gender Equity and the Boys Debate: What Sort of Challenge Is It?" *British Journal of Sociology of Education* 18 (3): 337–347.

———. 1985. "Is Girl Friendly Schooling Really What Girls Need?" In *Girl Friendly Schooling*, edited by J. Whyte, R. Deem, L. Kant and M. Cruikshank, 209–229. London, Methuen.

———. 2011. "Rethinking Knowledge, Rethinking Work." In *Australian Curriculum Dilemmas: State Cultures and the Big Issues*, edited by Lyn Yates, Cherry Collins and Kate O'Connor, 25–44. Carlton, Australia: Melbourne University Press.

Young, Iris Marion. 1986. "The Ideal of Community and the Politics of Difference." *Social Theory and Practice* 12 (1): 1–26.

———. 1995. "Mothers, Citizenship, and Independence: A Critique of Pure Family Values." *Ethics* 105 (3): 535–556.

Index

218   *Index*

and emotions, 7
feminism
    Anglo-American, 26
    and dualistic relationship, 13–16
    and individualism, 115–116
    and legal rights of women, 122
    standpoint, 24–26
Fesmire, S., 80–81
Flower, L., 170
Fraser, N., 26, 114, 116
freedom, 125
Freire, P., 22, 54–56, 73, 160–162,
    173–174
futurity, 116, 118, 158

G

Gardner, S., 56, 59, 61, 62
gender
    and behaviour, 144–145, 152–153
    categories, 15
    and communications skills, 150–152
    and curriculum, 141–144
    development theory, 26
    discrimination and, 2
    and inequality, 13, 14, 21
    and literary skills, 150
    psychological development of, 16,
        193n3
    stereotypes, 139
generalisation, 38, 84
gestures, 101
Gilbert, P., 140
Gilbert, R., 140
Gilligan, C., 6, 25, 27, 102, 110–111
Giroux, H., 173
giver/receiver relationship, 166
global community, 128
God, belief in, 64
Golding, C., 54, 57, 62
Goleman, D., 92
Gordon, L., 114, 116
Gradgrind, 85
Greene, M., 23, 86, 91
Gregory, M., 60
Grontowski, C., 18
growth, 43
Gustein, E., 171–172

H

habits, 42–43, 93, 96, 125–126
Hanna, P., 175
Harding, S., 6, 40, 53, 67–68, 73
Harry Stottlemeier's Discovery

Lipman, M., 106–107
Harvey, I., 185
Hass, M., 27
Haynes, F., 148
health education, 20
hearing, 18, 31
hierarchies, 14, 21, 166, 169
Highlander Folk School, 172–173
Hirsch, E., 1, 47, 54, 123
Holdsworth, R., 158–159, 159
Holt, J.
    Escape from Childhood., 119
homogenisation, 16
Hooks, B., 26, 173
Hoops, J., 174
Horton, Myles, 172, 173–174
Hull House, 129–131, 172
hunter and gatherer missions, 24
hyperseparation, 14
hypotheses, 63–65

I

ideas, 63–66
    defined, 34–35
    and imagination, 82
    testing of, 35–36, 36
imagination, 34, 110–111
    and the arts, 86
    Dewey on, 80–85
    and emotions, 7, 10, 111–112
    and inquiry, 33–34
    intelligent, 78, 82, 89–91, 91
    philosophy and, 87–91
    Platonic notion of, 79–80
    and Reason, 80
    in traditional education, 85–87
individual/community dualisms, 7,
    113–138, 148
individualism, 1, 36, 114–116,
    120–122, 146
indoctrination, 177–178
inequality, class and gender, 13, 21
inferences, 83, 84
inquiry
    activities based on, 47–48
    background factors of, 67–68
    collaborative, 48, 180
    communal, 27, 40, 42, 51, 66–70,
        73, 101, 127–129, 132, 155, 181
    Dewey on, 37–38, 46
    and emotions, 5–6, 99–102, 104
    goals of, 62–63
    intercultural, 61–62, 170
    selecting for, 31–33, 68

skills, 177
  as social reconstruction, 161
intellectual content, 96–97
intelligence, emotional, 92, 108, 110,
    194(chap.5)n2
intercultural inquiry, 61–62, 170
interdependency, 15, 43, 134
internalisation, 15, 41, 125
Internet, 23
intersubjectivity, 40, 74, 76

J
Jaggar, A., 6, 32, 97–98
James-Lange theory, 93
James, W., 64, 95–96
Jonas, H., 17–18
Jo, S., 150–151
judgments
  in perception, 32
  provisional, 74
  and the reasoning process, 35–36
justice/care dualism, 134
justice perspective, 25, 102

K
Kahne, J., 163, 164, 165, 175
Kant, E., 10
Keller, E., 6, 16–17, 18, 25, 27, 29
Kennedy, D., 23, 74
Kenway, J., 142
Kilpatrick, W., 175
knowledge, 74
  abstracting, 55
  attributes associated with, 13
  constructing, 123
  cultural, 54
  Dewey on, 36–38
  disciplinary, 48
  discovering, 123
  dualistic notions of, 19
  meaning and, 36–38
  visual metaphors describing, 18
knowledge transmission, 21, 46,
    54–55, 117–118

L
Laboratory School, 8, 45–47, 49, 51,
    154, 156, 175
language
  Dewey on, 39, 193(chap.2)n2
  of ideas, 19
  philosophy of, 151–152
Law, S., 59
learning

from an activity, 29
  experience and, 50, 71
  project based, 24
  rote, 123
  service, 51
LeDoux, J., 98–99
Lipman, M.
  on Community of Inquiry, 74–75,
    133
  on creative children, 90
  on emotional development, 111
  Harry Stottlemeir's Discovery,
    106–107, 148–149
  and learning materials, 105,
    148–149
  on logic, 74–76
  and Philosophy for Children, 3–4,
    70, 71–72, 88
  and philosophy in curriculum, 185
  on reading comprehension, 150–151
  on service learning, 167
  on theory/practice dualism, 154–157
Lisman, D., 185
literacy, 150–152
logic, 41–42, 51–52
  Dewey on, 70, 75–76
  imagination and, 89
  and inquiry, 66–70
  Lipman on, 75–76
  and thinking, 150–151
Lorde, A., 26
Lyotard, J., 26

M
Macoll, S., 147
male/female dualism, 139–153
marginalisation of males, 146
marginalised groups, marginalised
    social, 16
Marshall, T., 116
Marullo, S., 163, 164, 168, 169
masculinity, 140–144, 145–147
  attributes of, 2, 13
  moral perspective of, 25, 102
  and separate knowing, 25, 27
mastery and domination, 15–16
Matthews, G., 58, 105
McClintock, B., 25
McKay, E., 91
McLaren, P., 173, 175
McNeil, J., 22, 85
Mead, G., 101, 110
meaning
  Dewey on, 63–66